All the Queen's Men

The World of ELIZABETH I

Peter Brimacombe

SUTTON PUBLISHING

This book was first published in 2000 by
Sutton Publishing Limited · Phoenix Mill
Thrupp · Stroud · Gloucestershire · GL5 2BU

This new paperback edition first published in 2003

British Library Cataloguing in Publication Data
A catalogue record for this book is available from the British Library

ISBN 0 7509 3260 0

Typeset in 10/11pt Korinna.
Typesetting and origination by
Sutton Publishing Limited.
Printed and bound in Great Britain by
J.H. Haynes & Co. Ltd, Sparkford.

CONTENTS

Acknowledgements   v

Introduction   vii

1   *The Tudor Kingdom*   1

2   *At the Royal Court*   17

3   *Portrait of a Queen*   33

4   *The Statesmen*   44

5   *The Seafarers*   63

6   *The Explorers*   76

7   *The Suitors*   96

8   *Men of God*   112

9   *The Scholars*   129

10   *Cambridge Connections*   145

11   *The Creators*   151

12   *Men at War*   170

Notes   188

Bibliography   193

Index   195

ACKNOWLEDGEMENTS

While I was living in Plymouth several years ago, A.L. Rowse came to lunch, thereby introducing me to the world of Queen Elizabeth I. It is with considerable trepidation that I stumble in the footsteps of this acknowledged and much-regarded authority on the Elizabethan age – fortunately I have received considerable help.

I would like to thank the archivists of Burghley House, Hatfield House, Longleat, Sudeley Castle and Woburn Abbey together with Bonnie Vernon at Penshurst Place. My gratitude to the staff of the Bodleian Library, Oxford, Maritime Studies Library and West Devon Records Office, Plymouth, the Public Record Office, Kew, and Trinity College Library, Cambridge. Also to Crispin Gill, Alan Cotton and Phil Edwards, the assistant librarian in Devizes, Wiltshire.

I am particularly grateful to Dr John Adamson at Peterhouse, Cambridge, Professor Wallace MacCaffrey at Trinity Hall, Cambridge, Dr Pieter van der Merwe at the National Maritime Museum, Greenwich, Dr Robin Robbins at Wadham College, Oxford, Canon David Durston at Salisbury Cathedral, and Sir Roy Strong for kindly giving me so much of their time and knowledge.

Finally and most of all to my wife Jennie, without whose unflagging assistance there would be no book.

INTRODUCTION

E lizabeth I was the last English monarch truly to rule the nation – subsequently only Queen Victoria possessed the same majestic stature, yet by then royal power was no longer absolute but subject to the wishes of Parliament. Elizabeth had inherited a weak and divided kingdom yet relentlessly fashioned it into a major world power, having decisively defeated the mightiest invasion fleet ever to approach our shores. Her relationships with the key men in the kingdom, both in war and peace, were vital to the success of her reign.

The Queen coupled a shrewd judgement of human nature with the unerring ability to choose and motivate men: during her long and glorious reign, she surrounded herself with the ablest, most energetic and fearless minds in the kingdom. As with the majority of women who achieve power, her retinue remained entirely male – the Court of Queen Elizabeth I held no place for women except for their wit and beauty. The only man she did not choose was a husband, although there was certainly no shortage of suitors.

Elizabeth's England abounded with eminent statesmen, while wave after wave of sea captains became her swordbearers. Her charismatic reign produced brilliant scholars and creative talent, among them the world's foremost playwright. Elizabeth was devoutly religious and embraced the New Learning with fanatical zeal. She inspired magnificent architecture, while her sea captains sailed great oceans to discover new shores and found a mighty overseas empire. Centre stage in these heady days of new ideas and new horizons was the Royal Court, a colourful kaleidoscope of glittering courtiers and important foreign dignitaries, all trying to impress, all jostling for her favours – All the Queen's Men.

1

THE TUDOR KINGDOM

The Battle of Bosworth ended with Richard III a bloodstained corpse, his army completely destroyed. The long-running Wars of the Roses finally over, Henry Tudor was acclaimed King Henry VII of all England, marking the beginning of the Tudor age. Yet while 1485 is generally considered to signal the end of the Middle Ages, the Tudor monarchs who followed that decisive military encounter, continued to reign with the blissful assurance of the divine right of kings, in precisely the same manner as their medieval forebears. Elizabeth, the last and arguably greatest of the Tudor rulers, was no exception: divine right was a fundamental concept in which she wholeheartedly believed. She was chosen by God.

Henry Tudor, born at Pembroke Castle on the Welsh coast, was twenty-eight years old when he became king. His claim to the throne was questionable but in those days kingdoms could be won in combat and Henry had eliminated the opposition in time-honoured style when his heavily outnumbered Lancastrian army triumphed amid the rolling Leicestershire countryside outside the small town of Market Bosworth. Now that he was King, Henry was greatly determined to see a conclusion to the long-running civil wars between the Yorkists and Lancastrians which had grievously disrupted the kingdom for so many years. 'We will unite the white rose and the red,' declaims Henry triumphantly in the last act of William Shakespeare's great historical drama *Richard III*, written just over a century later. So it was to be, for no Yorkist head of any significance rose above the parapet ever again and peace was finally sealed when Henry married Elizabeth of York, the daughter of Edward IV, Richard's elder brother and the last head of the House of York.

The two dozen years of Henry VII's reign that followed were understandably almost entirely taken up with regaining royal authority, re-establishing much-needed law and order throughout the kingdom and ensuring that the hard-earned peace was maintained in the face of potential internal or external threat of renewed conflict. It was during this time that the great families which Henry's granddaughter, Elizabeth, was later to rely on so heavily came to prominence, such as the Cecils who found themselves on the winning side after Bosworth and benefited accordingly. Henry was necessarily preoccupied with internal domestic issues within the country while momentous events were occurring overseas that were to be of monumental consequence for England in the future. France had become unified after the French King Louis XI annexed the hitherto independent Dukedom of Burgundy following the death of Charles the Bold. The expulsion of the Moors from Granada in 1492 by King Ferdinand, followed by the Duke of Alba's conquest of Navarre, finally brought political unity to Spain. These unconnected, yet highly significant occurrences created two new larger and potentially hostile nations to menace England, posing an almost continual military threat during the ensuing centuries. The map of Europe was in a state of flux – even the Holy Roman Empire, a loose-knit group of states dating back to the Middle Ages and ruled by Emperor Maximilian I, was in relentless decline.

Meanwhile, the Renaissance and the Reformation were sweeping across the whole of continental Europe and a new age of discovery was pushing back the frontiers of the unknown world, pioneered by the epic voyages of that trio of Portuguese explorers, Diaz, Vasco da Gama and Magellan, and the Genoese Christopher Columbus's courageous journey across an uncharted Atlantic Ocean to the fringes of a hitherto unknown continent that later came to be known as the 'New World'. Throughout this time England took virtually no part in these historic activities, but remained isolated on the margins of Europe.

When Elizabeth's father, Henry VIII, inherited the English throne in 1509, he was eighteen years old, a magnificent figure of a man with a magnetic personality. His reign, like many, began amid high expectations, but as Henry began increasingly to treat the kingdom as a personal playground in which to indulge himself, the nation became progressively more isolationist, a minor kingdom on the fringe of Europe. Severing religious ties with the Pope and the Roman Catholic Church was done for personal reasons rather than national or religious motives, resulting in England being out of step and favour with a predominantly Catholic western Europe. His alternating tactics of being either friend or foe to France left that nation bemused and belligerent. Divorcing his first wife, Catherine of Aragon, youngest daughter of King Ferdinand of Spain, did not endear him to a country which had hitherto been a friendly nation. Defeating the Scots at the Battle of Flodden in 1513 achieved little of lasting benefit – Scotland remained a hostile nation in the wild countryside beyond the northern border, continuing to regard England as 'the auld enemy'.

Henry's dissolution of the monasteries, so expertly carried out in 1536 by his chief minister of the time, Thomas Cromwell, was a spectacularly ingenious exercise in asset stripping, popular with the fortunate nobility and gentry who acquired monastic land and property, but doing little in the long term to address the grave underlying financial and economic problems that beset the kingdom. All of these difficulties were to be inherited by Elizabeth on becoming queen. Henry is understandably best remembered for his gargantuan size and his six wives.

Elizabeth was not yet three years old when her father ordered the execution of her mother and barely into her teens when Henry died. At fourteen, she was sexually molested by her new stepfather and by twenty-one, the princess had been imprisoned within the grim fortress of the Tower of London. Not exactly an idyllic, carefree childhood, but an upbringing that was to mould the character of one of the greatest rulers Europe has ever known.

Henry VIII had been bitterly disappointed when he learned that the child born in September 1533 to his second wife, Anne Boleyn, was a girl, particularly having gone through the difficult exercise of divorcing his first wife, Catherine of Aragon, and later being excommunicated by the Pope. It was not long after Elizabeth's birth that Henry's roving eye alighted on the demure, young Jane Seymour, one of the ladies of his Court. The increasingly strident Anne was dispatched to the Tower, accused of adultery with several of Henry's courtiers, and soon lost her head to a swift blow from an executioner's sword which had been brought from France at her own request.

The young Princess Elizabeth then began a nomadic existence, shuttling between a number of houses in the Home Counties including Ashridge, Havering, Eltham and Rickmansworth, interspersed with spasmodic appearances at the Royal Court which she attended along with her half-sister Mary, Catherine of Aragon's only surviving child. Both princesses were present at ceremonies such as the christening of Edward, their new half-brother, son of the short-lived Jane Seymour, Henry's third and much-loved wife who died in childbirth.

Princess Elizabeth had limited direct experience of the Royal Court after the death of Jane Seymour in 1537. Anne of Cleves, Protestant but very plain, became Henry's fourth wife but was quickly replaced by the prettier yet promiscuous Catherine Howard. Both the lively young Catherine and the more stolid Anne behaved kindly to the young Elizabeth. Though Anne could not speak a word of English, she used to take Elizabeth riding in the grounds of

Hampton Court Palace. Elizabeth was eight at the time and loved riding horses; like many children of her age, she was observant and possessed an enquiring mind. She would have noted the happenings around her, particularly her father's procession of wives, events which could have shaped her view on the subject of marriage, which was to become such a vexed question for Elizabeth in the years to come.

Anne was soon to be divorced yet was thankful to remain alive, living on in England in quiet and contented retirement for another seventeen years. Anne of Cleve's demise was, however, to cause the downfall of the devious Thomas Cromwell in 1540, incurring Henry's wrath for arranging such a disastrous marriage. Cromwell was subsequently executed at the Tower of London, a fate previously suffered by Sir Thomas More, another of the king's capable ministers to fall from grace. Catherine Howard followed Elizabeth's own mother, Anne Boleyn, and died on the execution block at Tower Green.

It was not until Henry married Katherine Parr, his sixth and final wife, that Elizabeth began to settle into a more stable existence, albeit for a limited period of time. Katherine brought Elizabeth back to the Court to live with herself and the King until his death at the age of fifty-six in 1547, leaving his only son Edward to inherit the throne at the tender age of nine with his uncle, Edward Seymour, the Duke of Somerset and brother of Jane Seymour, as Regent and Lord Protector. Hitherto Elizabeth had enjoyed a relatively close relationship with her half-brother, but after he became King she saw little of him. A famous portrait of Elizabeth painted around 1546 by William Scrots, an official artist to both Henry VIII and Edward VI, is now part of the Royal Collection and can be seen at Windsor Castle. It depicts Elizabeth in her early teens, demure, pale complexioned with light auburn hair and a thoughtful, wary expression.

Katherine Parr scandalized the Court by remarrying a mere matter of months after the King's death. While she was still only thirty-five, Thomas Seymour was her fourth husband and Edward Seymour's younger brother. Thomas had been Katherine's lover before she was betrothed to Henry and was now Lord High Admiral with ambitions to climb to even greater heights; he was thoroughly unscrupulous in his endless pursuit for power and prestige using whatever means were available to him. Elizabeth lived with Katherine Parr and Thomas Seymour, dividing their time between Katherine's London house by the River Thames at Chelsea and the romantic Sudeley Castle in the Cotswolds, given to Thomas by Edward the boy king when he created him Lord High Admiral and Lord of Sudeley. The castle had been a royal property since Henry

VIII had first come to the throne and the King had visited there briefly in 1535 with Elizabeth's mother Anne Boleyn.

Thomas Seymour might well have married Katherine earlier if he had not been obliged to make way for the ageing Henry. A letter displayed in Katherine's bedroom at Sudeley Castle written to Thomas shortly after becoming Henry's sixth wife states, 'As truly as God is God, my mind was fully bent . . . to marry you before any man I know.'[1] With Henry dead she was now free to marry Seymour.

The Lord High Admiral represented an excellent early example of the type of man that most appealed to Elizabeth: tall, dark, extremely good-looking, aggressively masculine, possessing a commanding manner yet highly amusing and entertaining, qualities which were particularly appealing to an impressionable young princess, barely into her teens yet on the threshold of womanhood. The attraction would appear to have been mutual, as it was not long before Thomas Seymour, still wearing his night-shirt, began to appear suddenly and unexpectedly in Elizabeth's bedroom while she was still in bed, in order to indulge in playful, yet disturbing antics. Elizabeth appeared to quite enjoy being tickled and fondled, chased giggling around the room while uttering delighted shrieks. Katherine would sometimes join in these childish yet sexually suggestive games – on one occasion Katherine held down the struggling princess in the garden while Seymour cut her dress to ribbons with a dagger. These erotic romps only ceased after Katherine discovered her husband with Elizabeth clasped in his arms in a passionate embrace.

In September 1548, Katherine Parr died in childbirth at the age of thirty-six, barely eighteen months after Henry VIII's death. She was buried within the chapel at Sudeley Castle in spite of the King's dying wish that she should be laid alongside him at Windsor. It was not long before the irrepressible Thomas Seymour began pestering the Princess Elizabeth with proposals of marriage.

None of these activities involving Elizabeth and Seymour were mere Court gossip, for their relationship was publicly exposed when Seymour was subsequently tried on thirty-three counts of treason against the realm and later executed on Tower Hill; his elder brother Edward, the Lord Protector signed the death warrant. Elizabeth suddenly found herself subject to severe questioning from Sir Robert Tyrwhitt, the Privy Council's Special Commissioner, while Kat Ashley, Elizabeth's loyal yet indiscreet governess, revealed all under interrogation, in between complaining bitterly about the uncomfortable conditions of her prison cell. This situation was highly embarrassing for Princess Elizabeth and made a profound impression on her, considerably influencing her relationships with the opposite sex in the years to follow.

During this particularly bloodthirsty period, Lord Protector Somerset was deposed by John Dudley, the Duke of Northumberland, and beheaded. The Duke succeeded Somerset as Lord Protector but in turn met his executioner on Tower Hill, having foolishly proclaimed the tragically manipulated Lady Jane Grey as queen after Edward VI had died in 1553. Northumberland's foolhardy actions involving his young niece represented a desperate attempt to maintain England as a Protestant kingdom, but they were regarded as a revolutionary act, attracted little public support, and were quickly suppressed. Northumberland's young son Robert Dudley was also involved in his father's abortive attempts to elevate Lady Jane and, while escaping a similar fate to his father, he was imprisoned in the Tower before going into temporary exile in France. Dudley was destined to become one of the greatest figures of the Elizabethan era.

Elizabeth watched these dramatic events from the safety of Hatfield, wisely distancing herself from a course of action that was unlikely to succeed and in any case would have no material advantage for her. Amid the confusion of this extraordinary power struggle, Mary did exceptionally well to rally sufficient support from the Court and her citizens to successfully claim the throne. Posterity tends to overlook this achievement, preferring to concentrate on the plight of the teenage Lady Jane Grey and her short-lived husband Lord Guildford Dudley, the Duke of Northumberland's son, who was executed at the same time as Lady Jane, there being less than a year between altar and scaffold.

Edward VI had been a sickly child since birth and never seemed destined to occupy the throne for very long. His portrait, painted in 1546 and attributed to William Scrots, shows a slight, thin-faced figure with a wan complexion. He died at the age of fifteen, very probably of tuberculosis, in the summer of 1553, to be succeeded by Mary, half-sister to Edward and Elizabeth. Mary was as fervently Catholic as Edward had been Protestant and was eager to restore the 'True Faith' to her newly acquired kingdom. Initially, the relationship between the two half-sisters appeared reasonably amicable as Elizabeth rode in procession behind the new Queen to attend her coronation ceremony at Westminster Abbey. That autumn, however, Mary decided to marry Philip of Spain against the advice of her Council, causing a wave of discontent across the country which culminated in an uprising in Kent led by a local squire named Sir Thomas Wyatt. While this revolt was quickly suppressed, it was discovered that letters had been sent by Wyatt to

Princess Elizabeth, creating the suspicion that she was implicated in the plot against Mary together with Edward Courtenay, the handsome young Earl of Devon. At once, Elizabeth dispatched a highly emotional letter to the queen appealing to her better nature and pleading her innocence: 'I protest before God that I never practised, counselled, nor consented to anything prejudicial to you or dangerous to the state. Let me answer before I go to The Tower if not before I am further condemned.'[2] Her frantic plea fell on deaf ears and it was not long before a near-paranoid Queen Mary, heavily influenced by Simon Renard, the Spanish ambassador who saw an anti-Catholic conspiracy around every corner, ordered her half-sister to be taken to the Tower. Elizabeth was in grave danger.

The princess was conducted to the Tower from Whitehall Palace by barge down the River Thames, on 18 March 1554, Palm Sunday. It was a dark and dismal day, pouring with rain, the sky grey and heavily overcast. Elizabeth was escorted on the journey by two of Mary's Privy Councillors, the Marquess of Winchester and the Earl of Sussex, two astute peers who, with an eye to the possible future, were determined to treat the princess with scrupulous politeness, an action which proved highly beneficial, as both were to subsequently serve on Elizabeth's Privy Council when she became queen, while Sussex was later appointed to the significant post of Lord Chamberlain.

Negotiating the swirling tide under London Bridge with some considerable difficulty, they arrived at the Tower and entered the sombre fortress through the watergate below St Thomas's Tower, an entrance now known as Traitor's Gate, under whose wide arch had passed an ever-increasing number of state prisoners, many of whom never saw freedom again. Lady Jane Grey, granddaughter of Henry VIII's sister Mary, the tragic 'Ten Day Queen', had been executed on Tower Green only a fortnight earlier, in the same place as Elizabeth's mother Anne Boleyn and stepmother Catherine Howard had perished on the block. Elizabeth had known Lady Jane when both had been in Katherine Parr's care and the two girls had spent many happy childhood days together both at Chelsea and Sudeley Castle. Jane was another innocent young girl whose life had been imperilled when caught up in the dangerous plotting of ambitious older men. Now she had been beheaded and if the Spanish ambassador had his way, Elizabeth would surely follow. Never had she felt so utterly helpless, so alone or so vulnerable.

A huge phalanx of heavily armed guards towered above her on the quay, impassive yet acutely menacing to the frightened young princess. For a moment, Elizabeth's resolve deserted her. She stepped slowly out of the barge then sank down onto the wet flagstones and refused to go any further. When the kindly Lieutenant of the Tower, Sir John Brydges, tactfully suggested that she would benefit from coming in out of the rain, Elizabeth tersely rebuked him that she was better off remaining where she was. Mary was to give Sudeley Castle to Sir John Brydges, making him Lord Chandos. Elizabeth later made his son Edmund a Knight of the Garter. In turn Sir John's grandson Giles entertained the Queen at Sudeley: in 1592 to celebrate the anniversary of the Armada's defeat, a joyous feast and pageant was held in Elizabeth's honour that lasted three whole days.

The impasse outside the Tower was conveniently overcome when one of Elizabeth's manservants suddenly began to weep uncontrollably. Without losing face, Elizabeth was able to rise to her feet, loudly declare that as she was totally innocent, no man need shed tears on her behalf, then stride haughtily into the Tower, every inch a princess, albeit one in great peril. 'Let us take heed my Lords, that we go not beyond our commission for she was our King's daughter. Let us use such dealings that we may answer it thereafter, if it shall so happen for just dealing is always answerable,'[3] the ever-cautious Earl of Sussex warned his companions as burly guards marched Elizabeth towards the Bell Tower, close to the Lieutenant's lodgings and where Sir Thomas More had previously been imprisoned. Sir John Brydges followed the Earl's advice and treated Elizabeth well – she was able to dine in his lodgings and take exercise in the fresh air by walking under close escort along part of the battlements known today as Queen Elizabeth Walk. Sir Thomas Wyatt was also imprisoned in the Tower at the same time in much less salubrious surroundings, while undergoing torture in an attempt to make him confess that Princess Elizabeth had been involved in his plot to overthrow the Queen:

> We have this morning prevailed with Sir Thomas Wyatt touching Princess Elizabeth and her servant Sir William St Loe. Wyatt confirms his former sayings and says Sir James Croft knows more, Croft has been examined and confesses with Wyatt, charging St Loe with the same. Examine St Loe or send him to be examined by us. Croft will tell all. Sir John Bourne. Sir John Brydges.[4]

Thus runs a laconic report with sinister undertones recounting proceedings at the Tower while the hapless Wyatt was under interrogation. Sir James Croft was a country squire, thought to be one of the conspirators, but in fact was in Wales at the time of the uprising and so took no part in it. Arrested and brought back to

London under guard, he survived close questioning, revealing nothing that implicated either himself or the princess. Likewise, Elizabeth's servant St Loe, who was suspected of being an intermediary between Elizabeth and Wyatt, resisted all attempts to say anything which might incriminate her in any way.

Meanwhile, Elizabeth was closely interrogated by Stephen Gardiner, the stern-faced Bishop of Winchester, together with other Privy Councillors. She rebuffed all their efforts to make her confess and her inquisitors were unable to make any headway in establishing her guilt. Within Mary's Privy Council, Elizabeth had a powerful and sympathetic advocate pleading her case, her great-uncle Lord Admiral William Howard. Her case was further strengthened when Sir Thomas Wyatt made an impassioned speech prior to his execution on Tower Hill, exonerating the princess from any knowledge of his abortive uprising. Elizabeth's robust conduct throughout her ordeal displayed all the character of a future queen.

Whether or not Elizabeth really knew anything of significance about Wyatt's plans remains a matter of speculation; suffice to say that it would have been out of character for Elizabeth to conspire to replace the legitimate sovereign of the nation, particularly a plot organized by a person of Wyatt's lowly social standing. However, these events were pivotal to her conduct in later life, an important process in the shaping of the future Queen of England.

Sir James Croft and Sir William St Loe both survived their ordeal to take up important positions in the royal household when Elizabeth became Queen. She invariably rewarded those who had shown loyalty to her during her formative years, particularly in such desperate circumstances as her incarceration in the Tower. Sir James Croft was made Captain of Berwick, the key frontier town on the border with Scotland and later promoted to the Court post of Comptroller of the Household. He remained with Elizabeth for many years and in 1588 he was one of her negotiators with the Duke of Parma in the Netherlands, vainly trying to avert war with Spain. Sir James Croft, however, was always considered pro-Spanish and was even suspected of being an informer. Sir William St Loe was subsequently given the highly prestigious position of Captain of the Queen's Guard and later became the third husband of the formidable 'Bess of Hardwick', the builder of Hardwick Hall, one of the greatest of all Elizabethan houses situated just north of Derby.

Lord William Howard's support during her hour of need was rewarded by Elizabeth – she retained him as a Privy Councillor when she acquired the throne, while his son Charles was subsequently given command of the English Fleet against the Spanish Armada and later became the 1st Earl of Nottingham, one of relatively few peers which the Queen created throughout her reign. Edward Courtenay had also been confined in the Tower at the same time as Elizabeth. He was released in 1555 and went into exile on the continent but died in Italy the following year.

After a couple of very anxious months confined within the Tower, Elizabeth was taken to Woodstock in Oxfordshire to reside in a small house belonging to Queen Mary which stood in grounds now occupied by Blenheim Palace. Here Elizabeth found herself in the strict custody of the highly conscientious Sir Henry Bedingfield, a hitherto obscure country squire who was to take his duties so seriously that he would follow the princess around everywhere like a persistent guard dog. While this drove Elizabeth to distraction it was infinitely preferable to life in the Tower. The princess subsequently bore Sir Henry no malice whatsoever, for when he appeared at Court after she became Queen she would jokingly greet him as 'my gaoler', teasing him that if she ever had an important prisoner who needed close observation then she would know where to come!

After nearly a year in confinement at Woodstock, Sir Henry was commanded by Queen Mary to bring Princess Elizabeth to Hampton Court. Elizabeth's audience with the Queen was considerably delayed in the wishful hope that the princess might find the suspense unbearable and confess all. When summoned after several weeks of waiting, Elizabeth knelt meekly before the still suspicious Mary and was able to achieve an uneasy reconciliation in spite of giving no confession or even the vestige of an apology. This was a vital and anxious moment for Elizabeth and one she needed to handle extremely carefully to avoid being returned to the Tower, but finally Elizabeth was permitted to return to Hatfield where she spent the last three years of Mary's reign. While further plots against Queen Mary were frequently mounted, they always failed and numerous heretics were burnt at the stake at Smithfield in London, Oxford and elsewhere. Among those to perish amid the flames at Oxford in 1555 were the two ultra-Protestant Bishops Latimer and Ridley, to be followed the subsequent year by the aged and very frail Archbishop Thomas Cranmer, who had been godfather at Elizabeth's christening at Greenwich more than twenty years earlier and had survived the turbulent reigns of both Henry VIII and Edward VI.

'Be of good comfort Master Ridley, and play the man,' cried Latimer as the flames began to engulf him, 'we shall this day light such a candle by God's grace in England, as I trust shall never be put out.'[5] Bishop Latimer's death was mercifully quick but Ridley's suffering proved long and agonizing. Both the elderly Nicholas Ridley, formerly Bishop of London, and Hugh Latimer, whose bishopric had been Worcester, were tried for heresy after publicly preaching against Catholicism. Ridley had denounced both Mary and Elizabeth as bastards before a congregation which included the Mayor of London.

Thomas Cranmer had been Henry VIII's Archbishop of Canterbury and embodied that bewildering blend of idealist and opportunist so often prevalent in the Tudor era. He had originally ingratiated himself with Henry, when, as an unknown lecturer in divinity at Cambridge and friend of the Boleyn family, he had come up with the ingenious idea of submitting the King's claim for divorce from Queen Catherine to the major European universities. When the majority of these august seats of learning surprisingly told Henry exactly what he wanted to hear, the delighted King appointed the young Cranmer first as ambassador to the Holy Roman Empire and shortly afterwards Archbishop of Canterbury. He had been married twice, and since marriage of the clergy was illegal in England at that time, Cranmer's second marriage had to be kept well hidden – it was even rumoured that when the archbishop was on the move his wife accompanied him as part of the luggage in a large trunk![6] It was Cranmer who pronounced Henry's marriage with Queen Catherine null and void, supported the break from Rome and the king's desire to make Elizabeth rather than Mary his legitimate heir. Not surprisingly, when Mary became queen, Cranmer's days were numbered, particularly as he had introduced the Book of Common Prayer in English among a welter of Protestant reforms during the short but eventful reign of Elizabeth's half-brother Edward VI.

By the time Mary came to the throne, Cranmer was an old man, white-haired and bearded. The Protestant flame within him seemingly dimmed, he initially recanted and declared all other Protestants should renounce their faith and revert to Catholicism. However, Cranmer recovered his courage to preach a final sermon at St Mary's, Oxford, which bravely denounced the Pope as the enemy of Christ. When the time came for him to die, he stumbled to the stake and thrust the hand that had signed his recantation into the fire so that it burnt first.

Cranmer had been Elizabeth's godfather and chaplain to her mother Anne Boleyn. Had it not been for his death at the hands of Queen Mary, he could well have lived to be Elizabeth's first Archbishop of Canterbury. However, the princess was in a precarious position herself at the time and unable to help him in any way. Cranmer lived on in the hearts and minds of the Elizabethan age as a man of almost saint-like qualities, a man to inspire Elizabeth's successful efforts in the lasting establishment of the Church of England, one of the major achievements of her reign and something of which Cranmer would have whole-heartedly approved had he lived to witness it.

The barbaric deaths of prominent clergy such as Cramner, Latimer and Ridley together with some three hundred other Protestant martyrs during Mary's reign of terror ensured the hatred of Catholicism in England that was to follow, with unfortunate consequences for Catholic citizens who were loyal to their country, regardless of their faith. Mary unwittingly created a public perception in England that identified Roman Catholicism with foreign interference, ruthless persecution and traitorous practice. It was an image that was to haunt English Catholics for centuries to come.

Public burnings would rightly be condemned as appalling atrocities in today's society. In the context of a far more brutal sixteenth century, they were regarded as a fitting penalty for the crime of heresy and a large number of Catholics were burnt at the stake during the second half of that century when the Protestants were once more in the ascendancy. So-called 'Merrie England' had its dark side: other forms of execution included the horrific sentence of being 'hung, drawn and quartered', and the severed heads perpetually displayed on London Bridge were a gruesome reminder of a less compassionate age.

Queen Mary must surely go down in history as one of the saddest queens, suffering humiliation and deprivation during her childhood just like Elizabeth, but without any of the subsequent glory. She saw her mother, Catherine of Aragon, callously cast aside for Elizabeth's mother, the younger Anne Boleyn, while Mary was declared a bastard and no longer welcomed at Court. She and her mother were banished from the royal palaces and separated; they never saw each other again and were forced to live in much humbler circumstances in the country. Mary was sixteen years old at this time and therefore much more aware of events around her than Elizabeth, who had been a baby when Henry tired of Anne Boleyn. Catherine died of cancer at the age of fifty, her chaplain and Mary's tutor were both burnt at the stake and Mary's best friend, the Countess of Salisbury, was also executed, leaving Mary to an even lonelier existence.

By the time Mary acquired the throne in 1553, she was nearly thirty-eight, ten years older than Philip of Spain whom she chose to marry shortly after becoming queen, thereby making herself deeply unpopular with her subjects, many of whom were highly suspicious of both Catholics and foreigners. Philip later became King of Spain and Elizabeth's greatest foe.

A portrait of Mary by the Flemish artist Antonio Mor, possibly painted to enable Philip to preview his prospective bride, depicts a woman of no great beauty with a short-sighted stare and a faintly disgruntled expression, the mouth small and thin-lipped. Mor was known for his realistic likenesses, an artistic quality not to be appreciated by Elizabeth following her succession. A portrait of Mary by Hans Eworth, Mary's official court painter, which can now be seen in the National Portrait Gallery, conveys a similar image. In reality, England's last Catholic queen was short and to Spanish eyes, rather dowdy. She had a disconcertingly masculine voice, low-pitched and rather hoarse. Hardly surprisingly, it was not long before Philip left England never to return. The only man in the whole of her life who meant anything to Mary had quickly deserted her. Abandoned by both her husband and the people of her realm, Mary was to die at the age of forty-two from the same disease that had killed her mother. Having waited many years to ascend the throne, she achieved little of note during her short reign apart from acquiring the nickname 'Bloody Mary', the term by which posterity most remembers her.

The reigns of both Edward and Mary were a disastrous period for England, eleven years of further rapid decline in the nation's financial fortunes, leaving the treasury severely depleted and the country plunged deeply in debt. The windfall provided by the dissolution of the monasteries had long since disappeared through economic mismanagement, necessitating heavy borrowing at prohibitively high interest rates on the Antwerp money market. It was written of Edward's days on the throne: 'The misery of the people and the moral and social anarchy by which the nation was disintegrated . . . the government was corrupt, the courts of law were venal. The trading classes cared only to get rich. The multitude were mutinous from oppression.' Circumstances were not to improve appreciably in Mary's time.

In the meantime, Spain was reaping huge financial benefits from the exploits of the conquistadors in the New World. Colonizers such as Cortés and Pizarro had subdued the Inca and Aztec Empires in Central and Southern America and discovered untold riches. This resulted in vast amounts of gold and silver being shipped across the Atlantic by Spanish galleons, enabling Spain to appear at face value, the wealthiest and most powerful country in the whole of western Europe. England had achieved nothing remotely similar and had to exist within its own meagre internal resources.

Meanwhile, France was enjoying a period of unparalleled peace and prosperity following the end of the Hundred Years War and had enthusiastically embraced the full flowering of the Renaissance. Nowhere was this better reflected than in the magnificent châteaux that were appearing along the length of the Loire Valley in the first half of the sixteenth century. Masterpieces were constructed such as Chambord and Amboise where King François I of France had employed Leonardo da Vinci as his architect, Blois where he was married and Chenonceaux, which was given by Henry II of France, the son of François I, to his mistress Diane de Poitiers, only to be recovered by Henry's wife, the all-powerful matriarch Catherine de Medici, when Henry was killed in a jousting tournament in 1559, the year after Elizabeth had inherited the English throne from Mary. Catherine then became Regent of France and was destined to have considerable diplomatic dealings with Elizabeth.

No equivalent architecture appeared in England during this glorious period of creativity across the Channel. Thus England was outstripped both economically and culturally by its principal western European rivals and was in grave danger of becoming an irrelevant backwater, an offshore island of no great consequence to its richer and more sophisticated neighbours in continental Europe.

England had become a sad and bewildered nation, its citizens frightened and confused, ruled by Mary, an embittered and discontented monarch whose husband, having grown quickly disenchanted with her, left England and went first to the Netherlands and then returned to Spain. The Netherlands had become a Spanish possession when Philip's father, Charles V, decided to retire to a monastery in 1556 and abdicated in favour of his son. Charles was an expert linguist, reputed to speak to God in Spanish, to women in Italian, converse with men in French while addressing his horse in German.

Mary imagined herself to be pregnant, but her hopes proved groundless; in reality she had a tumour from which she eventually died. She suffered another devastating setback when Calais, the last fragment of a once extensive English Empire in France that had stretched from the Channel to the Pyrenees, surrendered to French troops in January 1558. The town had been an English possession for many centuries and its loss represented yet another major blow to England's dwindling international reputation. It seemed that Mary could do no right. She had lost her husband and her people's affection, she had forfeited the nation's pride and was losing the will to live.

All this time, Elizabeth watched and waited, careful to do nothing provocative yet remaining attentive to anything of material significance. It was during this long period of waiting at Hatfield that Elizabeth had first become acquainted with William Cecil, the man who was later to become her Chief Minister. She had learned the importance of maintaining control of herself and all of those around her and to trust only in her own judgement. In the future she was determined that nobody should control her in any way, even if this meant sacrificing her own personal happiness.

Cecil had become her land surveyor after Elizabeth inherited Hatfield, a royal residence she had lived in intermittently since early childhood. William Cecil was an extremely hard-working and conscientious individual, qualities which greatly appealed to the young Elizabeth and thus a long and fruitful relationship began.

Throughout the summer and autumn of 1558, Queen Mary's life remorselessly ebbed away. Both the Queen and her Court recognized this fact and Mary was reluctantly persuaded by her Privy Council to confirm Elizabeth as the legitimate successor to the throne. Mary died in the early hours of 17 November 1558. Sir Nicholas Throckmorton, later to be Elizabeth's ambassador in Paris, rode out to Hatfield, carrying with him the Queen's wedding ring as proof of her death. A number of courtiers had already galloped ahead and it is said that in spite of the winter's cold, they discovered Elizabeth in the garden seated under an oak tree quietly contemplating the Bible. Upon hearing the joyful news she fell to her knees and after a considerable pause was heard to murmur in Latin the words of the twentieth-third verse of the 118th Psalm, 'This is the Lord's doing: and it is marvellous in our eyes.'[7]

Elizabeth had trodden a perilous path to the throne, during which time she avoided numerous fatal pitfalls. These had been formative years, that were to prove highly beneficial in later life, for although Elizabeth had acquired no proper training in the art of ruling a kingdom, she had received an excellent formal education from William Grindal and Roger Ascham, two of the foremost scholars in the kingdom. Her intense experiences of life had taught her valuable lessons, given her a penetrating insight into human nature and prepared her for the loneliness and isolation that invariably accompanies supreme power. These factors were to stand her in good stead during the long and arduous reign ahead. Elizabeth was to rule significantly longer than her father and nearly twenty years more than her grandfather. Indeed, between William the Conqueror and Elizabeth I, only two monarchs had ruled England for a greater length of time.

Elizabeth displayed a number of natural attributes which were hugely beneficial to a successful ruler: an obvious regal presence, boundless energy, great intelligence, a fund of common sense and most important of all, the ability to capture her subjects' loyalty and then retain it. She had an instinctive grasp of how to rule a kingdom and motivate its subjects to best effect. This was just as well: England was in desperate need of a charismatic ruler to repair its fortunes and its shattered prestige. The nation floundered in the reign of her father and had sunk into gloomy mediocrity during those of her half-brother and sister. The glory days lay ahead.

2

AT THE ROYAL COURT

The centre of power and prestige in Elizabeth's kingdom continued to be the Royal Court, for while Parliament was becoming progressively more important than it had been in the Middle Ages, it was still those immediately around the monarch who set the political agenda and put it into practice. Thus any ambitious man seeking power and affluence came to Court in order to ingratiate himself with Elizabeth and those within her immediate circle who could be most beneficial to him in the pursuit and fulfilment of his desires. The perceptive young Queen was quick to appreciate the situation and fully exploit it for her own ends: 'The Queene did fishe for men's souls, and had so sweet a baite, that no one coude escape hir network.'[1]

The upward climb to fame and fortune could often prove to be a long one: even when fortunate enough to catch the monarch's eye, the expectant courtier could well wait many years before his high hopes were fulfilled. Sometimes this never happened or the rewards proved insignificant in relation to the service rendered. Sir Henry Sidney, owner of Penshurst Place in Kent, was one of the Queen's most faithful courtiers with over twenty years' service in Ireland, first as Vice-Treasurer of the Irish Council, then as Lord Deputy of Ireland. Throughout that time Sir Henry had received little royal recognition for his efforts apart from being made a Knight of the Garter in 1564. By 1583 he was more than £5,000 in debt and complained that he possessed 'not so much land as would graze a mutton'.[2] Sir Henry even had to turn down the opportunity of becoming a lord as he felt unable to support the expense that this rank would entail. Sir Henry's plight was a typical example of the manipulative Queen taking much and giving little, one of her most regrettable characteristics. Henry's first child was Philip Sidney. Born in 1554, he was destined to become one of the most charismatic members of the Royal Court, slender and red-haired just like the Queen and with the same fiery temper. Scholar, poet and soldier, he was doomed to die young when killed in the wars in Flanders fighting the Spanish. Ironically, Sidney's godfather was the King of Spain and thus he had been christened Philip.

The Queen loved men of wit, charming, attentive, crowding around her to amuse, to entertain, to provide a welcome distraction from the often all-too-tedious affairs of state – men such as Lord Robert Dudley, Master of the Queen's Horse, who later became the Earl of Leicester, Sir Christopher Hatton, Sir Walter Ralegh, young Edward de Vere, the 17th Earl of Oxford, and towards the end of her reign, Dudley's stepson Robert Devereux, the 2nd Earl of Essex. All of these men were cast in the same mould, tall, dark and handsome, all jostling for her attentions and favours, a place in the royal sun. 'When she smiled, it was a pure sunshine, that everyone did chose to bask in if they could',[3] noted Sir John Harington, a brilliantly witty, long-serving courtier and the Queen's godson. Yet Elizabeth's mood swings could be swift and notoriously unpredictable: 'but anon came a storm from a sudden gathering of clouds and the thunder fell in wondrous manner on all alike', wrote the same courtier. It was on these occasions that even the most eminent or well-regarded courtier could be publicly humiliated by the Queen, having their ears boxed like William Killigrew, her Groom of the Chamber, a fate that was also suffered by Essex. Others like Francis Walsingham had shoes thrown at them or were dismissed from her presence amid a barrage of oaths – there was never a dull moment at the Royal Court.

Elizabeth had inherited her father's commanding presence, his red hair and devastating temper. She used this last characteristic as an effective instrument of her authority. As a child she had seen how her father's outbursts could make strong men weep and she astutely realized that the risk of incurring the royal wrath, along with the distinct possibility of a speedy one-way ride to the Tower, could provide her with an effective control mechanism in the predominately male world she ruled. Though they were among her major royal favourites, Sir Walter Ralegh and the Earl of Essex were consigned to the Tower by an angry Queen. Essex never came out alive. Nevertheless, being a courtier in the reign of Elizabeth I endangered one's health far less than it had done when her father was on the throne. 'In King Henry the Eighth's time his doings for sure would have cost him his pate,'[4] remarked Dudley of Sir John Norris after one of their many disagreements – Queen Elizabeth invariably agonized long and hard before signing a courtier's death warrant.

The life of an Elizabethan courtier was an expensive business, even long-time royal favourites, such as Dudley and Hatton, were destined to die heavily in debt. Keeping up royal appearances inevitably proved to be a costly affair, as even those of minor rank needed to spend considerable amounts of money on themselves, particularly their clothing. The aspiring young courtier, eager to make an impression, could run up excessive bills with the tailor as well as those who fashioned the elaborate hats and intricate handmade boots that were so *de rigueur* at the Royal Court. It was an age of opulence and conspicuous consumption, one in which style was considerably more important than substance; indeed, so extravagant were the outfits on parade in the Court that visitors from the country sometimes found it difficult to distinguish between the sexes. Not that Elizabeth's Court ever became so outrageous as its counterpart across the Channel, where Prince Henry, Duke of Anjou, who later inherited the French throne, was accustomed to wafting about the French Court amid clouds of perfume, attired as a woman in low-cut dresses.

Vying for attention and possible advancement in Elizabeth's Court was a highly competitive affair – even the most expensive attire could suddenly become outmoded as the latest fashion swept in from continental Europe. A young Elizabethan courtier also needed to expend considerable sums of money in order to bribe court officials to gain entry into the exclusive circle of those who might be useful to him, and for gifts once he had successfully gained access to that inner sanctum.

Those who had achieved success found that the expense increased further, particularly if required to entertain the Queen at their home, a prestigious yet hugely costly affair, which at best could prove daunting, and at worst lead to bankruptcy, depending on the length of time Elizabeth chose to stay, or the size of the retinue which came in her wake and also expected to be royally entertained.

Elizabeth could prove markedly reluctant in granting honours or favours, even to those members of her Court who had provided outstanding service. Compared with other Tudor and Stuart monarchs, she granted remarkably few new peerages, less than a dozen throughout her entire reign, while at the same time she was both chary and capricious in handing out financial rewards, such as a share in custom dues, or a control over one of the numerous trade monopolies that proliferated during Tudor times. Sir Walter Ralegh began to prosper when the Queen rewarded him with the 'Farm of Wines', a device whereby every wine merchant in the country was obliged to pay Sir Walter one pound in return for an annual retail licence.

It was tacitly understood that a person was fully entitled to make as much as he could out of any particular government office which he had been granted – thus Sir William Cecil, Elizabeth's long-time Privy Councillor, was to benefit considerably out of the lucrative post of Master of the Wards, which the Queen had awarded him as a mark of her favour in 1561. The word 'sleaze' may have been unheard of in the Royal Court at that time, yet the practice was widespread. Conversely, other highly capable men such as Sir Francis Walsingham, the Queen's Secretary of State for many years, was never lucky enough to attract such favourable largesse and destined to die extremely poor. It could prove to be a thankless task even after becoming a highly successful member of the Court. Furthermore, what the monarch had given could just as easily be taken away: the Earl of Essex faced financial ruin when, as a result of falling out of royal favour, his right to collect import duty on sweet wines was not renewed.

The English Royal Court was traditionally divided into the Household, under the Lord Steward, this being the Hall and all the service areas, then the Chamber under the Lord Chamberlain, which included the Chapel Royal, Guard Chamber, and all the remaining areas of the Court that were open to the public. Finally, the monarch's private quarters were the domain of the intriguingly named Groom of the Stool. Henry Norris had been Henry VIII's Groom of the Stool and was executed after being accused of making love to Anne Boleyn, Elizabeth's mother. Under these august senior courtiers came an army of retainers: Yeomen of the Guard, Gentlemen Pensioners, carvers, cup bearers, ushers and grooms, right down to the humble, yet highly necessary, royal rat catcher, who, because of the constant risk of bubonic plague, had a vital full-time task to perform. The majority of these Court retainers were paid for their services and could expect to be fed and housed, even the most minor member of the Court. Another category of keen enthusiastic young men were the Esquires of the Body Extraordinary, unemployed and unpaid, invariably from a good family, in receipt of a good education, ceaselessly roaming the Court like so many well-bred marauding sharks, constantly seeking to be noticed and given a full-time position. In the meantime they ran errands, escorted visitors around the Court and generally helped with official Court correspondence. The most important rule for all courtiers to observe, from the most eminent Privy Councillor downwards, was to engage in the rather farcical game of appearing to be hopelessly in love with their highly desirable but unobtainable sovereign, something that was to become progressively more ridiculous as Elizabeth aged.

The fast track to success at the Royal Court could be considerably enhanced by patronage, the result of attaching oneself to a far larger fish in the golden pond. Ralegh had arrived at Court as an unknown soldier fresh from the Irish wars and had been fortunate enough to find favour with Sir Robert Dudley, by then the Earl of Leicester, an ageing yet still highly influential royal favourite. 'Leicester had then cast in a good word for him to the Queene, which would have done him no harme'.[5] wryly noted a contemporary historian. A more romantic account of how Ralegh came to the Queen's attention first came to light some forty years after his death:

> This Captain Ralegh coming out of Ireland to the English Court in good habit . . . found the Queen walking, till, meeting with a plashy place, she seemed to scruple going thereon, presently Ralegh cast and spread his new plush cloak on the ground. Whereon the Queen trod gently, rewarding him afterwards with many suits.[6]

Well, it makes a good tale.

Francis Walsingham's political ambitions were greatly assisted by Sir William Cecil, later Lord Burghley, who in turn ensured the rise and rise of his son Robert Cecil. Nepotism and favouritism were both familiar and acceptable in the Royal Court, representing a comfortable tradition practised by everyone from Elizabeth downwards, in which sons followed fathers down the corridors of power, while friends provided favours amid a warm glow of wealth and happiness for the privileged few in the inner circle of power and affluence.

Favouritism could in turn incur criticism and outright jealousy in the highly competitive Royal Court, where one man's advancement could be another one's impediment. The Queen's obvious enthusiasm for Ralegh was a case in point. 'He had gotten the Queene's eare in a thrice . . . which nettled them all',[7] wrote a contemporary historian, while one of Ralegh's own poems declared, 'for those reapes renown above the rest with heapes of hate shall surely be opprest'.

This incestuous trend of patronage bred and multiplied in the hothouse atmosphere of the Court, particularly as the Queen's reign lengthened and she became progressively more conservative in her appointments to high office and at the same time less conscious and critical of promotions made by her senior courtiers. As the Queen grew older and the key members of her Council aged with her, fewer fresh faces came on the scene to revitalize a by now jaded Court. Younger courtiers grew frustrated as they found themselves marginalized and their views ignored. This potentially explosive situation led ultimately to the Earl of Essex's ill-conceived coup in the twilight years of the last of the Tudors. Nevertheless, this Elizabethan system of promotion through patronage had hitherto worked extremely well amid a heady climate of opportunism, greed and the fear of failure.

Traditionally, the English Royal Court had been wholly male-dominated, but the arrival of a female monarch in 1553, when Mary succeeded to the throne, had led to some very significant changes in the way it was run. Some of the most important functions of the household hitherto carried out by men came to be undertaken by women. Elizabeth was therefore fortunate that when she became queen she was able to inherit arrangements within the sovereign's private quarters that were very different to those which had operated in her father's day. Henry VIII's entourage had included eighteen Gentlemen of the Privy Chamber and six grooms. By Elizabeth's time this had changed dramatically. The Queen only appointed two Gentlemen of the Chamber throughout her entire reign, one of these being the handsome young Thomas Heneage, whom the Queen would flirt with outrageously in order to make Robert Dudley jealous. Heneage was later knighted and went on to become Treasurer of the Chamber and then Vice-Chamberlain and finally a Privy Councillor in the final years of Elizabeth's reign.

The large number of Gentlemen of the Privy Chamber were replaced by four Ladies of the Bedchamber, eight Gentlewomen of the Privy Chamber and some half-dozen Maids of Honour. While the majority of these received their board and lodgings, not all of them were paid. A number of these posts were honorary and usually occupied by the wives or sisters of the members of Elizabeth's Privy Council or those holding other important positions in the Court. Some were members of the nobility such as Margaret, Lady Howard of Effingham, wife of the Queen's Lord High Admiral, and Mary, Lady Sidney, sister of Robert Dudley. Lady Frances Cobham, wife of Lord Henry Cobham, Lord Warden of the Cinque Ports, complained constantly of the amount of time she was separated from her husband, but nevertheless still managed to give him six children.

The Maids of Honour were enticed into royal service by the delicious prospect of meeting and marrying a rich and famous member of the Court; however, husband-hunting could prove to be a perilous course of action unless conducted with the utmost discretion. These nubile young ladies were considered fair game for a temporary fling by any hot-blooded male of the Court, while Elizabeth was very possessive of her lady attendants and envious of sexual pursuits that she had denied herself. Thus, Beth Throckmorton, the homely-looking daughter of Sir Nicholas Throckmorton, was permanently banished from Court after being discovered conducting a clandestine affair with Sir Walter Ralegh, even though she later became his wife. Lady Mary Fitton, a luscious brunette thought by some to be Shakespeare's 'Dark Lady of the Sonnets', fell into disgrace after being made pregnant by the new Earl of Pembroke, the Queen's godson. In this particular instance, noblesse declined to oblige and make an honest woman of her, so the unhappy Lady Mary, still heavily pregnant, was sent back to Cheshire from where she had originally come to Court with such high hopes. Lady Mary Grey, sister of the ill-fated Lady Jane, had been appointed one of Elizabeth's Maids of Honour but had the temerity to marry Thomas Keys, the Queen's portly Sergeant Porter, without royal permission. The angry Queen consigned Keys to prison and the distraught Mary was destined never to see her husband again. Nevertheless, she was more fortunate than Anne Vavasour, the luckless Maid of Honour who became pregnant by the lusty young Earl of Oxford. She was sent to the Tower. In many respects, the term 'Maid of Honour' in Elizabeth's Court seems to have been somewhat of a misnomer.

In the earlier days of the male-dominated royal private quarters, the Groom of the Stool was in charge of the bedchamber. This function was now fulfilled by the Chief Gentlewoman of the Privy Chamber. The first person to hold this position after Elizabeth became Queen was her long-time servant Kat Ashley. When she died in 1565, her replacement was Elizabeth's long-serving Welsh attendant, Blanche Parry. Blanche's tomb in St Margaret's, Westminster, carries the inscription 'Chief Gentlewoman of Queen Elizabeth's most honourable Privy Chamber and Keeper of Her Majesty's jewels'.

The other key position in the Privy Chamber was that of Mistress of the Robes, a post that was normally filled by a person of noble rank, such as Lady Frances Cobham who was responsible for all items of clothing within the Privy Chamber. The Queen was a dedicated follower of fashion, and her wardrobe grew continually throughout her reign, bulging with increasingly more exotic outfits that were said to total several thousand in number towards the end of her reign.

A female monarch in command of the Court, destined never to bring a royal husband into the household, resulted in the King's side of the Court being scaled back to purely ceremonial status; the important administrative and financial function which it previously fulfilled passed into the hands of the ever more powerful Sir William Cecil, Elizabeth's Principal Secretary and later her Chief Treasurer. While there was a male monarch on the throne, the Privy Chamber had competed with the Council in an endless power struggle, which saw fortunes fluctuate according to the strength of the individuals involved in either Council or Chamber. However, in Mary and

Elizabeth's reigns a predominantly female Chamber ensured that the Council found themselves now in total control. While a degree of 'petticoat power' lingered on in Court, this did not impinge on affairs of state in the way it had done throughout the time of the male Tudor monarchs. Instead, the Privy Chamber became an exclusive inner sanctum, populated solely by the Queen and her lady attendants, with admittance only to be granted to the privileged few at the behest of the Gentleman Usher, thereby providing an oasis of calm for Elizabeth away from the frenetic atmosphere of the Court. On one particularly notable occasion, even the Queen's long-time favourite Robert Dudley was refused admission; Dudley was greatly upset but the Queen upheld the decision.

One of the important benefits of these new arrangements was that the Royal Court became less prone to the disruptive factions and internal intrigue that had existed in earlier reigns, and while Court rivalries still existed, particularly between such powerful personalities as William Cecil and Robert Dudley and later the Earl of Essex and Robert Cecil, there was to be far greater harmony in Court during the Elizabethan era, particularly in the late 1570s and 1580s, when England was most at peril as the nation moved remorselessly towards war with Spain.

After Elizabeth had ascended the throne in 1558, it was not surprising that she unceremoniously removed most of the members of Mary's Court in order to replace them with those of her own family, together with those who had stood by her during her long and dangerous journey to the throne. 'The old flock of Hatfield', as they were sometimes derisorily referred to, included people like Kat Ashley, her husband John Ashley and Blanche Parry, who had known the Queen as a child.

This family stemmed from that of her mother Anne Boleyn, so Elizabeth created her cousin, Henry Carey, to be Baron Hunsdon, at the same time appointing him Captain of the Gentlemen Pensioners, a gorgeously attired body of young nobles eager to make their mark. Part military, part ceremonial in function, the group strutted around the Court looking mean and magnificent. Thomas Parry, who had also been with Elizabeth since she was a child, was made Treasurer of the Household, while the strikingly good-looking Robert Dudley, whom she had also known since childhood, was created Master of the Queen's Horse.

The Queen's lady attendants were similarly drawn from the great Tudor families – the Howards, Careys and Knollys. These were related to Elizabeth on her mother's side and only death terminated their position at Court, whereupon invariably they would be replaced by their daughters. In this way membership of both the Privy Chamber and the Court was virtually a closed shop of long-serving, loyal and hard-working servants dedicated to Elizabeth's well-being with fanatical enthusiasm. In return, the Queen was endlessly demanding in her requirements. Constant attendance at the Court was mandatory unless the Queen gave specific leave of absence, something that could prove particularly irksome to those whose husbands had duties away from the Court. This was something that the Queen appeared blissfully ignorant of, being particularly self-centred, selfishly unaware and uncaring of her courtiers' welfare. The confined nature of the Court meant that it soon became a web of intermarriage and family connection, wherein most of the Court's key members eventually were all relatives, one big Elizabethan family with a matriarchal Queen at its head. Thus Sir Robert Cecil married Lord Cobham's daughter Elizabeth, while Sir Walter Mildmay took Francis Walsingham's sister as his wife and Sir Philip Sidney's wife was Walsingham's daughter, Frances, who went on to marry the Earl of Essex after Sir Philip had been killed in battle.

On her accession, Elizabeth had acquired more than two dozen palaces of varying shapes and sizes ranging from the vast, sprawling Palace of Whitehall, the largest and ugliest in Europe according to one visiting foreign ambassador, down to smaller palaces tucked away in the depths of the country, places such as Eltham and Hatfield, which Elizabeth had inherited while she was still a princess, and Woodstock where she had once been held as a prisoner. Whitehall Palace, spreadeagled along the banks of the River Thames like an enormous Gothic beached whale, was originally the property of Cardinal Wolsey but had been seized by Henry VIII after the original central London Palace of Westminster was badly damaged in a fire. Henry rapidly redeveloped Whitehall at vast cost, creating a complex labyrinth of narrow, winding corridors and a bewildering variety of rooms, more than two thousand in number, big and small, covering many acres, from which earnest government bureaucrats administered Tudor England. The Privy Council invariably met at Whitehall but occasionally at Hampton Court Palace or Greenwich. Elizabeth was never very keen on Hampton Court, as it held so many bad memories from her childhood.

Whitehall Palace continued to be much used throughout Elizabeth's reign and subsequently by her successors up to the time of the serious fire in 1698 which destroyed very large parts of it, never to be rebuilt. At Whitehall the main corridor of power was the Privy Gallery, a broad thoroughfare running straight through the heart of the palace from the Holbein Gate and King Street past the Privy Garden. The Bedchamber, the Queen's private quarters, faced the Council Chamber across this gallery and at the far end lay the Privy Chamber, Presence Chamber, Guard Chamber, the Hall and Royal Chapel and then finally the Privy Stairs and Whitehall Stairs leading down to the Thames, the river still providing the best form of transport in those days.

Along the riverbank lay Hampton Court Palace, another palace which had originally been built by Cardinal Wolsey, and Richmond Palace, the Queen's favourite which she referred to as 'my warm little box'. Beyond this was Windsor Castle, at that time sited right out in the country. Downstream lay the Tower of London, by now little used as a royal residence, and Greenwich Palace, where the Queen had been born some twenty-five years before she had ascended the throne. One of her other favourite palaces was located deep in the Surrey countryside at Nonsuch, described by the contemporary historian, William Camden, as 'the highest point of ostentation'. Here the Queen greatly enjoyed hunting and hawking, together with other country pursuits which she continued to partake in almost up to the time of her death in 1603.

Elizabeth had inherited her father's relentlessly energetic nature and so the Court was constantly on the move between these various royal palaces, like a hugely colourful travelling circus orbiting elegantly through the countryside of southern England, to her citizens' delight and her courtiers' dismay, being highly irritated by this disruption to their well-ordered lives which these royal peregrinations were to cause. Elizabeth was to build no new palaces in her lifetime, not that she required any more, nor was she to carry out much in the way of alteration or addition to those already in existence. The conservative Queen was content with what she already possessed and highly reluctant to indulge in a spending spree; only at Windsor Castle did a limited amount of work take place during her lifetime.

Elizabeth waged a constant running war on what she regarded as the extravagant cost of maintaining the Royal Court. 'I will not suffer the dishonourable spoil and increase that no prince before me did to the offence of God and the great grievance of my loving subjects,'[8] thundered Elizabeth during one of her many memorable outbursts. She was assisted in her periodic economy drives by William Cecil who was every bit as miserly in state expenditure as his sovereign, being acutely conscious of the parlous state of the nation's finances. Controlling the spiralling cost of the Court was to be a hopeless task. Elizabeth ruled in an opulent age, one in which ostentation had been elevated to an art form, where the glittering royal courts of Europe constantly strove to outdo each other in ever-increasing magnificence. Trying to curb her courtiers' excesses proved an uphill struggle: indeed, Elizabeth's royal progresses around England in order to display herself to her loyal subjects, were to prove counter-productive in attempting to control expenditure, adding considerably to royal expense. One of the main reasons the Queen never travelled west of Bristol or north of Stafford, thereby never seeing towns as important as Plymouth and York, was the sheer cost of these royal walkabouts as well as the time expended to travel there.

Another source of self-indulgent extravagance was the introduction of colourful events such as the Accession Day 'tilts', which were part of the annual nationwide celebration of the Queen ascending the throne, involving spectacular tournaments, re-enacting the jousting of medieval knights in which the more macho members of the Court fought valiantly before their beloved Queen. These events were part of the cult of Elizabeth as Gloriana, which emerged towards the end of the sixteenth century – Venus descended in England's green and pleasant land. These Arthurian antics were supervised by Elizabeth's Master of the Armoury, Sir Henry Lee, who had styled himself Queen's Champion of the Tilts in order to renew a romantic concept of chivalry. They were held before several thousand excited spectators, with the gorgeously attired Queen surrounded by the ladies of her Court in all their finery. Similar events had been held in her father's reign, and Henry had participated energetically in his younger days. In Elizabeth's reign, the accent was more on the elaborate ceremony rather than the skill of combat – the Earl of Essex used Francis Bacon as his scriptwriter, to concoct flamboyant speeches heralding his grand entrance into the arena.

Sir Henry Lee was the enthusiastic patron of one of the most outstanding portrait painters of the Elizabethan era, Marcus Gheeraerts the Younger. Lee resided at Ditchley in Oxfordshire and commissioned Gheeraerts to paint the so-called Ditchley Portrait, one of the classic portrayals of Elizabeth painted around 1592, depicting the Queen in all her glory astride a map of England, in command of her kingdom, Queen and country, one and the same. This work is the largest portrait of Elizabeth ever painted and can now be found in the National Portrait Gallery in London. In 1592 it would have hung in the Long Gallery of Sir Henry's house at Ditchley, when the Queen came to stay with him for a couple of days' elaborate entertainment, which included an allegorical play which Sir Henry had written and in which he also acted. Sir Henry's unruly nephew, Thomas, later took part in the Earl of Essex's abortive uprising against the Queen and was subsequently executed at Tyburn. Marcus Gheeraert's fine portrait of Essex hangs in the Long Gallery at Woburn Abbey. When Sir Henry retired as Champion of the Tilts, his place was taken by George Clifford, the 3rd Earl of Cumberland. Nicholas Hilliard's portrait of the Earl, which is now part of the National Maritime Collection at Greenwich, shows a giant of a man proudly clutching a huge lance and wearing an exotic plumed hat. Cumberland would enter the arena at the head of other challengers such as the Earls of Essex, Sussex and Oxford. The latter had first come to the Queen's attention because of his spectacular performances at the Tilt Yard. Cumberland entered in his guise as Knight of Pendragon, a mythical warrior of legendary reputation. In real-life combat, Cumberland proved considerably less successful as a naval commander whose forays against the Spanish achieved little of military significance, but helped supplement his own purse to some extent, thereby recouping the gambling losses he incurred at Court.

The Tilt Yard tournaments were, like the annual Knight of the Garter ceremonies at Windsor Castle, part of a skilful Tudor public relations exercise that projected an image of the Queen as someone who had become a heavenly creature returned to earth in order to be passionately worshipped by her adoring subjects: 'all those loves meet to create but one soul. I am of her own country and we adore her by the name of Eliza,'[9] enthused the poet Thomas Dekker.

Sunday was always an important day in the life of the Royal Court, an essential time for any aspiring courtier to be in attendance, a day for meeting and greeting, perhaps an opportunity to attract the attention of the Queen herself, albeit momentarily. A magnificent procession would wend its stately way from the Presence Chamber to the Royal Chapel for morning service. First came the nobility in strict order of precedence, then the Lord Keeper bearing the Great Seal, followed by other senior courtiers carrying the Sword of State and the Sceptre. Finally Queen Elizabeth would appear, fabulously befrocked and bejewelled, surrounded by her Ladies-in-Waiting and her Maids of Honour elegantly attired in their Sunday best. This colourful procession moved majestically through crowds of visitors who knelt reverently as the monarch swept past in shining splendour into the chapel. After the service, dinner would be served promptly at noon. Elizabeth was not a noted gourmet and the food served was known rather more for its quantity than for its quality: plenty of roast meat of every conceivable kind, together with poultry and game, followed by copious helpings of sweet meats and rich puddings, for the Queen was well known for her sweet tooth. Elizabeth ate relatively little and drank even less, preferring beer to wine which she only drank heavily diluted with water. Very often she would dine alone in her private apartments served by her lady attendants, and at the glittering state banquets she was observed to merely pick at her food, pushing it around her plate until the meal was over and the music and dancing began.

Musical entertainment was much more to Elizabeth's liking than wining and dining and the normally economical Queen spared no expense either on her large group of court musicians or her choir which numbered more than fifty singers and whose expert performances greatly impressed the normally sceptical foreign envoys visiting the Court. Like press-ganged sailors, young boys with promising voices would be plucked from the countryside to be brought to the Court for expert tuition before becoming part of the choir. The Queen employed William Byrd and Thomas Tallis as both musicians and composers and Dr John Bull was her chapel organist. Elizabeth played the virginals very proficiently, possessing one of these popular sixteenth-century harpsichords; she practised regularly and diligently whenever the opportunity arose, and enjoyed showing off her skill to visitors at the Court.

Dancing was another of the Queen's great passions, one that was to remain with her throughout her lifetime. As the French diplomat de Maisse reported to King Henry IV towards the end of the sixteenth century:

she takes great pleasure in dancing and music, in her youth she danced very well, and composed measures and music and had played them herself and danced them. She takes such pleasure in it that when her Maids dance she follows the cadence with her head, hand and foot. She rebukes them if they do not dance to her liking and without doubt she is a mistress of the art, having learnt in the Italian manner to dance high.[10]

A painting by an unknown artist hangs at Penshurst Place which shows the Queen dancing in the 'high style' with her favourite Robert Dudley, watched by Sir Philip Sidney and other members of the Court. The dance is the *Volta*, Italian for 'running turn', the only dance in Elizabeth's time that involved the man clasping his lady partner in his arms in order to lift her high into the air. The *Volta* caused a sensation the first time it was performed at Court, as it was considered decidedly *risqué* in those days. Elizabeth loved dancing, particularly with Robert Dudley.

The two other most popular dances of the day were the *Gaillard*, French for 'a gay dance', performed briskly in triple time involving jumps, termed *capriols* from which the word 'capers' was derived, and the *Pavan*, a processional dance with an underlying marching rhythm. Although there was a fairly elementary format to these dances, the more skilful participants such as Robert Dudley, Christopher Hatton and the clever, rather obnoxious Earl of Oxford would introduce their own more elaborate variations in order to demonstrate their superior expertise as Lords of the Dance. The Queen was to continue to dance almost up to the time of her death in 1603 and it was an activity that was a constant and enjoyable feature of her Court.

In spite of the Queen's well-publicized royal processions around the countryside, Elizabeth never travelled outside southern England. She never visited Wales or Ireland and certainly never went to continental Europe. 'Foreign parts' definitely began at Calais ever since that last outpost of English territory in France had been recaptured by the French at the end of her half-sister Mary's reign. Unlike other English monarchs, Elizabeth never led a conquering army overseas: '. . . my mind has never been to invade my neighbour or usurp any. I am content to reign over mine own and to rule as a just prince,'[11] she was to declare in one of her periodic addresses to Parliament. Unlike her father Henry, there were no elaborate summit meetings with other heads of state, no royal razzmatazz such as the Field of the Cloth of Gold when Henry VIII and François I of France preened and postured before each other in dazzling splendour. Elizabeth was never to meet a ruler of another nation throughout the entire time she was on the English throne, not even her cousin, Mary, Queen of Scots, who lived in exile in England for nearly twenty years, or Mary's son James VI of Scotland, who was ultimately to succeed her as James I of England.

Elizabeth's main contact with the rest of the civilized world was through her various ambassadors and diplomats stationed in places such as Paris and the numerous foreign envoys who frequented the Royal Court. The fact that Elizabeth had never been abroad presented no handicap to her grasp of foreign affairs or in formulating foreign policy. She had once held a foreign ambassador, visiting her Court for the first time, in open-mouthed admiration as she delivered a lengthy, highly accurate discourse analysing the current political situation, which revealed an astonishing insight into the complex, constantly shifting scene that characterized Europe in the second half of the sixteenth century. The Queen's understanding of events abroad was derived from careful listening to her own overseas emissaries, men such as Sir Nicholas Throckmorton, Sir Francis Walsingham and Sir Thomas Smith, together with the various foreign diplomats living in London such as Don Guerau de Spes and Don Bernardino de Mendoza, successive Spanish ambassadors to the Royal Court, also Bertrand de Salignac de la Mothe-Fenelon, the urbane French ambassador who professed a high opinion of Elizabeth as Queen while at the same time sneering that she ruled over the dullest Court in the whole of Europe.

Fluent in French and Spanish and well versed in a variety of foreign languages, Queen Elizabeth was in her element during her frequent audiences with these royal representatives, immensely enjoying their visits, chattering effortlessly in their own language. When all else failed, she fell back on her classical education. 'I swear that Her Majesty made one of the best answers extemporare in Latin, that I have ever heard,'[12] declared a highly impressed Sir Robert Cecil to the Earl of Essex in July 1597, following an audience with a visiting ambassador who spoke no English.

Inevitably, these ambassadors were drawn into intrigues within the Royal Court or tempted to meddle secretly in the nation's internal affairs, particularly those that involved the Catholic cause in England. Mendoza never disguised his fundamental contempt for the English nation as a whole and had a particularly active dislike of Sir William Cecil, by then Lord Burghley, one of England's principal ministers throughout most of Elizabeth's reign. In turn, Burghley saw Mendoza as the prototype Spaniard, both arrogant and completely impossible. He was therefore delighted when the Spanish ambassador was ordered to leave England after he had been discovered implicated in the 'Throckmorton Plot', one of the many Catholic conspiracies to threaten Elizabeth's well-being during her long and eventful reign. The Queen invariably received ambassadors in the Presence Chamber, a room which was often a place of high drama. When Mothe-Fenelon came to present the official French version of the St Bartholomew's Day Massacre in Paris in which thousands of Huguenots were slaughtered, he had the unnerving experience of being received by the Queen together with her large retinue in total silence. On another occasion, Elizabeth swore loudly at a Polish ambassador in Latin. She could be either imperious or totally charming, flirting with an embarrassed ambassador, while constantly gesticulating with her hands in a highly theatrical manner. 'She drew off her glove and showed her hand which is very long and more than mine by more than three broad fingers. It was formerly very beautiful but is now very thin, although the skin is still most fair,'[13] observed de Maisse, the King of France's envoy towards the end of the sixteenth century. Elizabeth's hands feature strongly in many of her portraits, notably George Gower's celebrated *Armada Portrait*, now in the Long Gallery at Woburn Abbey and William Segar's *Ermine Portrait*, currently to be seen at Hatfield Palace. A visiting ambassador to Hampton Court noted:

> In one chamber were several excessively rich tapestries, which are hung up when the queen gives audience to foreign ambassadors: there are a number of cushions ornamented with gold and silver. Here is besides a certain cabinet called Paradise, where besides that everything glitters so with silver, gold and jewels, as to dazzle one's eyes, there is a musical instrument made all of glass, except for the strings.[14]

Sometimes Elizabeth developed a surprisingly close relationship with one of these distinguished overseas visitors to her Royal Court, as appeared to be the case with Monsieur Andre de Maisse towards the end of her reign. The personable, highly impressionable young French diplomat attentively listened to the Queen's long rambling reminiscences, acutely conscious that he was closeted alone with one of the great legendary figures of western Europe, a unique privilege he would treasure to the end of his days. De Maisse's detailed written observations convey a fascinating insight into the state of the English nation during Elizabeth's declining years, when stirring actions were fast becoming faded memories: 'Her Government is fairly pleasing to the people, who show that they love her';[15] 'She thinks highly of herself and has little regard for her servants and Council, being of the opinion that she is far wiser than they';[16] 'When some expense is necessary her Government must deceive her before embarking on it little by little . . .';[17] such is the hubris of history, as Tudor England was coming to an end, seen through the perceptive eye of Andre Hurault Sieur de Maisse, special envoy of the French King Henry IV, to the Court of Queen Elizabeth I.

At all times the Royal Court of Elizabeth I was living theatre, with the Queen centre stage in the starring role surrounded by a huge and glittering cast: 'A kingdom for a stage, princes to act and monarchs to behold the swelling scene'[18] as William Shakespeare so memorably observed.

3

PORTRAIT OF A QUEEN

Elizabeth was twenty-five years old when she first ascended the English throne in the winter of 1558. She had received no formal training for governing her newly acquired kingdom, yet was intelligent and well educated, while the long period of waiting and watching as Mary's health progressively declined had enabled Elizabeth to be psychologically prepared to assume the trappings of power. Few English citizens mourned her half-sister's death: there was widespread optimism in the Court and across the country as Elizabeth inherited the throne. The political climate was right and the nation rejoiced.

In many respects the new young Queen was remarkably like her father, with a naturally regal appearance that positively radiated authority. Elizabeth was physically striking, tall, auburn-haired, extremely charming and highly energetic. Like Henry VIII, she loved hunting, dancing and the undivided attention of the opposite sex. She was also very vain and adored flattery, but shrewd enough not to succumb to it when serious issues arose. Not surprisingly, it was not long before murmurs of approval began to reverberate around the Court, making favourable comparisons with her father who many still fondly remembered.

In reality Elizabeth was no great beauty: 'her face is comely rather than handsome, but she is tall and well formed; with a good skin, although swarthy; she has fine eyes and above all a beautiful hand',[1] reported Giovanni Michael to the Doge in Venice the year before Elizabeth became Queen. She had her father's prominent nose and her mother's lovely dark eyes. She was lively and to her new Court, completely enchanting. It was love at first sight.

The majority of today's art historians consider most of the early portraits of Elizabeth to be desperately mediocre in quality. William Scrots, who had painted the striking picture of the young princess now to be seen at Windsor Castle, had died four years before she came to the throne. Elizabeth chose not to retain the services of the distinguished Flemish painter Hans Eworth, whom Queen Mary had employed as her unofficial court painter and whose powerful rendering of Henry VIII can now be found at Trinity College, Cambridge. So the early years of Elizabeth's reign are recorded by a series of indifferent paintings by unknown and best-forgotten artists. The clearest indication of the physical appearance of the new young Queen rests with the portrait of her that was produced at the time of her coronation on 15 January 1559, crown on head, orb and sceptre to hand, looking confidently straight ahead, relaxed, dignified and supremely assured. This likeness is currently to be found at Warwick Castle.

Elizabeth was the third of Henry VIII's children to become monarch in less than a dozen years. Merely surviving to inherit the throne represented a major achievement, having endured the disgrace of being the daughter of Anne Boleyn, the animosity of her half-sister Mary and imprisonment in the Tower of London. Elizabeth was a complete novice in the affairs of state and had inherited a weak, divided and dispirited kingdom with a long list of problems awaiting a solution. The new Queen, however, was astute, highly conscientious and hard-working, and she immediately demonstrated an instinctive grasp of how to rule a kingdom and motivate its subjects to best effect. Furthermore, whereas her predecessors had ruled by fear, Elizabeth was to reign with love. It was to be a long and successful affair.

Her experiences on the long and perilous journey to the throne had instilled the new Queen with considerable caution and bred an inclination for making a lengthy assessment of any situation before coming to a decision or taking any specific course of action. Impulsive gestures, hasty conclusions or instinctive reactions were simply not part of Elizabeth's character. It was as if she was a new batsman in a game of cricket, determined to settle down and play a long and successful innings, patient, careful and highly focused. The Queen normally listened very carefully to her Privy Council and rarely embarked on a move of any consequence before she had consulted its members often both individually and collectively. Sir William Cecil, later Lord Burghley, exercised a profound influence over her for nearly forty years until he died, still in office, not very long before the end of her reign. However, while Elizabeth was usually appreciative of the advice of her Privy Council, she always knew her own mind and was rarely open to persuasion or prompted to adopt a course of action contrary to her own instincts or which differed from her strongly held beliefs. 'Though very capable of Council, she was absolute enough in her own resolution, which was ever apparent even to her last',[2] a contemporary historian was to note not long after her death.

Mary's short reign, unsatisfactory though it may have been, had at least been advantageous in accustoming the English kingdom to the novel concept of a female monarch, an institution which was becoming increasingly prevalent in Europe. In the initial period of Elizabeth's reign, Catherine de Medici became Regent in France and Mary, Queen of Scots had inherited the Scottish crown. Only Elizabeth, however, possessed the necessary ability as well as the opportunity to be a successful female ruler of a kingdom which, in the second half of the sixteenth century, was essentially a man's world. Elizabeth was able to use her sex as a potent weapon in this overtly masculine society and skilfully turn a perceived disadvantage into one that could be cleverly exploited to both her own and her kingdom's benefit. In particular, she realised that the marriage card was a useful one to hold, leaving the Court to wonder when it might be played and what the possible consequences of such a move might be. Elizabeth shrewdly realized it was not a card to use in a hurry – in many respects, its greatest value lay in it being kept in hand. She was relaxed. Time was on her side. She was young, barely twenty-five years of age, yet old enough to know her own mind. She had a confident and mature outlook, was completely self-possessed and still in the full bloom of youth. The Queen was a woman with no parents or dominant elder brother to command her or put pressure on her to do her duty – she was free to make her own decisions. Furthermore, she was cool and unemotional, rarely one to let her heart rule her head, one characteristic that Elizabeth definitely did not inherit from her father. Henry's younger daughter tended to adopt an altogether more pragmatic approach towards most matters, particularly affairs of the heart.

In many respects, twenty-five was a highly appropriate age to come to the throne as a healthy single person, footloose, if not entirely fancy free. Both her father and her half-brother Edward had been considerably younger when they inherited the English throne, the latter not in the best of health, a characteristic shared by her half-sister, Mary, who had also been a good deal older when she had become Queen. Elizabeth was to enjoy remarkably good health for most of her life, which was not the case in a surprisingly large number of the male courtiers who surrounded her. It was of course an unhealthy age: diseases such as bubonic plague and smallpox were rife and consistently proved fatal. Many other illnesses had no known cure. Medical facilities and treatment were far less sophisticated and even a simple chill could prove fatal, as it was to prove with Roger Ascham and Francis Bacon, two of the great Elizabethan scholars. Ascham was Elizabeth's teacher in her formative years and Bacon became a trusted legal and political adviser who the Queen nicknamed her 'Young Lord Keeper'. One of Elizabeth's inexplicable traits was a compulsive urge to give those closest to her a pet name; very often this could be one that was at best banal and at worst extremely hurtful, but consideration for men's finer feelings was never one of Elizabeth's attributes.

The Queen was very image-conscious, acutely concerned about how she was perceived at home and abroad. For somebody who always appeared very robust, she could at times be remarkably thin-skinned and susceptible to wounding criticism in an age that specialized in short yet eloquent pithy put-downs, something that a Pope or person such as Catherine de Medici could excel at with devastating effect.

Elizabeth's reign had got off to a solid if unspectacular start when suddenly, in the autumn of 1562, the Queen succumbed to the dreaded disease of smallpox. In the sixteenth century this was often terminal. The wife of the 2nd Earl of Bedford, a member of the Queen's Privy Council, had died of it only a few weeks earlier, so great gloom descended on the entire Court. 'Last night the people were all in mourning for her as if she was already dead',[3] gloated the Spanish ambassador, Alvaro de la Quadra, to King Philip. The Queen lay at Hampton Court Palace for several days with a very high fever, drifting in and out of consciousness, while distraught members of her Council gathered around her bedchamber. Ever practical in the hour of crisis, they discussed in hushed tones possible successors to the Queen, mindful of the awesome, but very real prospect of Elizabeth failing to recover. The Queen suddenly regained consciousness and staring up at their anxious faces, feebly croaked that she would like them to appoint Robert Dudley as Lord Protector of the Realm at a salary of £20,000 a year, a colossal sum in those days. Sensing their astonished reaction to this amazing suggestion, she quickly went on to reassure them that although she loved Robert Dudley dearly and would always do so, there had never been anything untoward in their relationship. 'The Queen protested at that time that although she loved and had always loved Lord Robert dearly, as God was her witness, nothing improper had ever passed between them,'[4] commented the Spanish ambassador. Elizabeth then lapsed back into a coma, leaving her Privy Councillors in stunned silence. 'Everything she asked was promised but will not be fulfilled,'[5] was the Spanish ambassador's cynical comment.

Desperate measures were called for to alleviate the Queen's suffering and, having heard of an ancient remedy which supposedly cured smallpox, the Councillors had the Queen wrapped in a scarlet cloth and laid down in front of the fire which burnt brightly in her bedroom. Miraculously, this improbable sounding cure was successful and Elizabeth made a complete recovery, even her fabled fair skin was left completely unmarked. Her attendant, Lady Mary Sidney, wife of Sir Henry and sister to Robert Dudley, who had been at the Queen's side throughout her illness, was not so fortunate. She too contracted smallpox and although she recovered, Lady Mary was left so disfigured she felt compelled to leave the Court and never show her face again. 'As foul a lady as the small pox could make her',[6] Sir Henry was sadly to tell Sir Francis Walsingham many years later.

This traumatic event made the more far-sighted members of the Council give further serious consideration to the vexed matter of the succession, for, in spite of constant urging, there was still no sign of the Queen's intention to marry. She was approaching thirty, virtually past the time when a healthy child could be delivered safely in an age of high infant mortality. As members of the Council redoubled their efforts to find the Queen an appropriate husband, others were already beginning to contemplate the possibility of her never becoming a bride, and pondering precisely what the consequences of such a situation might be. Some were even evaluating the merits of preserving the status quo. Later, when there was still no obvious successor in sight, Sir William Cecil even drew up plans for the establishment of a republic in the event of the Queen's death, in order to avoid the nation being plunged into political turmoil. If the Queen had died of smallpox in October 1562, posterity would have looked back on an unremarkable reign of no particular consequence; as it was, through a mixture of the Queen's robust nature and strength of purpose, coupled with sheer good luck, she survived to go on to far greater things. This combination of circumstances typified the essential nature of Elizabeth's time on the English throne. As Elizabeth's reign developed and she weathered the initial trials and tribulations, she grew in stature and confidence, her authority no longer based on hopeful anticipation but on solid achievement acknowledged by all her subjects. Both the perceptive Queen and her largely supportive Council shared an awareness of the concept of the divine right of kings, as well as an acknowledgement of Bracton's celebrated dictum of the monarch being subject only to God and the Law. Nevertheless, there was an unspoken caveat which required the monarch to perform satisfactorily as a ruler after ascending to the throne through God's blessing, together with an invisible subtext demanding that the monarch should be seen to be successful –

otherwise a replacement would be swiftly found. Elizabeth was acutely aware of the number of occasions in history that a monarch had been replaced, from Edward II to Richard III, usually in painful circumstances for the individuals concerned. The divine right of kings might assist a monarch to acquire the throne but gave no guarantee of maintaining it, something that Elizabeth's Stuart successors ignored at their peril. Even the most forceful of kings, such as Henry II and her father Henry VIII had faced serious insurrection during their time on the throne, something the astute Elizabeth never forgot. She had an almost Churchillian sense of history and her place within it, being extremely determined to rule successfully and leave her mark for posterity.

There was something of a sea change taking place in the England of the second half of the sixteenth century. The population increased by more than a million during Elizabeth's reign, the largest growth being in an expanding middle class, which was better educated and more affluent than in medieval times, and representing an important new strand in the nation's social strata. A perceptible shift was developing in the nation's power base, away from its traditional aristocratic origins towards the landed gentry and prosperous merchants. It was a situation that was later to climax in an explosive confrontation between King and Parliament in the middle of the seventeenth century. While in most respects Elizabeth was the last of the medieval monarchs, she could equally be said to be the first constitutional ruler on the English throne, not by desire, but by force of circumstance. Elizabeth, conservative by nature, did not seek to originate change, but was conscious of its occurrence and acknowledged its significance. She was a great observer and listener and had a good grass-roots appreciation of her kingdom. How fully aware Elizabeth was of the consequences of the sweeping changes taking place throughout her kingdom and the whole of the civilized world is a matter of pure conjecture; what is certain is that the Queen was always careful not to antagonize Parliament and was continually able to retain the goodwill of her people. Elizabeth was always conscientious and industrious, and consistently demonstrated an infallible ability to read the small print of any document or grasp the most minute nuance of debate, together with an appreciation of the implications of the likely outcome of any chosen course of action. To this end, the Queen would sit for long hours studying state papers or mulling over advice she had received. While this undoubtedly avoided unforced errors, it invariably infuriated those who awaited patiently on the monarch's decision. Any attempt to persuade her to hurry or contemplate doing something that was contrary to her basic beliefs was inevitably cut short by one of her notorious temper tantrums. Logical discussion would be abruptly terminated as her advisers were summarily banished from her presence, often for weeks on end, until the royal rage subsided.

The Queen could be extremely stubborn and hated the idea of change in the established order of things – she would vacillate endlessly and happily grasp at any straw to avoid making a decision and, while adoring flattery, was rarely open to individual or collective persuasion, unlikely ever to succumb to emotional blackmail or subtle manipulation. Above all, she never gave in to threats or external pressure at times of extreme crisis, always demonstrating great resolution. Queen Elizabeth I was totally in command and needed to be in control and respected. Shrewd men such as William Cecil were always conscious of these facets of Elizabeth's character and acted accordingly. Others less perceptive or more headstrong, such as the Earl of Essex, ignored them at their peril and paid the ultimate price. Few chose the latter path. It led only to the scaffold.

Although Elizabeth was undoubtedly a strong personality, she was rarely dogmatic and remained remarkably devoid of preconceived notions. She consistently approached problems calmly and rationally – solutions were to be reached by the use of logic rather than by force of arms, as she had the traditional feminine distaste of the horrors and vainglories of war. She regarded war as a ridiculously masculine preoccupation, unfailingly costing a great deal of money but achieving little of lasting benefit. Fluttering flags and marching bands, days of greatness and glory were not for her. She urged Sir Francis Drake and Sir John Norris, two of her more combative military commanders, 'not to suffer themselves to be transported with any haviour of vain-glory'.[7] Elizabeth would not have been impressed by Clausewitz's celebrated military maxim of war being diplomacy by other means, preferring nations to settle their differences by diplomacy. She considered that the Tudor pen should be mightier than medieval sword.

Elizabeth displayed an equal dislike of extremism, particularly in connection with religious beliefs. She constantly chided Sir Francis Walsingham about his extremist Protestant views, while similar ones expressed by another Privy Councillor Sir Francis Knollys led to some blazing rows, regardless of the fact that Sir Francis was her cousin. Conversely, the Queen was not automatically anti-Catholic. Thomas Tallis, William Byrd, and her chapel organist, Dr John Bull, were all Roman Catholics. She employed them for their outstanding musical abilities not their religious beliefs. Her suspicions of Roman Catholicism derived from her experiences and observations during the time her half-sister Mary was on the throne. Subsequently, it was the Pope and Catholic Spain which became antagonistic towards *her*, rather than the other way round.

Elizabeth was equally wary of the rising tide of Puritanism that was threatening to engulf Europe and becoming such a strident voice within her own Parliament. The anti-feminist utterances of the Scottish Presbyterian John Knox were to rouse her to a particular fury. Although Knox's *The First Blast of the Trumpet against the Monstrous Regiment of Women*, was essentially directed at Mary, Queen of Scots, the fact that this book had been published in the year that Elizabeth came to the throne meant that she always regarded Knox's diatribe as a personal attack on herself.

More fundamentally, it was the Queen's pragmatic nature, coupled with a deep-rooted conservatism that guided her thinking on religious issues in as far as they affected her kingdom. On the one hand, her personal inclination to adopt a largely secular view on religious matters induced a revulsion towards what she saw as the slavish dogma of Roman Catholicism. On the other hand, her instinctive desire to maintain the status quo on almost everything led her to regard with acute alarm the radical concepts that had first been unleashed in continental Europe by Martin Luther and Jean Calvin.

As her reign progressed, philosophical considerations were overtaken by practicalities as Catholic Spain developed into England's greatest enemy and provided the biggest threat to her national security. The dividing lines between religion and politics became confused and blurred – indeed, both Philip of Spain and Elizabeth's own Principal Secretary, the abrasive Sir Francis Walsingham, regarded the approaching conflict between their respective nations not so much as a titanic military encounter between two major powers but as a new crusade between the forces of goodness and light and those of eternal darkness as ideological adversaries manoeuvred endlessly for the moral high ground.

In many respects, the late 1570s and 1580s represented Elizabeth's finest years, particularly the euphoric period after the defeat of the Spanish Armada. The image of Elizabeth at the height of her reign is brilliantly captured in the magnificent icon-like portraits of her painted during this glorious period, pictures such as George Gower's Armada Portrait, the Ermine Portrait by William Segar and Marcus Gheeraert's sumptuous Rainbow Portrait which Sir Robert Cecil had commissioned and has remained in the possession of the Cecil family ever since. Today it hangs at Hatfield

House, Robert Cecil's former home. These works, together with Nicholas Hilliard's outstanding miniature painted around 1595, now in the Victoria and Albert Museum, all convey a universal glorification of the Queen, full of shimmering imagery, allegorical detail and all-powerful majestic splendour.

Though Elizabeth was essentially the last of the great English medieval monarchs, the last of the nation's rulers able to control the kingdom by sheer force of personality and unchallenged authority, she never had to put that authority on the line. Her success came essentially through adopting middle-of-the-road policies on all the important issues and avoiding extremism or confrontation with her loyal subjects at all costs. Conservative and cautious she may well have been, sometimes to a maddening degree, yet patience, persistence and supreme fortitude in the hour of maximum danger inevitably paid off, as under her guidance England progressively moved from being a medieval kingdom into a modern state. At the same time, pride in the nation and a sense of patriotism became a collective feature of her citizens, particularly in the glory years that followed the defeat of the Spanish Armada in the summer of 1588. This was a major event during Elizabeth's reign, where fortune favoured the brave and victory was achieved as much by luck as judgement. It was a crucial military encounter that was to have monumental significance, in the short term ensuring that the threat of imminent invasion no longer existed. In the long term, the English fleet's epic victory was to have even more far-reaching consequences, as it heralded the beginning of the decline and fall of the Spanish Empire. The eminent twentieth-century Elizabethan historian A.L. Rowse commented succinctly that, as well as Central and South America, the whole of North America might have ended up speaking Spanish, an interesting and altogether plausible theory.

Elizabeth was a 'drama Queen' in a highly dramatic age: charismatic, inspirational, effortlessly able to motivate otherwise cynical men into glorious achievements for the collective good of her kingdom – to circumnavigate the globe, to defeat the mightiest of her enemies, to create the finest literature the world has ever seen. She had an uncanny ability to inspire not only the great and the good but also the ordinary people in her kingdom, to capture the hearts and minds of her citizens regardless of class or calling. Blessed with the common touch, she captured the affection of those that she encountered on her famous 'Royal Progresses', when the Queen and all her retinue passed in slow and stately manner across the English countryside in high summer. Though the immediate purpose of these progresses was to visit important towns in her kingdom, it was also part of an elaborate propaganda exercise to project a favourable image of the Queen to her public in the days before the existence of any form of instant wide-scale communication. Although Elizabeth did not invent the concept of 'the progress', she certainly exploited it to maximum effect throughout her reign. The Queen's temperament was ideally suited to these occasions as she loved an audience. Whereas her half-sister Mary had been rather shy and hated crowds, Elizabeth was in her element. Although a 'Royal Progress' could be regarded as a piece of cynical stage-management, it nevertheless brought a touch of glamour into the ordinary world, and great pleasure to the local dignitaries of each town the Queen visited. Elizabeth might stop to talk with people in the crowd or out on the open road, a brief moment in time that would remain with them for the rest of their lives. 'Progresses' could be arduous and even boring for the Queen, dutifully listening to local mayors droning on with tedious orations, or enduring yet another amateurish local pageant. Yet throughout these occasions she behaved impeccably, listening in apparent rapt attention before paying a gracious comment or a word of heart-felt thanks in Norwich, Coventry, Bristol, Southampton or any of the other towns she descended on in a blaze of glory. She cleverly recognized that this was all part of being a successful Queen of England, maintaining the love and loyalty of her subjects.

Even during the normal course of Court activity in London, the Queen's movements appeared highly impressive to the casual observer:

> When the Queen goes abroad in public the Lord Chamberlain walks first, being followed by all the nobility who are in Court, and the Knights of the Order that are present walk after, near the Queen's person, such as the Earl of Essex, the Admiral and others. After come the six heralds who bear maces before the Queen. After her march the fifty Gentlemen of the Guard, each carrying a halbard, and sumptuously attired; and after that the Maids and Ladies who accompany them very well attired.[8]

The French envoy de Maisse's graphic description beautifully conveys the vibrancy of the Royal Court, together with the Queen's love of pageantry on every conceivable occasion, a trait that she had acquired from her father. This endeared Elizabeth to the majority of those who filled her kingdom: the members of her Court were themselves on one long ego trip and appreciated star quality when they saw it, and the ordinary people enjoyed a star that every now and again could sparkle among them. Elizabeth was universally popular as a 'People's Queen', adored by her friends and impressive even to her enemies. 'She is a great woman, and were she only Catholic she would be without her match,' enthused her arch adversary His Holiness Pope Sixtus V. 'Just look at how she governs; she is only a woman, only mistress of half an island and yet she makes herself feared by Spain, by France, by the Empire, by all.'[9]

4

THE STATESMEN

The guiding force behind Elizabeth's illustrious reign was her Privy Council, a group of wise men meeting on a regular basis in a room located immediately adjacent to the monarch's private quarters within the royal palace. The Privy Council is said to have been only formally constituted subsequent to the downfall of Thomas Cromwell during the reign of Elizabeth's father, Henry VIII.

The Queen displayed excellent judgement in her choice of Councillors and while she could be excessively demanding, often harsh in her criticism and not particularly generous in her rewards, she nevertheless managed to hold their loyalty. In turn, the Queen returned this loyalty thus creating a unique bond of confidence between Queen and Council, whereby the majority of its key members served for a lifetime, a state of affairs in marked contrast to her father, who disposed of his most prominent advisers, eminent men such as Cardinal Wolsey, Sir Thomas More and Thomas Cromwell, with monotonous regularity. Elizabeth's conduct in Council was altogether different from her half-sister, Mary, who during her mercifully short reign berated them constantly yet ineffectually. Elizabeth's custom was to listen quietly to the debate, but ultimately the decision was always hers and everyone present was under no illusion as to who was in charge.

The Queen's initial Council of 1558 was significantly smaller than Mary's – only some twenty men were chosen, aiming at greater cohesion. She retained ten of its previous members in the interest of continuity, men such as the highly experienced Sir William Petre, a former Secretary of State, and the aged Marquess of Winchester who she maintained as Lord Treasurer. Her new Council was an eclectic mixture of privileged peers, earls like Pembroke, Bedford and Arundel contrasting with self-made professional men such as William Cecil and his brother-in-law, the corpulent Sir Nicholas Bacon, both lawyers. Then there were Elizabeth's relatives including Lord Howard of Effingham, Sir Richard Sackville and Sir Francis Knollys, the Queen's cousin, who shared the Earl of Bedford's rigidly Protestant views. Knollys's extremist religious beliefs, coupled with a somewhat tactless manner, led to some sharp exchanges between himself and the Queen. Unlike previous Councils there was no room for the clergy: the power of the Church, which had been so prevalent in the Middle Ages, was in decline and throughout the whole of Elizabeth's reign the sole cleric to serve in the latter years of her Council was Archbishop Whitgift, whom she dubbed 'her little black husband'.

The veteran peers, Bedford and Pembroke, had both benefited from Henry VIII's dissolution of the monasteries. Pembroke, originally William Herbert, a minor Welsh squire who had been befriended by Henry, married Katherine Parr's younger sister Anne, and built the magnificent Wilton House on former monastic lands near Salisbury. After, Henry's son, Edward VI, had bestowed an earldom on Herbert. Throughout his life, the Earl remained totally illiterate, something of which he was curiously proud.

Francis Russell, the 2nd Earl of Bedford had been granted Woburn Abbey by Henry. Today the magnificent *Armada Portrait* of Elizabeth can be seen in the Long Gallery alongside a picture of Philip II of Spain, Mary's husband, who was to become the Queen's most formidable adversary, and opposite the Earl of Essex, a royal favourite towards the end of her reign. Their presence at Woburn is due to Lucy Harrington, married to the 3rd Earl of Bedford, who was an avid collector.

While this initial Council lacked the men of stature and the powerful array of personalities which later characterized her Councils, it was nevertheless a carefully considered and balanced collection of individuals, ideal for the initial period of Elizabeth's tenure, when making a good steady start was more desirable than striving for ill-considered spectacular achievements which could so easily backfire at a later date.

'I mean to direct all my actions by good advice and council,'[1] the new young Queen had solemnly declared during her coronation, when the enormity of the task that lay ahead was becoming all too apparent. Throughout the duration of her reign, Elizabeth rarely took a decision without consultation, sometimes taking the process to excessive lengths. It could well be argued that her reign might not have been nearly so successful without the continual benefit of such impeccable guidance from a Council whose influence in turn, may not have been so great had the monarch of the day not been a woman destined to remain unmarried throughout her lifetime. Certainly, the disastrous Stuart era which followed, marked by civil war, Charles I's execution, England a republic for the first and only time, and James II deposed, was largely attributable to successive arrogant male monarchs ignoring what little good advice they received, during a period of time conspicuously lacking in the capable statesmen which Elizabeth so fortunately possessed during the whole of her lifetime. These Privy Councillors were skilfully able to persuade the Queen to embark on courses of action that were sometimes contrary to her personal inclinations and which a more autocratic male monarch might therefore have refused to contemplate yet alone undertake: traumatic events such as the execution of Mary, Queen of Scots, a relative as well as a royal personage, or war with Spain, a nation with such manifestly larger resources.

Faced with a powerful and persuasive Council, backed by a Parliament becoming more conscious of its role as the voice of the people, Elizabeth might be said by force of circumstance to have become the first ever democratic English monarch. The decisions that she finally and habitually reluctantly made were indeed very much her own, but had to be acted on swiftly before she predictably changed her mind. Invariably these had come about as a result of continual political pressure mixed with the gentle art of persuasion from skilful statesmen grown well accustomed to her mysterious ways. 'That deep and inscrutable centre of the Court which is Her Majesty's mind,' declared Francis Bacon, the perceptive son of Sir Nicholas, Elizabeth's long-time Privy Councillor and Lord Keeper.

Left to her own devices Elizabeth's reign might have been one of masterly inactivity, as the Queen was happiest in the safe haven of indecision. Costly mistakes were avoided by simply adopting the principle of waiting in the anticipation of complicated issues being overtaken by events. 'I am greatly discouraged with her lack of resolutions,' complained William Cecil on one occasion.

Notorious for her indecisive nature, the Queen was extremely slow to make up her mind, exceedingly quick to change it. Yet this irritating facet of her character could well have been merely one of many weapons in an extensive armoury used in dealings with her Council. It kept them guessing, disrupting their logical, predictable thinking processes in a way that was infuriating and frustrating in the extreme, yet could be highly effective, a feminine ruse to neutralize all-male opposition. Her Privy Council could do little else but wait upon her pleasure. By a combination of innate caution, an occasional push from behind and perhaps a bit of guile, the nation's destiny was well assured and Elizabeth's reputation secured throughout her lifetime and maintained to the present day.

Elizabeth made the first appointments of her embryonic Council within just three days of becoming Queen when she chose William

Cecil as her Principal Secretary of State on 20 November 1558 while she was still living at Hatfield. It was to be an inspired choice. Cecil was to be Elizabeth's faithful civil servant for the next four decades, a rock of dependability on which to build a successful kingdom and one of the nation's great statesmen.

Cecil was only thirty-eight at the time of his appointment, yet exuded a reassuringly avuncular air, a feeling of reliability and trustworthiness that was greatly appealing to women, particularly a new young Queen, outwardly calm but inwardly desperately anxious to meet the high expectancy of her subjects. The astute, dependable Cecil would enable her to fulfil her objectives. Above all, in an age bedevilled by deceit and corruption he was both discreet and honest. 'This judgement I have of you,' Elizabeth famously told him at the time of his appointment, 'that you will not be corrupted with any manner of gift and that you will be faithful to the state and that without respect of my private will, you will give me that council that you think best.'[2] It was to prove an assessment that typified Elizabeth's clear-sighted judgement of human nature. Cecil was later to profit greatly from the post of Master of the Court of Wards, given to him by the Queen in 1561, which enabled him to live in considerable style, constructing several magnificent houses such as Burghley, close to his home town of Stamford in Lincolnshire and Theobolds in the Home Counties, where he lavishly entertained Elizabeth on a number of occasions. There is, however, no evidence that his judgement in matters of state was in any way impaired or influenced by material gain, even on Cecil's grand scale.

The relationship between the monarch and her principal minister was a political marriage of considerable convenience – they suited each other admirably, complementing one another in almost every facet of human behaviour. Both were innately cautious, conservative in the extreme. It is one of the strange paradoxes of Elizabeth's reign that amid such a dazzling age of achievement, rapid change and advancement in virtually every aspect of life, the Queen invariably preferred to maintain the status quo. She was rarely proactive and deeply suspicious of the many profound changes happening around her, characteristics she shared with William Cecil.

Cecil, like the Queen, had Welsh origins; his grandfather David Cecil, or 'Cyssell' as it was then spelt, had fought alongside Henry Tudor, Earl of Richmond, Elizabeth's grandfather, against Richard III at the decisive Battle of Bosworth in 1485. It was at this battle that victory enabled Henry to claim the Crown as Henry VII, thereby founding the Tudor dynasty of which Elizabeth was to be the fifth and arguably the greatest monarch of the line.

Elizabeth was fortunate, for although Cecil was by far the youngest member of her first Council, he had already gained considerable political experience, first under the Duke of Somerset and then the Duke of Northumberland as part of Edward VI's Council. Although keeping a low profile during Queen Mary's reign, he had undertaken some minor diplomatic missions while patiently awaiting in hopeful anticipation Elizabeth's arrival on the throne. For the eight years before she became Queen, he had served in the young princess's household as her Land Surveyor. Both Elizabeth and Cecil survived the turbulent years that ensued following the death of Henry VIII in 1547 by adopting a thoroughly pragmatic approach, eschewing any romantic idealism and avoiding risk at all cost. So while Somerset and Northumberland were executed at the Tower of London, Elizabeth and Cecil lived on, despite a period of time incarcerated in that great fortress on the Thames originally created by William the Conqueror. Graduating from the same survival school, they forged a unique bond during the many years of her reign, enduring the inevitable trials and tribulations along the way. They admired each other's intellectual abilities and Cecil became progressively more impressed with Elizabeth's growing political acumen.

If William Cecil had ever nourished any thoughts of becoming the power behind the throne, an Elizabethan *éminence grise*, pulling the strings of a puppet princess who had become apprentice Queen, he was soon to be disappointed. Elizabeth proved to be a quick learner, combining this with an exceedingly demanding nature. She displayed an intuitive grasp of politics coupled with an instinctive appreciation of the art of statesmanship, rarely taking a wrong turning in the complex sixteenth-century corridors of power. So when Cecil returned from Scotland in 1560, delighted with his unexpected yet successful achievement of the Treaty of Scotland, thereby removing the threat of a hostile neighbour on England's northern border, he was both surprised and dismayed to be received coolly by a monarch keen to demonstrate a determination not to be over-dependent on the abilities and actions of any one person, not even one as energetic and capable as Cecil. It was a salutary lesson for her new Secretary of State and a foretaste of a relationship which was to continue in a similar vein for many years to come.

William Cecil was the consummate bureaucrat and administrator, qualities which Elizabeth greatly admired and exploited shamelessly throughout his long and distinguished career, even summoning him to Court for official business within days of the death of his wife. Like several of her key Councillors, Cecil continually suffered from poor health. He was severely stricken with gout from his early thirties, an affliction which left him in old age unable to walk unaided. This is possibly why the well-known portrait of him in the Bodleian Library, Oxford, shows him astride a mule. Elizabeth was unmoved, 'my Lord, we make use of you, not for your bad legs, but for your good head,'[3] she urged her hard-pressed adviser, who was also becoming rather deaf.

Cecil was the only one of Elizabeth's Privy Councillors to receive a peerage: the Queen made him Lord Burghley in 1571. Surprisingly, he later declined the Earldom of Northampton, not long after the defeat of the Spanish Armada, 'being too old and too poor for higher honour',[4] as he was to write to his fellow Privy Councillor, the 6th Earl of Shrewsbury in January 1589.

William Cecil's early dominance of the Queen's Council was to be short-lived: two years after his own appointment he was joined on the Privy Council by the hugely handsome Lord Robert Dudley. Dudley, who had already exercised considerable influence over the Queen as a royal favourite and ardent suitor for her affections and was now attempting to reinvent himself as a politician, having failed in his bid to become Elizabeth's husband. While his royal romantic ambitions were to come to nothing, his political aspirations were rewarded when the Queen elevated him to her Privy Council in the autumn of 1562, additionally appointing him a Knight of the Garter and granting him the generous gift of Kenilworth Castle in Warwickshire, together with extensive estates.

At the same time Elizabeth perversely appointed to her Council Thomas Howard, 4th Duke of Norfolk, Earl Marshal of England and the nation's only Duke at that time, the latest member of a powerful family that had long influenced English affairs of state. He was also a sworn enemy of Robert Dudley. His appointment to the Council was a typical tactic of the Queen, and one for which she was well known. The concept of complete harmony on the Privy Council was simply not Elizabeth's style – she continually appointed members whom she knew held opposing views and different agendas. Intriguingly, this strategy worked remarkably well most of the time, although it was not long before Dudley and Norfolk began to dress up their respective followers in distinctive colourful outfits, to roam in noisy gangs through the Royal Court like rival modern-day football supporters. No doubt it kept the Queen amused, but not William Cecil, who had little time for the dashing Dudley, whom he saw as an irrelevant but dangerous distraction both for the Queen and the nation as a whole. Yet their uneasy relationship on the Council lasted for twenty-five years, during which time they complemented each other well, Cecil's gravitas contrasting with

Dudley's more glamorous image, all to the Queen's satisfaction and the nation's benefit.

Lord Robert Dudley's unpopularity with some of the Privy Council members arose rather unfairly from a collective jealousy of his intimate relationship with the Queen, coupled with the undoubted chequered history of his family. Both his father and grandfather were Dukes of Northumberland who had been executed for high treason under previous monarchs. Dudley himself had spent time in the Tower, imprisoned on suspicion of plotting against Queen Mary. Thus the sins of the fathers coupled with his own rumoured carnal sin with Elizabeth prejudiced his initial attempts to be viewed objectively as a trustworthy member of the Council. Even his swarthy good looks were held against him: 'beware of the gypsey, for he will be too hard for you all, you know not the beast so well as I do',[5] the Earl of Sussex, another implacable enemy, supposedly warned on his deathbed. Robert Dudley was also wrongly suspected of being implicated along with the rather dim and misguided Duke of Norfolk in the 'Ridolfi Plot', one of the endless Catholic conspiracies, real or imagined, which involved removing Elizabeth from the throne in order to replace her with Mary, Queen of Scots.

Dudley was singularly unsuccessful as a military commander in the Netherlands, one of a number of royal favourites seemingly more successful in the bedroom than on the battlefield. Yet Dudley was a political survivor and served for more than a quarter of a century as a trusted Councillor to the Queen, who created him Earl of Leicester in 1564. His consistently upbeat approach made a refreshing counterbalance to William Cecil's sometimes depressingly ingrained caution, an attitude which served Elizabeth very effectively, particularly during the long war years.

It was not long before the Queen and her Council knew each other intimately. The Councillors understood her character. Recognizing her violent mood swings, they became masters of timing and manipulation, well rehearsed in the art of subtle persuasion, soothing when the Queen became strident, reassuring when she was anxious or depressed. Naturally, Elizabeth fully comprehended this and treated them accordingly. 'I perceive they deal with me like physicians who administering a drug, make it more acceptable by giving it a good aromatical savour or when they give pills to gild them all over,'[6] she once sardonically declared to a foreign envoy.

After the early years of her reign, the Queen rarely attended the Council while it was in session except during times of crisis, preferring to consult its key members on an individual basis, a classic case of divide and rule. In turn, the Council cleverly adapted its strategy in response to the Queen's actions and declared intentions. Having long experienced Elizabeth's reluctance to pay little more than lip service to marriage, and despairing of ever hearing the welcome chime of royal wedding bells, they began to appreciate the advantages of an unmarried monarch without a consort to interfere in the affairs of state or confuse the Queen with conflicting advice. A husband drawn from another country could lead to political alliances, which might seem a good idea at the time but could later become inexpedient amid the shifting political climate of sixteenth-century Europe. Thus the Queen became hoist with her own petard when she famously declared that she was already bound unto a husband named the kingdom of England. When, almost into middle age, Elizabeth finally appeared serious about marriage with a French prince, the Council poured cold water on the idea, causing her to leave the Council Chamber in floods of tears. It was not long before some Tudor spin doctor coined the phrase 'The Virgin Queen'.

To a certain extent, Elizabeth's behaviour was a reflection of the environment in which she found herself, a situation in part of her own making. Her decision not to marry had left her curiously isolated in the claustrophobic atmosphere of the Court, never alone, yet nevertheless rather lonely, with no husband or sympathetic non-partisan shoulder to lean on in times of need. There was no Denis Thatcher, no Prince Albert, not even a Mr Brown with whom to unwind, to offload stately cares and woes, to discuss quietly the problems of the day or plan the agenda for tomorrow. True, there were confidantes like Anne, Countess of Warwick and the likes of the Earl of Oxford, Sir Walter Ralegh, the Earl of Essex and other Tudor sycophants for an ageing Queen to relax with and temporarily cast off the pressing cares of state while making song and dance, but this was not the consistant, sympathetic support needed by a head of state under constant pressure. In short, the Queen lacked a man about the house to give moral support in her dealings with an all-male Council.

Many of Elizabeth's Council were highly ambitious men seeking power and authority and material gain, yet for some of her royal subjects merely to serve was sufficient honour in itself. The Earl of Sussex was such a man, one whom posterity conceivably underrates as an Elizabethan Councillor. He was brought onto the Council by the Queen after many years of thankless service as her Deputy in Ireland, having later performed a decisive part in quelling the Northern Rebellion of 1569 while Lord President of the North. This revolt, led by the Earls of Northumberland and Westmorland, was the only potentially serious large-scale internal threat to

Elizabeth's rule, a forlorn attempt to turn back the clock and restore England to Catholicism. It failed dismally and Sussex was rewarded with a seat on the Council and the post of Lord Chamberlain, remaining a Councillor until his death fourteen years later. The failure of the Northern Rebellion finally saw the demise of the influence of two of the nation's oldest families, the Nevilles, Earls of Westmorland, and the Percys, the Earls of Northumberland. Since the Middle Ages the north had 'known no other Prince than a Percy'. This noble state of affairs had finally drawn to a close.

It was occasionally possible to become a Privy Councillor by more unorthodox means. Christopher Hatton was said to have literally leapt to prominence when he caught the eye of the Queen while energetically performing the *Gaillard*, one of Elizabeth's favourite dances, at a masque at the Inner Temple in 1561, thereafter becoming a member of the Royal Court. He was subsequently made a Privy Councillor in 1577 and Lord Chancellor ten years later, inevitably to be christened, 'The Dancing Chancellor'. Hatton was the archetypal Elizabethan courtier whose good looks and obvious adoration of the Queen quickly made him a royal favourite almost on a par with Robert Dudley, another expert at the *Gaillard*. Unlike Lord Robert, Hatton was never a serious suitor, for while he willingly took part in the elaborate game of playing court to the Queen, this was always conducted on an abstract plane, causing little harm and collecting no enemies. He studiously avoided involvement in the various cliques or causes that bred and multiplied in the frenetic atmosphere of the Court, a quality that served him well in a career progression that was less meteoric than Dudley's but just as enduring, due entirely to his own political acumen coupled with royal patronage, a combination not necessarily possessed by all royal favourites. Ironically Hatton, who never married, was possibly in love with the Queen, who was seven years older than himself. He was a vital link between the Queen and her Parliament, being a regular attender of a House of Commons which was steadily growing in stature. He made a number of important speeches including a particularly stirring oration following the defeat of the Armada.

Hatton had a kindly nature and was invariably the soothing voice of reason when discussions on matters of state were in danger of becoming overheated. At the same time, he possessed a welcome ability to dissuade the Queen from any unwise course of action, such as her sudden whim to appoint Dudley, by then the Earl of Leicester, to be Lieutenant General of the Realm at the time of the Armada, effectively making him her supreme military commander.

This was a decision which could easily have proved disastrous in view of Dudley's lacklustre combat record. Hatton was yet another of the Queen's Privy Councillors who was to die while still in office, after nearly fifteen years' faithful and effective service.

Being a royal favourite did not necessarily guarantee promotion to the Privy Council. The Westcountryman Sir Walter Ralegh was indeed blessed with the same good looks and charm as Dudley and Hatton, becoming 'the darling of the English Cleopatra'. Hatton in particular was wildly jealous of the attentions paid by the Queen to this Devonian newcomer. Ralegh rose rapidly in the Royal Court to become Captain of the Guard, yet progressed no further, the Queen finding his company delightful but his judgement highly questionable, a characteristic which was finally to prove fateful to him after Elizabeth's death. During his lifetime, the Queen noted Ralegh's actions rather than his attributes and never invited him to join her Privy Council. Ralegh was the great underachiever of the Elizabethan age: soldier, sailor, poet, courtier, explorer, he was Renaissance Man *par excellence*. Sadly, though promising much, he produced little, the epitome of the Jack-of-all-trades syndrome.

The celebrated tale of Ralegh gallantly casting his cloak in a muddy pool, 'that plashy place', in order that the Queen could step safely across is manifestly absurd, yet of all his exploits it probably sums up Ralegh best – a man of more style than substance. There is no doubt that Ralegh was very clever, but he knew it well and could rarely resist the opportunity to demonstrate it. Even the closest of his friends could be frequently upset by a well-chosen, yet tactless, remark. Ralegh continually alienated his limited number of supporters while further antagonizing his growing number of enemies, including that other great royal favourite, the Earl of Essex and his powerful coterie of well-connected followers. Even the Queen, who used to affectionately call him 'Wather' on account of his strong West Country accent, became deeply angered when she discovered that Ralegh was conducting a secret affair with Beth Throckmorton, one of her Maids of Honour. Ralegh was temporarily consigned to the Tower and Beth was never allowed to return to the Court even after becoming Ralegh's wife.

Little escaped the attention of a highly observant Queen – she was well aware of how Ralegh was perceived within her Court and thus ensured that he was omitted from many of the important missions and events of her reign. He was doomed to spend much of his life banished from Court or languishing in the Tower. While Ralegh was no politician, he even managed to antagonize Robert Cecil, William

Cecil's second son, who was to become Elizabeth's most prominent statesman late in her reign. This time, Ralegh never came out of the Tower but perished on the executioner's block, like so many high profile courtiers before him.

Patronage was vital for any politician or would-be statesman. While the Queen chose and appointed Privy Councillors, a word or so of approval from someone she trusted and respected invariably proved more than helpful. Thus Francis Walsingham was indeed fortunate to be a protégé of William Cecil. Walsingham, like the Queen, was a gifted linguist, fluent in both French and Italian. He had been Elizabeth's ambassador in France at the time of the notorious St Bartholomew's Day Massacre in Paris on 24 August 1572, when several thousand Huguenots were slaughtered by Catholic extremists. Walsingham was also a religious fanatic, a die-hard Protestant who had been in exile on the continent during Mary's reign and who the contemporary historian William Camden described as 'a most sharp maintainer of the purer religion'.[7] Walsingham took his religious zeal to the ideological edge and mistakenly perceived England's growing quarrel with Spain to be not so much a simple confrontation between nations but an all-out conflict between Protestantism and Catholicism. No wonder then, that when it was ultimately reported to King Philip of Spain that 'Secretary Walsingham has just expired, at which there is much sorrow', the King wrote in the margin, 'there, yes, but is good news here!'

A man of inflexible principle, Walsingham lacked William Cecil's patience and he was fearlessly outspoken, even to the Queen, who could be surprisingly inhibited by him at times – not without cause. 'For the love of God Madam, let not the cure of your diseased state hang any longer in deliberation!'[8] he harangued her on one memorable occasion.

Dark and brooding, Walsingham invariably dressed in sombre black, in stark contrast to most of the more colourfully attired courtiers – the Queen nicknamed him 'her Moor'. A fine portrait of Walsingham in the National Portrait Gallery attributed to John de Critz, who had come from the Netherlands as a child and attracted Walsingham's patronage, brilliantly projects the appearance of Elizabeth's formidable Secretary of State, who had been appointed to the Privy Council in 1573. The position of Secretary combined the modern-day ministerial post of Home Secretary with that of Foreign Affairs. During his time in office, Walsingham set up and financed a network of spies in order to provide intelligence for the Queen, maintaining out of his own pocket more than one hundred secret agents both at home and abroad, one of whom was Christopher

Marlowe. It is even thought that William Shakespeare was employed by Walsingham in an undercover role in the Queen's Secret Service at one time.

Walsingham was highly intelligent, wily, authoritative and astute, all essential qualities for a successful Privy Councillor at the Court of Elizabeth. Initially as Cecil's protégé, he worked in close harness with this great patrician whom Elizabeth called 'her spirit', and by that time had become Lord Treasurer and the senior statesman of the Elizabethan era. Yet as Walsingham established himself and gained confidence in his abilities, their contrasting beliefs and attitudes, particularly in the conduct of relationships with Spain, tended to make them draw further apart. Walsingham's confrontational stance made Elizabeth uneasy, while William Cecil found such belligerence towards Europe's most powerful nation most alarming. Nevertheless, they developed enormous respect for each other and were united in unswerving loyalty to the Queen and the well-being of her nation. Like Cecil, Walsingham suffered poor health throughout most of his life, just as Hatton was to develop a serious kidney complaint. Considering the long and excellent service he was to give the Queen over so many years both as Privy Councillor and Principal Secretary, Walsingham was scantily rewarded. Eventually he was given a knighthood, but no further honour followed. Unlike some other less able, but more favoured courtiers, Walsingham was not granted any lucrative sinecures and thus far from becoming very wealthy like many of his colleagues, he was extremely poor when he died and had so many creditors that he was supposedly buried in secret.

Walsingham was one of Elizabeth's more devious Councillors, economical with the truth, as a modern diplomat was famously to declare. He could be both deceitful and obstructive in his dealings with the Queen, who became well aware that some of the policies which she wished to pursue were subtly but effectively turned aside by her long-time Principal Secretary. Naturally, such high-handed yet difficult-to-substantiate actions were resented and while Elizabeth did not want yes-men around her and actively encouraged independent thinking and advice, Walsingham's lack of material reward was to some extent of his own making.

To be one of Elizabeth's Councillors by no means guaranteed a peaceful and prosperous career. Elizabeth's criticism of them could be very public and brutally humiliating. 'Her Majesty's unkind dealing towards him hath so wounded him as he could take no comfort to stay there',[9] wrote Walsingham to Cecil in 1586, explaining his own sudden departure from the Court. Grown men resorted to sometimes pathetic tactics when confronted by

Elizabeth's fury: they would retire from the Court in a huff, sulking, feigning illness like Lord Robert Dudley or threatening to resign as William Cecil did on numerous occasions, 'to serve her Majesty elsewhere, be it in kitchen or garden', as his most famous letter of resignation stated. Cecil had served three decades before becoming Lord Burghley.

Even the longest-serving royal favourite, Sir Robert Dudley, later Earl of Leicester, was upset by her wrath. 'After having had so many months sustained by her indignation, beseeches her to behold with the eyes of her princely clemency his wretched and depressed estate and to restore him some degree of her Majesty's former grace and favour',[10] ran his plaintive letter to the Queen in January 1588.

Surprisingly her incredibly harsh words which flew around the Royal Court like hordes of angry hornets could create a curious feeling of camaraderie. The beleaguered courtiers would shake their heads and chuckle to each other how much like her father the Queen was and carry on as if nothing had happened. In this respect her legendary temper sometimes proved counter-productive. Perhaps that was all part of the act: '*Per ardua ad astra*'.

Burghley, Leicester, Hatton and Walsingham were the four major long-serving members of Elizabeth's Privy Council and she was indeed fortunate to have such a formidable quartet of statesmen at her disposal during the critical years in the countdown to inevitable conflict with Spain. By the time the Spanish Armada had been sighted off the Cornish coast in the summer of 1588, they had collectively served on her Council for more than a decade and thus knew each other intimately. They recognized one another's strengths and weaknesses and had developed a strong mutual understanding. In turn, the Queen was wholly confident of their abilities, having known Burghley as a Councillor throughout her reign, while Leicester had served for more than a quarter of a century, Walsingham for seventeen years and Hatton more than a decade. Elizabeth by then was into her fifties, a highly experienced monarch on a very secure throne.

However, the Queen displayed an irritating tendency of being quick to take the credit for the actions of her Privy Council, while being equally agile at distancing herself from anything that went wrong or might be seen by the world at large as unpopular, being extremely conscious of her image, particularly overseas. A classic example of this was the execution of Elizabeth's cousin, Mary, Queen of Scots in February 1587. Mary had sought political asylum in England in 1568 but had progressively become the focus of Catholic conspiracies and had ultimately been confined at Fotheringhay Castle in Northamptonshire. There existed the unthinkable scenario of Elizabeth being assassinated and an attempt mounted to place Mary on the throne, being the most obvious claimant by virtue of being the granddaughter of James IV of Scotland, whom Henry VIII's sister Margaret had married. There was a grave risk of civil war in the event of this happening, something the Council were determined to avoid at all costs; this was an aim shared by everyone concerned, rapidly uniting all those of differing viewpoints.

Walsingham's agents had unearthed first the Ridolfi Plot, then the Babington Plot, both conspiracies implicating Mary, Queen of Scots. Once more, the Council was strongly motivated in its thinking by the fact that Elizabeth was unmarried, with no obvious direct successor within England. Hatton and Sir Walter Mildmay, another shrewd Privy Councillor and friend of Lord Burghley, holding similarly strong Protestant beliefs, mustered parliamentary support for Mary's execution. Burghley masterminded the trial at Fotheringhay and subsequently persuaded Elizabeth to sign the death warrant. The Council then acted with great speed, carrying out Mary's execution before the Queen could change her mind and countermand her own order.

When Elizabeth discovered that the axe had fallen on her cousin's head, she predictably fled into one of her famous rages. Burghley was berated, 'traitor, false dissembler and wicked wretch, and all about the death of the Scottish Queen'.[11] A huge display of grovelling by Burghley was to no avail – the Queen was unimpressed and it was many months before the chastened Lord Treasurer was allowed back into favour. Burghley was more fortunate than the hapless Secretary, William Davison, who had brought the death warrant for Elizabeth to sign. In classic 'shoot the messenger' mode, the wretched Davison was thrown in the Tower and although released some eighteen months later, his political career was in ruins. While the Queen might rant and rave against her advisers for the execution of her cousin and fellow queen, these tantrums, partly brought about by guilt, were mainly play-acting in an attempt to quieten public opinion, particularly abroad. In this instance her theatrical posturing proved effective. Reaction from the rest of Europe was relatively muted. Even in Scotland, the mood was surprisingly low-key as James VI appeared more mindful of his prospects of succeeding Elizabeth than the fate of his mother. It was the clever, yet politically naive James whom the French King Henry IV later dubbed, 'the wisest fool in Christendom'.[12] Ultimately it was Elizabeth's failure to marry and produce an heir that had sealed her cousin's fate.

These were, however, desperate times: the Armada was gathering at Cadiz and both Queen and Council needed to maintain a strong united kingdom in the face of this mounting external threat, one to which nobody knew how the extensive Catholic population in England would react. 'The cutting away of the Queen of Scots has wonderfully eased the body of the state',[13] was the satisfied Council's collective view after the Queen's rage had finally subsided; sometimes it was difficult to know precisely who was pulling the strings.

Ultimately, the burden of office, coupled with the passage of time, ended the lives of the Queen's key Councillors in the golden years of her reign. The Earl of Leicester died, probably from malaria, in the autumn of 1588 not long after the defeat of the Armada, closely followed by Sir Walter Mildmay, her astute Chancellor of the Exchequer in 1589. Walsingham exited a year later, then Sir Christopher Hatton in 1591 and finally Lord Burghley in 1598. The Council was never to be quite the same again. The loss of so many of her long-standing trusted advisers in such a short period made the Queen very cautious in her choice of replacements. She developed an unfortunate tendency to replace fathers with their sons, in a hopeful belief that ability was somehow hereditary. Thus Sir Francis Knollys was succeeded by his son William, and Lord Admiral Howard and the Barons Hunsdon and Buckhurst by their offspring. None of them were the men their fathers were. Paradoxically, the Queen stubbornly refused to countenance the possibility of either of Sir Nicholas Bacon's sons becoming Councillors, particularly the highly talented Francis who was not destined to be a member of the Privy Council until the reign of James I. He was then made successively Attorney General and then Lord Chancellor, but later was accused of accepting bribes and dismissed from office in disgrace, thereby belatedly justifying Elizabeth's judgement of him.

Francis Bacon had been constantly touted for office by Robert Devereux, the 2nd Earl of Essex, Leicester's stepson, who towards the end of the sixteenth century had become a major influence on Elizabeth, the last of a long line of good-looking young men to catch her eye and become a royal favourite. He was created a Privy Councillor in 1593, arguably one of the few bad mistakes in a major appointment that Elizabeth ever made, although to his credit Essex initially tried hard to assimilate the demands of his new post, thereby justifying his appointment. It is difficult to try and visualize precisely what Elizabeth had hoped to achieve with this uncharacteristically precipitous action. If it was an attempt to repeat her success upon elevating Essex's stepfather and former royal favourite, the Earl of Leicester, to the Council all those years ago, then her actions failed miserably. Essex was the ultimate spoilt child, handsome, pampered, privileged, doted on by parents and a besotted aged Queen. Perhaps she was nostalgic for her own lost youth and unconsummated love. If she regarded Essex as a child substitute and wished to indulge him, she was to be bitterly disappointed, muttering disconsolately that it would be most fitting if someone could teach him some manners.

On one occasion Essex insolently turned his back on the Queen, an unpardonable breach of Court etiquette. The outraged Elizabeth boxed his ears, Essex in turn lost his temper and instinctively reached for his sword to the consternation of the watching courtiers who quickly hustled him away. The Queen may be seen to be at fault: like many long-serving rulers, her reign had gone on too long and, like many of advancing years, she was out of touch with current thinking, unable to identify with the younger generation, happy for them to adorn her Court but not prepared to listen to their advice – 'she said that they were young and had no experience in affairs of state'.[14] Essex was a typical young man in a hurry, despising the old ways, contemptuous of his elders and betters, impetuous, emotional, irrational, absurdly jealous often for no particular reason, and prone to sulking when thwarted in his endeavours. If all this was not bad enough, Essex was faced with a formidable adversary, equally young and determined, yet different in all respects – Robert Cecil, the diminutive younger son of Lord Burghley.

Robert Cecil was the total antithesis of the usual Elizabethan stereotype who rose to prominence in the Royal Court. Barely five feet tall with a disproportionally large head, he also suffered from a curved spine, giving him the appearance of a hunchback, the result so it was said of being dropped as a baby. In Elizabethan days those who were particularly small were at a distinct disadvantage, unless seeking a post as a court jester. Dwarfs were either objects of derision or depicted as the embodiment of evil. Furthermore, Tudor historians had branded Richard III as a hunchback, something Elizabethans were reminded of every time Shakespeare's play was performed.

The Queen nicknamed Robert Cecil 'my pigmy'. 'I mislike not the name she gave me, only because she gives it',[15] he dolefully wrote to his father, who lobbied the Queen endlessly on his son's behalf, once for ten whole days when Elizabeth visited him at Theobolds. Robert Cecil was disliked and mistrusted by most of the Court and Council and was under no illusion in that respect. 'The world is not apt behind one's back to speak well,'[16] he said to fellow courtier Sir John Puckering in 1592. 'Robert the Devil' was one of many unkind nicknames Cecil was given in his lifetime and history continues to view him in the same light. 'One of the ablest yet at the same time nastiest members of Elizabeth's Privy Council', says a modern historian, conjuring up a vision of an Elizabethan Joseph Goebbels. Even today, prominent politicians of diminutive height are often disparaged.

Cecil was a loner who would have to succeed by sheer ability and dedication rather than grace and favour. He was, however, supremely self-confident: John de Critz's portrait, commissioned by Cecil himself, captures a quite handsome face with a coldly inquisitive stare, elegant, fastidious and rather arrogant. In Council, he was an eloquent speaker, both articulate and succinct in marshalling his argument; these qualities stood him in good stead in Parliament where he was in regular attendance while in session. At all times, the inscrutable Cecil elevated discretion to an art form, 'so subtle is the Secretary that hardly can it be judged which way he will take',[17] observed an admiring onlooker of this Elizabethan prince of darkness.

If Burghley was a pragmatist, then his son took the art of pragmatism to its outer limits. The description 'Machiavellian' which is often applied to Robert Cecil is highly appropriate, for like his father he had read Nicolo Machiavelli's definitive *Discorsi* published in 1531, a revolutionary exposition of the art of statesmanship. Robert Cecil firmly embraced Machiavelli's fundamental principle that a ruler holds a kingdom not by grace of God, but by proficiency in government. While Burghley had a profound love and reverence for the Queen as a person, his son regarded her merely as a symbol of the Head of State, part of the apparatus of power but not its defining element, to be judged like anyone else in government, purely by performance. What the Queen made of Robert Cecil is impossible to fathom – their relationship is possibly best summed up in Cecil's classic comment on his sovereign, 'More than a man and in truth sometimes less than a woman',[18] one of those pithy short phrases for which the Elizabethan era is justly famous and which may well have delighted the Queen had it come to her ears.

Not surprisingly Essex and Robert Cecil hated one another. This time the Queen's well-used stratagem of placing opposites on her Council came violently unstuck. The snobbish Earl of Essex branded Cecil as an upstart newcomer, the latter responding with a rare flash of humour by incorporating the phrase, '*Sero Sed Serio*' – 'Late But Earnest', on his coat of arms. In turn, Cecil disliked Essex's privileged background, his unwarranted promotion to the Council and the characteristics displayed by his impetuous rival which were so fundamentally opposed to everything that Cecil believed in so fervently. Most of all, Robert Cecil was alarmed by the disenchanted and dangerous faction of impressionable young courtiers who were collecting around the charismatic Earl, which he considered threatened both the Queen and the security of her kingdom. Essex's wanton behaviour and headstrong actions became so outrageous that Cecil was able to persuade the Queen to act without too much difficulty. Essex was arrested and tried for treason, having led an armed march through the city of London demonstrating against the Queen. One of the state prosecutors was his erstwhile friend and protector, Francis Bacon. The Earl of Essex was executed at the Tower in the early spring of 1601, the Queen declaring, more in sorrow than in anger, that he should not have touched her sceptre. This tragic episode clouded the last few years of an otherwise glorious reign, causing the very thing that the Queen most dreaded – unpopularity with her subjects, many of whom had held the Earl in considerable regard. Characteristically, Elizabeth tried to shift the blame onto Robert Cecil. Not that he cared: Essex's demise had left him in total control. 'Little Cecil trips up and down, he ruleth both Court and Crown',[19] ran a popular poem of the day.

Though physically short in stature, Cecil intellectually towered above his fellow Privy Councillors in the final years of Elizabeth's reign, in a manner which was to the detriment of the nation. The dynamic blend of passion and *realpolitik* characterizing the days of Burghley and Leicester that had served the Queen so admirably were well and truly past – Elizabeth was a spent force. 'A notable decay of judgement and memory, in so much as she cannot abide discourses of government and state, but delighteth to hear old Canterbury tales to which she is very attentive',[20] wrote a courtier to a friend in Venice. It was almost as if senility was beginning to manifest itself in the sovereign. 'The Queen is wholly directed by Mr Secretary who now rules all as his father did,'[21] bemoaned another courtier.

By now Cecil's coldly penetrating gaze had moved northwards, away from a Queen in the sunset of her reign as he happily orchestrated something Elizabeth had never been prepared to contemplate – her successor on the English throne. The well-being of the state combined with self-interest had supplanted everything else in Cecil's cool and calculating mind. No longer the Queen's man, he had begun directing all his energies into ensuring that James VI of Scotland became James I of England. 'All are in a dump at Court. Some from present danger, others doubt that she will not continue past the month of May, but generally all are of the opinion she cannot overpass another winter',[22] wrote Antony Rivers to Giacomo Creleto in Venice.

Elizabeth, the last and most successful of all the Tudor monarchs lay on a pile of cushions in the Privy Chamber at her favourite Palace of Richmond staring into space, saying nothing. 'Madam,' said Cecil, 'to content the people you must go to bed.' 'Little man,' retorted the Queen frostily, 'the word "must" is not to be used to Princes.'[23] Perhaps, like the rest of her Court, Elizabeth did not like Robert Cecil very much either.

5

THE SEAFARERS

D rake, Hawkins, Ralegh, Grenville, Frobisher – these names still reverberate down the centuries, names that feature proudly on modern-day warships and naval bases, the memories of their exploits remaining inspirational to sailors of the present day. They were the leading figures among a host of professional seafarers whose swashbuckling actions initiated the nation's long tradition as a major naval power yet raised many eyebrows at the time and, viewed from today's different moral perspective, are constantly open to question. John Hawkins had begun life as a slave trader, 'being amongst other particulars assured that negroes were very good merchandise in Hispaniola'.[1] The Spanish regarded Francis Drake as a pirate '*El Draques*', 'master thief of the unknown world', viewing Frobisher and Grenville in much the same vein, constantly immersed in piratical enterprise. At times, the collective exploits of Elizabethan seafarers could prove highly embarrassing to both the Queen and her Privy Council; judged by today's standards these activities would be seen as highly questionable, in many instances totally illegal. Elizabeth alternated between encouraging their efforts and distancing herself from them as her policies towards Spain oscillated wildly between aggression and appeasement. Generally, England benefited from the adventures of these seafarers and the Queen was fortunate to have so many available for her services, yet their aggressive actions towards Spain, most particularly those of Drake, were one of the major factors which inevitably led to war – the seafarers could indeed be a two-edged sword.

Many of these seafarers were from the West Country, sailing out of the Port of Plymouth. Hawkins, Drake and Ralegh were all born in Devon, tough, resourceful, determined to use their seafaring qualities to acquire both fame and fortune aided by the improved technical knowledge of deep-sea shipping, by then more readily available in Elizabeth's kingdom. Hawkins came from a seafaring family – his father, William Hawkins, had been an enterprising maritime merchant during the reign of Henry VIII. Drake came from farming stock on the edge of Dartmoor and Ralegh was descended from impoverished gentry in East Devon.

Hawkins and Drake were cousins; the younger Drake came under the more experienced Hawkins's influence and they voyaged offshore together to the west coast of Africa, then across the Atlantic Ocean to the Caribbean in order to seek rich pickings in the Spanish colonies which had become well established in that region. It was here in 1568 in a small coastal port named San Juan de Ulua, on the shores of Mexico, that an incident occurred which was to haunt Drake for the rest of his life and cast a massive stain on his reputation. Hawkins's and Drake's ships, anchored together in harbour, were subject to a sudden surprise attack by the Spaniards, causing Drake to seek his own safety and sail away into the night on his ship *The Judith*, leaving Hawkins to his fate. The latter, on *The Minion*, was very lucky to escape and his subsequent bitter comments put Drake in a very poor light: 'So with The Minion only and The Judith, a small bark of 50 tons, we escaped, which bark the same night forsook us in our great misery.'[2] Hawkins never asked Drake to sail with him again.

John Hawkins prospered and became both a Member of Parliament and a friend of Lord Burghley, subsequently coming to the attention of Queen Elizabeth, who with a characteristic flash of inspiration appointed him her Navy Treasurer responsible for the development and maintenance of her fleet. This appointment was made in 1577, by which time Elizabeth had come to realize that a strong navy was essential for the defence of her realm against the growing threat from Spain, a view shared by Lord Burghley. 'Her Majesties special and most proper defence must be her ships,'[3] declared the Queen's most influential Privy Councillor. Today Hawkins's transformation from slave trader to government civil servant might seem extraordinary, a classic case of turning the poacher into a gamekeeper; quite an unorthodox move yet nevertheless one which showed the Queen's acute perception of human nature together with an appreciation of a man's essential qualities to fulfil her requirements in important matters affecting the security of her nation.

Hawkins discovered corruption to be rife among many of those directly responsible for the building and repairing of Elizabeth's ships, which, combined with inefficient practices, meant that the whole process of maintaining the navy was costing considerably more than necessary. Warships were being constructed with unsuitable or even rotten timbers which, together with many other questionable methods, greatly prejudiced the construction of a sound and suitable fleet. Hawkins fearlessly routed out corruption to the highest level, even accusing Sir William Wynter, at the time Surveyor of the Queen's ships. Hawkins was able to reduce costs considerably and to produce far better quality ships but in the process he made some very powerful enemies and in turn was accused of malpractice. The Queen convened a high-level inquiry to examine these grave charges. The inquiry board, consisting of Burghley, Walsingham, Earl Lincoln, Lord Hunsdon, the Lord Chamberlain and Sir Walter Mildmay, Chancellor of the Exchequer, met in order to enquire into 'the articles of discovery in the unjust mind and deceitful dealings of John Hawkins'.[4] His accusers were numerous: 'I was also an eye witness of a great abuse committed in the store house by the said Mr Hawkins,'[5] proclaimed one of his many detractors. The charges proved groundless and Hawkins was completely exonerated, much to the Queen's great delight, as by then he was engaged in the vital task of preparing her navy to meet the Spanish Armada.

A man of considerable vision, Hawkins both revolutionized maritime construction and pioneered naval warfare. *The Revenge*, a warship that Francis Drake was to command against the Armada, became the model for successive generations of English fighting vessels. His concepts for the tactical deployment of the English fleet ushered in a totally new approach to war at sea, which was still in use during Nelson's time, three hundred years later.

Bold and brilliant in his approach, Hawkins was a consummate seaman and a hugely competent navigator, yet at the same time both cautious and methodical in the execution of his plans. Above all, he was deeply patriotic, a fanatical Protestant and fiercely loyal to the Queen, to whom he was deeply devoted. 'There is hardly any time left to serve God,'[6] he declared towards the end of his life. As he lay dying, Hawkins commanded one of his subordinates, Captain Troughton, to write a long letter to the Queen on his behalf, its contents eloquently conveying the sentiments of Elizabeth's veteran commander at the end of his days: 'Sir John Hawkins upon his deathbed willed me to use the best means I could to equate your highness with his loyal service and good meaning towards your majesty . . .'[7] He apologized to Elizabeth for the failure of his last mission, yet another attack on the Spanish Main, and left her a considerable sum of money in his will to compensate for her lack of financial return from this voyage. Hawkins's loyalty was unquestionable – he was modest but at the same time hugely ambitious, astute and utterly fearless, with a profound belief in his Maker. He commanded his crews to serve God daily, love one another, preserve their victuals, beware of fire and keep good company. He was always one of the most serious and scholarly of Elizabeth's seafarers, educated, articulate, meticulous both in appearance and action. His relationship with Elizabeth was at all times punctilious yet persuasive and in turn she held him in great regard during all his years of service.

The defeat of the Spanish Armada proved a high spot for both Queen and country and so it was for John Hawkins, Vice Admiral of Elizabeth's fleet in this epic sea battle. The English commander, Lord Charles Howard of Effingham, exercised his right to knight a number of his officers on the spot for supreme gallantry while on active service. Hawkins was among those chosen and on a bright summer's day as the fleet drifted slowly on the morning tide off the coast near Dover, it seemed that the Royal Court had come to sea, as with due pomp and ceremony Lord Howard dubbed Hawkins with his sword before an assembled crowd of captains and nobility, the *Ark Royal* dressed overall and everyone in their finery. Other recipients of knighthoods included Lord Sheffield and Lord Thomas Howard, for whom the award was an equally great honour – their titles had been hereditary, but a knighthood had to be earned and to be created a knight on the field of battle was a singular honour even for the aristocracy.

Francis Drake had achieved his knighthood via an altogether different route after he had parted company with Hawkins on the Spanish Main in such ignominious circumstances and returned to England. Drake was also a supreme seaman, arguably the greatest of the age, but a very different character to his mentor Hawkins, in many respects the total opposite. Unlike Hawkins, Drake was impulsive and impetuous, most of his actions being wholly unplanned and many of his most daring manoeuvres purely instinctive. Whereas Hawkins was a modest man, modesty was never among Drake's attributes, being a tremendous self-publicist. He was quick-tempered, opportunistic, imaginative and boundlessly self-confident, with a deeply held hatred of Catholicism and Spain, against whom he had waged a relentless one-man Holy War ever since the time of the San Juan de Ulua incident, when Drake was still in his early twenties.

Drake developed an easy rapport with the Queen, who regarded him as a winner, an all-purpose action man to be fully exploited to suit her own needs, yet he was viewed with misgiving by many of her Privy Councillors who were jealous of his direct access to Elizabeth. They regarded him as too much of a maverick, a loose cannon, capable of single-handedly blowing apart the nation's fragile relationship with

Spain. 'The Queen shows extraordinary favour to Drake and never fails to speak to him when she goes out in public, conversing with him for a long time,'[8] muttered Mendoza. The Spanish ambassador's distrust of Drake was one of the few things that he would have shared with the peace-loving Lord Burghley. A feature of the middle period of Elizabeth's reign was the rise of a growing number of aggressive Privy Councillors – men like Walsingham and Hatton – coinciding with the belligerent actions of seafarers like Drake, Frobisher, Grenville and their followers, linking up to constantly goad Spain. Hatton was Drake's major patron, and Walsingham shared Hawkins's belief that the enemies of England were the enemies of God. This abrasive combination of statesmen and seafarers proved a mixed blessing for the Queen: when hostilities with Spain began, she could count on a resolute government and a combative group of seafarers to become her swordbearers, yet it may well have been that without Spain being continually harassed and antagonized there might never have been a war. Drake's personal contribution to this scenario was immense. His voyage around the world, his plundering on the Spanish Main, his surprise attack on Cadiz, that celebrated 'singeing of the King of Spain's beard',[9] were all seen as acts of supreme provocation by Philip II of Spain. To brand Drake as a pirate is conceivably too harsh, yet he was undoubtedly a privateer, licensed by the Queen to carry out unprovoked attacks on Spanish ships and territories at a time of peace between the two nations.

In many respects Drake and the Queen were made for each other, and suited each other's purposes. She gave Drake a licence to kill, launching him like a long-range guided missile to strike with terrifying suddenness on the far side of the world – and he became extremely wealthy in the process. Yet if Drake grew rich then the Queen became even richer, while basking in the glory of his achievements. It remained a convenient partnership for a considerable number of years, but the price was a costly war lasting until after both of them were dead. Drake's value to the Queen, both actual and psychological, was immense in those distant days before radar, satellite observation or any scientific spotting aid other than a telescope. Drake was the sixteenth-century forerunner of the nuclear submarine, cruising vast, empty oceans, to appear undetected, suddenly and unexpectedly with devastating effect. The Spanish possessed no effective remedy against him, no seafarer equivalent to him who could be launched in retaliation. No comparable Spanish reprisal raids were launched against the English coast until towards the end of the century, and even these were on a small scale compared to the savage assaults mounted by Drake.

Drake was short and stocky with a jaunty stance and a cocky, rather arrogant face, sharing a similar stature with other men of military genius – Alexander the Great, Julius Caesar, Napoleon, Nelson and Montgomery. However, while Drake possessed many of their warrior attributes, he displayed considerable shortcomings as a commander on any scale. Drake was at his best commanding a single ship or at most a limited strike force such as that used for the 1587 raid on Cadiz. Unlike Nelson, he lacked strategic vision, and was a poor planner, without any sense of detail or the ability to remain focused. He could easily be diverted from the task in hand by secondary considerations and his sense of patriotism was almost always accompanied by an insatiable pursuit for personal profit; for example, when Lord Admiral Howard had instructed the English fleet to follow Drake's stern lantern in pursuit of the Armada at night. Drake extinguished the light in order to go off and capture a crippled Spanish galleon. Frobisher was one of Drake's fellow seafarers who was deeply incensed by his actions at this time, 'calling him a cowardly knave or traitor and that he only remained by the great Spanish carack to have the spoil of her'.[10] Frobisher vowed Drake should eat his words, 'or he should make him spend the best blood in his belly'.[11] Fortunately Drake's diversion had no detrimental effect on the outcome of the battle but certainly furthered his personal fortune once victory had been secured. He had wanted to introduce to the Queen, Don Pedro de Valdès, commander of the *Nuestra Señora del Rosario*, the flagship of the squadron of Andalusia which Drake had captured. Elizabeth declined to meet Don Pedro, but indicated to Drake that he was free to extract as much ransom from the Spaniard as possible.

Drake's shortcomings as a commander on a large scale were fully exposed during the disastrous expedition to Portugal and the Azores in 1589, when the Queen had hoped to exploit the victory over the Armada. A combination of poor organization and leadership, accompanied by sheer bad luck, led to the complete failure of this ill-conceived venture and a very angry Elizabeth accused Drake of going to places, 'more for profit than service'.[12] Earlier she had suspected that her favourite, the Earl of Essex, had joined the venture and warned Drake, together with the expedition's army commander, Colonel John Norris, that, 'if Essex had joined the fleet they are forthwith to cause him to be sent home . . . if they do not they shall look to answer for the same, at their smart, for these be no childish actions'.[13] The Queen was just as capable of treating her seafarers like naughty schoolboys as her statesmen.

Drake was always circumspect in his dealings with the Queen;

nevertheless he was never afraid to take issue with her on matters of importance. So when an ever-parsimonious Elizabeth wished to disband the fleet too soon after the Armada's departure from the English shores purely as an economy measure, Drake tactfully disagreed. 'My poor opinion is, that I dare not advise her Majesty to hazard a kingdom with the saving of a little change,'[14] he carefully yet firmly cautioned. The Queen readily accepted Drake's view.

Drake's last expedition on the Queen's behalf, a joint attack with John Hawkins on Panama, was equally unsuccessful, as a combination of inadequate preparation and ill luck caused them to lose the vital element of surprise. Elizabeth had realized this before the expedition had even set sail: 'by your own delays you have made your journey and purposes so notorious that the Spaniard has had sufficient warning to provide for your descent,'[15] she raged at an unusually subdued Drake and Hawkins while they were still in Plymouth. Elizabeth proved to be correct and the Spanish easily beat off the English attack when Drake and Hawkins eventually arrived off the coast of Panama. This proved to be the final voyage of the two greatest seafarers of the Elizabethan age. Hawkins died aboard his ship *The Garland*, off Puerto Rico in the late autumn of 1595. He was followed not long afterwards by Drake as he 'yielded up his spirit like a Christian to his creator quietly in his cabin',[16] aboard his ship *The Defiance*, anchored near Nombre de Dios off the isthmus of Panama – 'amidst a lament of trumpets and the thunder of the guns, the sea received her own again'.[17] Drake passed away in the early hours of 28 January 1596 and was buried at sea in a lead coffin off the small harbour of Portobello. He was fifty-one and by then looked an old man.

Drake was one of the great English folk heroes whose fame was to spread on an international scale, an archetypal man of the people who emerged from obscurity by virtue of his own endeavours to become a person of substance in Elizabethan society. He was the most dazzling of the Queen's seafarers, though he had a darker side, lacking the nobler qualities of his colleagues. There is no necessity for a supreme seaman to be a saint – Nelson certainly was not. Furthermore there is the problem of judging events of some four hundred years ago from a less religious, but paradoxically more moral and humane age in western Europe.

Not surprisingly, when the news of Sir Francis Drake's death reached Spain, it was greeted with wild enthusiasm. Lope de Vega, who had survived the ill-fated Armada expedition in 1588 to become one of Spain's leading dramatists, composed a triumphant poem, *La Dragontea*. In England, the reaction from both Queen and country to the passing of the nation's two most famous seafarers was understandably more muted. It had been a low-key ending for the pair who had caused so much mayhem during their lifetime. The attack on Panama had cost both Hawkins and Drake their lives, as well as costing the Queen a considerable amount of money – she had invested heavily in the expedition. It was impossible to comprehend which she mourned the most. Perhaps in her eyes they had served their purpose and were now expendable.

Drake's success had been achieved by his incomparable skill as a seafarer, his ruthless opportunism and more than his fair share of good fortune. The same could not, however, be said about another of the illustrious seafaring heroes of the Elizabethan era, Sir Richard Grenville. Despite an undoubted ability as a seaman coupled with a fierce determination to succeed, Grenville invariably seemed doomed to lurk in Drake's shadow, Grenville contemptuously regarded Drake as both a braggart and an upstart, simply not in his class, either socially or as a seafarer. The Grenville family collectively appeared to be unlucky – Sir Richard's grandfather was captured by Cornish rebels protesting against Henry's break with Rome and thrown into a cell at Launceston Castle. Sir Richard's father, Roger, had been drowned at sea when, as captain of the *Mary Rose* in 1545, he had gone down with almost all hands as Henry VIII's flagship had foundered in the Solent off Portsmouth before the horrified sovereign's eyes. It was Sir Richard in 1574 who had first devised the scheme for the voyage to the southern ocean which eventually led to Drake's circumnavigation of the globe. Unfortunately, Sir Richard had approached the Queen during one of the periodic moments in time when she did not wish to antagonize Spain, and his plan was rejected as being far too provocative. When the enterprise was revived by Drake, Elizabeth was in a more aggressive mood towards the Spanish, so the adventure was entrusted to Drake instead of Grenville. Timing is all.

Drake had prospered enormously from the voyage and was able to purchase Buckland Abbey in the winter of 1580 from an impecunious Grenville, who was forced to sell the property that Henry VIII had originally given to his grandfather subsequent to the dissolution of the monasteries. It was galling for Sir Richard that the purchaser was his arch-rival Drake, by then knighted by the Queen and wealthy – and in Grenville's eyes more puffed up and insufferable than ever before. To Grenville's understandably jaundiced view there was simply no justice in life. His fortunes only worsened further. First, Drake rescued the demoralized settlers that Sir Richard had taken to Virginia in 1585 in partnership with Sir Walter Ralegh in order to set up a colony in the

New World. Two years later, when the English fleet assembled in order to meet the Armada in 1588, both Grenville and Ralegh were dispatched for duties elsewhere and were unable to take part in the famous victory or share in the glory of one of the most celebrated triumphs in the history of maritime warfare. Elizabeth's image-conscious seafarers were desperately anxious to be in the centre of the action and to be seen performing heroic deeds. When after an exciting close-quarter encounter with the Armada, the commander of the English fleet returned Lord Henry Seymour to the humdrum task of patrolling the Straits of Dover, Seymour was furious and promptly sent a dispatch to the Queen signed sarcastically, 'Your Majesty's most bounden and faithful fisherman'.[18]

Sir Richard Grenville had originally come from an old aristocratic family and undergone legal training at the Inner Temple in London before becoming a Member of Parliament. Always hankering after action and glory, he had fought with distinction in both Hungary and Ireland. Grenville was incredibly brave to an almost suicidal degree, mercurial, explosive. Like Drake, he was wholly unscrupulous when it came to the pursuit of his own interest, but similar to Hawkins in that he was totally loyal to his sovereign, Elizabeth. Grenville would go to ridiculous lengths to enhance his macho image: one of his favourite party tricks was to eat wine glasses at the dinner table, chewing and devouring the splinters while the blood dripped out of his mouth before horrified and bemused fellow diners. Throughout his lifetime Grenville always seemed to be in the wrong place at the wrong time and this trait proved his ultimate downfall. In 1591, his ship *The Revenge*, which he had inherited from Drake, became isolated from the English fleet and surrounded by a large group of Spanish warships under Martin de Bertendona, who had commanded the Levant squadron at the time of the Armada. Bertendona's ships were part of Philip of Spain's newly built fleet which included twelve huge galleons symbolically named after the twelve apostles.

Despite being hopelessly outnumbered, Grenville predictably yet stupidly elected to stand and fight rather than beat a discreet retreat. He then engaged the Spaniards for more than twelve hours in one of those heroic yet pointless encounters which, like the Charge of the Light Brigade, the British are prone to involve themselves in from time to time. Fighting went on throughout the night, during which time two large Spanish warships were sunk and two more very seriously damaged. By dawn Grenville had exhausted his powder and shot and *The Revenge* lay at the enemy's mercy, while, 'round her in a silent ring lay the Spanish ships scored with the marks of her teeth'.[19] As Grenville lay helpless and dying, his decimated and exhausted crew surrendered to the Spanish. 'Here die I Richard Grenville, with a joyful and quiet mind; for I have ended my life as a true soldier ought to do, that hath fought for his country, Queen, religion and honour, whereby my soul most joyfully departeth out of this body, and shall always leave behind it an everlasting fame of a valiant and true soldier.'[20] Grenville, the most unlucky of Elizabeth's seafarers, must be one of the few people to have composed their own epitaph on their deathbed. He had finally achieved the everlasting recognition he so desperately desired. The Revenge sank shortly afterwards along with more than a dozen Spanish ships in a sudden violent gale off the Azores.

Thomas Fenner was another Elizabethan seafarer to be caught alone by a superior force yet managed to fight them off. His encounter with a much larger Portuguese squadron was also off the Azores and his survival was secured by superior seamanship and gunnery. Fenner often sailed with Drake, accompanying him on the epic West Indian raid in 1585, taking part in the assault on Cadiz in 1587 and Drake's Azores expedition in 1589 when he was Vice-Admiral. Fenner had commanded the 500-ton warship The Nonpareil against the Armada the previous year.

Martin Frobisher had also accompanied Drake on his frequent assaults on Spanish ports and shipping, being his second-in-command during the 1585 West Indian campaign. Frobisher was to spend a great deal of time and money in a vain attempt to discover an alternative route to China via the Northwest Passage. He was wholly unsuccessful and the Queen eventually lost patience with him, having originally been an enthusiastic backer of his pioneering efforts. Frobisher was an extremely accomplished navigator, in spite of being virtually illiterate and barely able to write his name. He captained Triumph against the Armada, the largest English warship, well over 1,000 tons, equivalent to any vessel in the Spanish fleet. Along with Drake and Hawkins, he commanded one of the individual squadrons which Howard, the English fleet commander, had formed during the second half of the encounter with the Armada and was always in the thick of the fighting, thoroughly deserving the knighthood awarded to him during the battle: 'For hee had valiantly and discreetly behaved himselfe.'[21]

Walter Ralegh's fame as a seafarer is largely illusory. Unlike Drake, Hawkins, Frobisher and Fenner, he was essentially an amateur sailor in a part-time capacity, unable to make up his mind whether he was a courtier, warrior, suitor or even a poet. In most matters concerning Ralegh, there was inevitably a noticeable credibility gap between aspiration and achievement. His one true moment of glory came as joint commander with the Earl of Essex in the attack on Cadiz in 1597, yet even then Essex took most of the credit for the limited success achieved.

William Borrough, Edward Fenton and John Davis, together with members of the nobility such as the Earl of Cumberland, Lord Thomas Howard, Lord Sheffield and Lord Henry Seymour, were also part of the distinguished company of seafarers who served the Queen so well during her many years on the throne and became her swordsmen in the time of war. Earlier in her life, men like Richard Chancellor, Hugh Willoughby and Anthony Jenkinson distinguished themselves in voyages of exploration. Chancellor sailed so far that he 'came at last to the place where hee found no night at all, but a continuall light and brightnesse of the sunne shining clearly upon the huge and mightie sea.'[22]

By the time of the crucial encounter with the Armada, the key seafarers in the English fleet, men such as Drake, Hawkins, Frobisher and Fenner, were in their prime, whereas the veteran Spanish commander, Don Alvara de Bazan, the Marquis of Santa Cruz, a man who had possessed a formidable seafaring reputation, had recently died, 'that light of war, the father of these soldiers, that valiant and unconquered leader'.[23] Santa Cruz left no obvious replacement, and his second-in-command, Juan Martinez de Recalde, was in his sixties and suffering from very poor health. This was to have a very significant effect when battle commenced.

The English fleet commander, Lord Charles Howard of Effingham, has always been conceivably one of the most underrated of Elizabeth's seafarers, so much so that the Spanish had assumed that Drake was really in command and Howard purely a figurehead. This was certainly not the case as the Lord Admiral was always firmly in control, and at all times made the crucial combat decisions. Howard's qualities as a leader of men in times of war could be compared with Eisenhower, that highly successful Supreme Allied Commander-in-Chief in the later stages of the Second World War. Like Eisenhower, Howard was a perfect conduit between anxious politicians in London and the fighting force under his command. Howard had the ability to get the best out of seafaring prima donnas such as Drake and Frobisher who had crucial roles in his fleet, massaging their egos whenever necessary, swiftly settling disputes and directing his volatile commanders against the enemy rather than each other.

Howard was invariably calm under pressure, displaying an excellent sense of humour during times of stress: 'we have danced as lustily as the gallantest dancers in the Court',[24] he reported to the

Queen as the fleet rode uneasily at anchor in Plymouth Sound, buffeted by strong winds, unprotected by the breakwater that now exists, during a time when 'the oldest fisherman could not remember such a summer season'.[25] The English naval commander dealt patiently with the anxious Queen's request for information about the whereabouts of the Armada. 'I am very sorry to perceive by your letter that her Majesty doth think that we have not sufficiently sought to understand some certainty of the Spanish fleet',[26] he communicated to Walsingham. Howard was at all times acutely aware of the quality and requirements of his men. 'My good Lord, there is here the gallantest company of captains, soldiers and mariners that we have ever seen in England,'[27] he told Lord Burghley, while constantly badgering the Council for extra food and other supplies, continually caring for the needs of his crews and ships.

Charles Howard was particularly appreciative of his Vice-Admiral, the volatile Drake, and anxious to maintain his support. 'Sir, I must not omit to let you know how loving and kindly Sir Francis Drake bareth himself and also how dutifully to her Majesty's service and unto me, being in the place I am in, which I pray you he may receive thanks for, by some private letter from you,'[28] he requested Walsingham.

Howard was equally supportive of his other senior commander, Sir John Hawkins, conscious of the fact that his Rear Admiral had been subject to criticism while building and maintaining the fleet. Thus Howard was at pains to point out that, 'the four great ships, *The Triumph*, *The Elizabeth Jonas*, *The Bear* and *The Victory* are in most Royal and perfect state'.[29] These were the four biggest vessels in his fleet and their successful performance was vital to English prospects in the coming encounter with the Spanish. *Victory* was Hawkins's ship, *White Bear* was commanded by Lord Sheffield, *Triumph* by Martin Frobisher and the *Elizabeth Jonas* by Sir Robert Southwell.

Howard's dry sense of humour was maintained when hostilities finally commenced after the agonizingly long wait for the Armada to appear off the Cornish coast. 'I will not trouble you with any long letter we are at present otherwise occupied than with writing',[30] was his laconic dispatch to Walsingham as the English fleet manoeuvred to engage the Armada from a favourable vantage point. The dispatches between Howard and the Queen and her Council have all the authoritative urgency of a modern-day television newscast and brilliantly capture the mood of the moment. Like Eisenhower more than 300 years later, Howard had lacked previous combat experience but this proved to be no handicap when it came to war. He was a natural leader of men, firm yet courteous, approachable, always keen to seek out advice from his more experienced commanders, yet he alone always made the ultimate choice of action. Howard was crisp and decisive, but never impulsive or headstrong, and he successfully avoided any major mistakes. The history of warfare invariably demonstrates that great military encounters are usually won by the side which commits the fewest errors.

Howard always maintained the Queen's confidence along with that of her most senior ministers. Equally importantly, he commanded the respect of his own senior commanders together with the confidence of the rest of the fleet. Elizabeth was indeed fortunate to have such a capable leader during this crucial conflict and his undoubted qualities ensured he obtained the best from his men with the limited resources at his disposal, thereby achieving ultimate success in one of the most decisive battles in the history of our island nation. Here was a commander destined to become supreme among the greatest of Elizabeth's seafarers, a talented yet temperamental bunch of buccaneers whom the Queen skilfully used in order to further her fortune and fight her cause. England had stood alone against the might of Spain and rose from a nondescript second-rate power to become the envy of the civilized world. However, Elizabeth lacked soldiers of equal skill to her seafarers, possessing no outstanding generals to command her armies, no Marlborough or Wellington to achieve dazzlingly decisive victories in continental Europe. Battles could be decided at sea but wars were normally won on dry land, so the stirring deeds of Elizabethan sailors were never fully consolidated or exploited during her reign with a Crecy, Agincourt or Waterloo. Perhaps that is how the Queen would have wished it; she had no desire to conquer the world yet was fiercely protective of her own kingdom, ably guarded by her seafarers.

6

THE EXPLORERS

Our island kingdom has long enjoyed a well-justified reputation as a seafaring nation, so it is perhaps surprising that English sailors had seemed so reluctant to voyage far beyond their shores during the early part of the sixteenth century. The Portuguese, Spanish and French navigators were far more keen to journey into the unknown, leaving the English floundering in the wake of Columbus, Cortés, Pizarro, Magellan, Bartolomeu Diaz, Vasco da Gama and Jacques Cartier, as they voyaged across great oceans to discover new lands far beyond the horizon while England's sailors remained largely in home waters.

Christopher Columbus's pioneering journey across the Atlantic Ocean inaugurated a great age of discovery which considerably extended the frontiers of the known world. At the same time, the financial fortunes of the nations involved were greatly benefited, as overseas empires were created and important new sources of wealth came into existence. A few years after Columbus had arrived in the New World, the Portuguese navigator Vasco da Gama followed his fellow countryman Diaz around the Cape of Good Hope and, on Christmas Day 1497, landed on the south-eastern coast of Africa, naming it Natal. Vasco da Gama then crossed the Indian Ocean, reaching Calicut on the subcontinent of India the following year, thereby paving the way for Portuguese colonies in Africa and the East.

At this crucial period in the history of exploration, England had been preoccupied with the War of the Roses and although Elizabeth's grandfather, Henry VII, had commissioned John Cabot to conduct exploratory voyages westward across the Atlantic, little was to transpire. Like Columbus and Amerigo Vespucci, the Florentine merchant who gave his name to America, Cabot was of Italian extraction, born in Venice, Giovanni Caboto. When Cabot arrived at Cape Breton Island on 24 June 1497, he was the first European to reach the North American mainland. The journey was made without maps, where none had previously ventured, so it was not surprising that Cabot believed he was in north-east Asia, an area of the globe long familiar to Venetians on account of Marco

Polo's extensive journeys overland to that region several centuries before. The cautious Henry was too involved with the internal matters of his kingdom to follow up Cabot's pioneering efforts with any degree of seriousness. Elizabeth's father, Henry VIII, employed Sebastian Cabot, John's son, who was living in Bristol at the time, to undertake a number of expeditions on his behalf, but Henry displayed little enthusiasm for this type of venture and Sebastian soon transferred his services to the Spanish.

A greater degree of English enterprise had begun during the short reign of Elizabeth's half-brother Edward VI, when the newly formed Company of Merchant Adventurers dispatched three ships under the command of Richard Chancellor and Hugh Willoughby to try and find a north-east passage around Europe in order to develop trade with the Orient. Willoughby was the Captain General sailing in the *Bona Esperanza*, while Chancellor was Pilot General captaining the *Edward Bonaventure*. The pair reached the Court of Ivan the Terrible in the spring of 1554 and successfully initiated trade with Russia, thereby breaking the monopoly of the German Hanseatic towns on the Baltic. Another fearless explorer, Anthony Jenkinson, carried on the pioneering activities which had been initiated by Willoughby and Chancellor, visiting Russia on three occasions during Elizabeth's reign, travelling down the Volga to Astrakhan and the Caspian Sea: 'The nineteenth day the winde being West, and we winding east south east, we sailed tenne leagues, and passed by a great river, which hath his spring in the lande of Siberia.'[1] Jenkinson travelled widely on the Queen's behalf, while in Syria he encountered the Turkish sultan, Suleiman the Magnificent, whose Ottoman Empire stretched from Persia to North Africa and the Balkans:

I have travelled forty daies journey beyond the said sea, towards the Oriental India, and Cathaia, through divers deserts and wildernesses and passed through five kingdomes of the Tartars, and all the lands of Turceman and Zagatay, and so to the great city of Bokhar in Bactria, not without great perils and dangers sundry times.[2]

These journeys were hazardous in the extreme, across trackless wastes, often among hostile tribes or in places where new and unforeseen dangers could loom suddenly and unexpectedly:

The same day, at a southwest sunne, there was a monstrous Whale aboard of us, so neare to our side that we might have thrust a sworde or any other weapon in him, which we durst not doe for feare hee should have overthrown our shippe: and then I called my company together, and all of us shouted, and with the crie we made he departed from us.[3]

Other explorers were not so lucky. Hugh Willoughby and his crew froze to death in Lapland during the winter of 1554. His ship, containing the ice-encrusted bodies, together with Willoughby's diary, was discovered by Russian fishermen the following spring. Richard Chancellor was drowned off the coast of Scotland. Ferdinand Magellan, the Portuguese navigator, credited with being the first person to circumnavigate the globe, was massacred by islanders in the Philippines, and Francisco Pizarro, the Spanish explorer who conquered the Inca Empire in Peru, was assassinated in 1541. Vasco da Gama perished in the Portuguese colony of Goa, while John Hawkins and Francis Drake died aboard their ships anchored off the coast of Puerto Rico. However, the nomadic Arthur Jenkinson was to outlive Elizabeth by eight years, having begun his foreign travels when she was merely thirteen years old.

Explorers needed rich patrons and people in high places with an enthusiasm for discovery, together with an appreciation of the benefits that it might bring. Portuguese exploration had originally been masterminded by Prince Henry the Navigator, whose inspiration led to the progressive colonization of Madeira, the Cape Verde Islands and the Azores. He was also able to persuade Portuguese seafarers to voyage down the west coast of Africa as far as Sierra Leone. Christopher Columbus had been fortunate enough to attract the support of the Spanish King Ferdinand and Queen Isabella, the parents of Catherine of Aragon. This was fairly remarkable as the last of the Moorish invaders had only just been expelled from Granada, and Spain was not a fully unified nation at that time. The elaborate tomb in the Cathedral of Seville shows 'Christobal Colon' as he is known in Spain, guarded by the Kings of Leon, Castille, Aragon and Navara. The French King François I employed the Italian Giovanni da Verrazano to explore the North American coastline on his behalf. Jacques Cartier was in the services of François when he sailed up the St Lawrence River and established Canada as a French possession.

To some extent, England's late entry into the field of exploration may have been the result of geographical accident, which gave Spain and Portugal a decided advantage. Being much further south, the Spanish and the Portuguese navigators could depart from their home ports of Oporto, Lisbon, Lagos and Cadiz on the long transatlantic voyage to the New World, wafted westwards on a warm and favourable tradewind. On reaching the far side, they would have encountered plenty of suitable harbours in the West Indies or Central and South America, together with a welcoming climate. The less fortunate English would usually find themselves punching into the teeth of a westerly gale towards a much bleaker northerly shore: 'The very same day in the afternoone about foure of the clocke, so great a tempest suddenly arose, and the seas were so outrageous that the ships could not keepe their intended course, but some were peforce driven one way, and some another way, to their great perill and hazard.'[4] The direct route across the Atlantic Ocean would bring them into that treacherous area of the Newfoundland Banks where thick fog concealed the icebergs that continually drifted down from polar regions on the cold Labrador counter-current. These icebergs could be as high as the tallest top mast of a Tudor ship; they would loom out of the fog with such speed that if a sharp lookout was not being kept, the ensuing collision would very likely take the ship down to the bottom of the ocean with all hands.

Ashore there were no hoards of silver or mountains of gold awaiting them, as there had been for the early Spanish and Portuguese explorers further south. The barren coastline held no such promise, nor did the interior of the continent, impenetrable forests full of hostile Indians, far more difficult to overcome than the Incas or Aztecs with which the Spanish conquistadors had to contend.

The decided lack of enthusiasm for exploration that had been displayed by England's monarchs prior to Elizabeth's arrival on the throne produced considerable difficulties when the English finally did become predisposed to journey offshore on any meaningful scale. By then, the Spanish and Portuguese had established a virtual monopoly over the majority of the New World, the French were firmly entrenched in Canada and the Portuguese exercised a similar control over the sea routes to India and the Far East. This led to the heroic, yet futile, attempts by the Yorkshire-born Martin Frobisher to try to find an alternative way to the Orient. Frobisher was an orphan who had become the ward of Sir John York, Master of the Mint and a merchant venturer in the Muscovy Company trading with Russia. York had been involved in the abortive attempt to have Lady Jane Grey crowned Queen of England in 1553 and had lost both his freedom and his fortune as a result of supporting this foolish venture. Young Frobisher was sent to sea at the age of eleven on a voyage to Guinea, an experience not uncommon in those days. Drake was a similar age when he first went to sea, as was Horatio Nelson when he joined the Navy. Frobisher traded along the North African coast as far eastward as the Levant in various enterprises that were not always completely lawful. Later, he was closely questioned, 'on suspicion of having fitted out his vessel as a pirate'. Frobisher was merely one of many English sea captains of the Elizabethan era suspected of being involved in piracy, among them John Hawkins and Francis Drake.

In 1576, the Queen granted Martin Frobisher a licence to undertake a transatlantic expedition in order to try and discover a north-west passage to Cathay, as China was known at that time. He sailed with two small ships of 25 tons and one of less than half that size. When he returned to the east coast port of Harwich, Frobisher brought back with him a cargo of black pyrites thought to contain gold, together with an Eskimo – both aroused considerable excitement in England. His next voyage took place a year later when:

. . . on Whit Sunday, being the six and twentieth of May in the yeere of our Lord God 1577, Captaine Frobisher departed from Blacke Wall with one of the Queene Majesties ships called the Aide, of nine score tunnes . . . accompanied with seven score Gentlemen, souldiers and sailers, well furnished with victuals, and other provisions necessarie for one halfe yeere, on this his second voyage for the further discovering of the passage to Cathay, supposed to be on the North and North West part of America . . . by west and northwest navigations where through our merchants may have course and recourse with their merchandize . . . in much shorter time, and with much greater benefite than any others, to their no little commoditie and profite.[5]

Herein lay Elizabeth's interests in exploration: not a noble desire to open up hitherto uncharted waters in the manner of the idealistic Henry the Navigator, but a far more prosaic quest for wealth and alternative markets, commercial considerations which were so often to be the driving force behind the establishment of the British Empire and the efforts of the great empire builders such as Clive of India and Cecil Rhodes.

This desirable aim could have its dangerous side; it was not long before, 'we met great islands of yce, of half a mile, some more, some lesse in compass . . . we tasted the most Boreal blasts mixt with snow and haile, in the moneths of June and July . . .'.[6] When Frobisher and his men landed on the bleak, inhospitable shoreline the natives were decidedly unfriendly: 'They fiercely assaulted our men with their bowes and arrowes, who wounded three of them with our arrowes: and perceiving themselves thus hurt, they desperately leaped off the Rocks into the Sea, and drowned themselves.'[7]

There was little of note to be found in this unfriendly environment which could be taken home to recoup the cost of the voyage and satisfy expectant investors. Ominously it was observed that, 'the stones of this supposed continent with America be altogether sparkled, and glister in the sunne like golde, so likewise doth the sand in the bright water, yet they verifie the old proverb: all is not gold that glistereth'.[8] Notwithstanding this laconic lower-deck assessment of the realities of the situation, as soon as Frobisher returned from this voyage, he hastened to the Court, which at that time was at Windsor, to acquaint the Queen with the success of his expedition and to inform her that plenty of gold ore had been discovered. Elizabeth was greatly pleased and Frobisher was warmly congratulated by the most eminent members of the Court while Her Majesty commended the rest of the gentlemen on the voyage for their skill and courage during this hazardous but apparently profitable adventure.

It was therefore with high hopes that a third voyage was undertaken by Frobisher towards the end of May 1578, the general and all his captains coming to the Court at Greenwich to take their leave of their Queen. Elizabeth presented Frobisher with a gold chain, as the rest of the sea captains kissed her hand and received her gracious encouragement for their forthcoming endeavours.

Back at sea Frobisher's problems mounted rapidly. First, the *Salamander* hit a whale with such force that she was stopped dead in the water. Then the 100-ton vessel *Bark Dennis*, struck a huge piece of floating ice and sank rapidly, within sight of the entire fleet. Finally, a sudden and terrible tempest blew in from the south-east and threatened to trap Frobisher's ships in the ice. His small fleet continued to be dogged by atrocious weather conditions: a foot of snow lay on the decks of the vessels, their ropes and sails were completely frozen and the mariners' clothing continually wet, conditions which caused considerable sickness throughout the fleet. Despite these appalling experiences, Frobisher's ships survived to return to England but with little to show for all their suffering. The Queen's initial enthusiasm for Frobisher's trips to the Arctic wastes rapidly cooled and he was not permitted to undertake further expeditions to this singularly inhospitable part of the world.

The quest to discover the elusive north-west passage to Cathay also fascinated Sir Humphrey Gilbert, the Devon-born half-brother of Sir Walter Ralegh. Gilbert was a well-educated man who had studied at Eton and Oxford University and had been part of Elizabeth's household before she ascended the throne. He later became a soldier and served under Sir Henry Sidney in Ireland where Walter Ralegh had also campaigned before coming to Court. Gilbert had previously written a book entitled *A Discourse of a Discoverie for a new Passage to Cataia*, while vigorously petitioning the Queen to be granted a licence to seek this north-west passage which he was fully convinced would give access to the Orient. However, Elizabeth had awarded this doubtful privilege to the more experienced Martin Frobisher. The Queen did later grant Gilbert a charter in 1578 to undertake a voyage for the purpose of establishing a colony in the New World:

> Elizabeth by the grace of God, Queen of England . . . to all persons whom these presents shall come, greeting. Know ye that . . . we have given and granted and by these presents for us our heirs and successors, do give and grant to our trusty and well beloved servant Humphrey Gilbert of Compton in our County of Devon, knight, and to his heirs and assigns for ever, free liberty and license from time to time and at all times for ever hereafter to discover, search, find out and view such remote heathen and barbarous lands, countries and territories, not actually possessed of any Christian prince or people, as to him, his heirs and assigns . . . shall seem good, and the same to have, hold, occupy and enjoy to him, his heirs and assigns forever, with all commodities, jurisdiction and royalties both by sea and land. . .[9]

Sir Humphrey Gilbert was one of the first people in England to appreciate the potential of establishing settlements overseas in order to provide fresh opportunities for the nation's rapidly expanding population and at the same time develop new markets abroad for English merchants. His was a visionary concept that anticipated the English colonies that were later to be founded in New England on America's Atlantic coastline. However, like so many visionaries, Gilbert was not very practical, and his expedition ended in failure, being poorly planned and underfunded. The disconsolate Gilbert returned to England heavily in debt much to the Queen's amusement, who laughingly exclaimed that Sir Humphrey appeared to be 'not of good hap at sea'. Elizabeth liked her men to be successful, and failure of any sort received little sympathy from either the Queen or her courtiers.

Undeterred, the energetic Sir Humphrey set forth once more with the Queen's authority on a venture financed by members of the Court and the City of London, in an attempt to fulfil his vision of establishing a colony across the Atlantic Ocean for his beloved Queen. Gilbert was a brave and resourceful man, but not a particularly experienced sailor. Although he possessed great intellect and considerable imagination, he was obstinate and self-opinionated, being impetuous, overbearing and reluctant to seek assistance or listen to advice from more capable navigators than himself. After he had airily brushed aside the judgement of Master Cox, his chief pilot, as to the correct course to adopt, Gilbert's largest vessel, the 120-ton *Delight*, foundered off the treacherous coast of Newfoundland. 'This was a heavy and grievous event, to lose at one blowe our chiefe shippe freighted with great provision . . . but more was the losse of our men, which perished to the number almost of a hundred soules',[10] noted Edward Haye aboard the *Golden Hind*, one of Gilbert's other ships. As they were now perilously short of provisions, Gilbert reluctantly decided to abandon the expedition yet foolishly remained determined to take the homeward voyage in a small vessel named *The Squirrel*, which he had been using to explore various creeks and inlets impassable to a larger ship. Edward Haye considered that Gilbert's rash decision to risk his life undertaking a transatlantic voyage using a craft of a mere 10 tons was motivated by overhearing a derisory comment that he was afraid of the sea. Gilbert's daring gesture proved fatal:

> The same Monday night, about twelve of the clocke, or not long after, the frigat being ahead of us in the Golden Hinde, suddenly her lights were out, whereof as it were in a moment, we lost the sight, and withall our watch cryed out, the general was cast away, which was too true. For in a moment, the Frigat was devoured and swallowed up of the Sea.[11]

It was a brave yet foolhardy and unnecessary death, Sir Humphrey Gilbert's undoubted courage proving insufficient to compensate for his numerous shortcomings as a leader. Gilbert's expeditions were poorly conceived and executed, under-financed and hopelessly lacking sufficient resources. He simply did not have the necessary maritime experience to achieve success in so hazardous adventure. Perhaps Gilbert saw death by drowning preferable to facing the ignominy and ridicule that he would encounter when he returned to Elizabeth's Court after yet another failure: 'All the men tired with the tediousnes of so unprofitable a voiage to their seeming . . . much toyle and labour, hard diet and continuall hazard of life was unrecompensed.'[12] The Gilbert family still live at Compton Castle, the South Devon home of Sir Humphrey during the Elizabethan era. A young member of the family born in 1983, the 400th anniversary of Gilbert's last voyage, is named Walter Ralegh Gilbert.

The first Walter Ralegh, who had been one of the investors in

Gilbert's enterprises, took up the challenge to colonize the New World and established the first English colony outside Europe two years later in 1585 on Roanoke Island, christening it 'Virginia' in honour of Queen Elizabeth. The colony was not to last long and a few dispirited survivors were rescued by Francis Drake some years later, yet these faltering efforts of Gilbert and Ralegh initiated the long process which eventually led to a British Empire which at its peak covered more than a quarter of the entire globe.

Ralegh was also a Devonian, born near Budleigh Salterton around 1552, into a family of impoverished country gentry who also were devout Protestants. He was totally obsessed by the sea from a very early age and as a boy constantly sought the company of fishermen and retired sailors. Millais's rather sentimental painting *The Boyhood of Ralegh* shows him on the beach near Budleigh listening intently as an old salt regales Ralegh and a young friend with highly exaggerated tales of adventure on the high seas. Ralegh was enthralled and determined to taste the ventures of life afloat for himself. He was to take part in Gilbert's first voyage to Newfoundland in 1578, and financed Gilbert's second expedition in 1583 which eventually led to the foundation of the colony of Virginia, sending two ships under the command of Philip Amadas and Arthur Barlowe. They reached Roanoke Island in midsummer, to discover a very different land to that encountered by Frobisher and Gilbert much further to the north:

> This island had many goodly woods full of Deere, Conies, Hares, and Fowle: even in the midst of summer in incredible abundance . . . the woods are the highest and reddest cedars of the world . . . beyond this Island there is the maine lande, and over against this island falleth into this spacious water, the great river called Occam . . . we brought home also two of the Savages being lustie men, whose names were Wanchese and Manteo.[13]

The Queen's interest in all these stirring adventures was entirely mercenary – not for her a spirit of pioneering, she was only interested in profit. Elizabeth regarded exploration purely as a potential source of much-needed additional revenue for her cash-starved kingdom and therefore encouraged adventurers such as Frobisher, Gilbert, Jenkinson, Davis, Hawkins, Ralegh and Drake to pursue their dreams in the hope that fanciful tales of untold treasure in far-away places might indeed turn out to be true and benefit her accordingly. Pizarro had discovered a mountain of gold in Peru and Cortés unearthed incredible riches in Mexico – perhaps some of her fearless

Englishmen might do the same. It was well worth trying, and there was little risk in her encouraging these activities, as eager members of her Court or enterprising City merchants could usually be persuaded to underwrite the cost of these voyages, an early example of the public purse being assisted by private enterprise.

In this manner, the pace of Elizabethan exploration gathered momentum. Yet again, the Queen had men around her ready, willing and able to rise to the occasion. They wished to impress their sovereign and needed her stamp of approval to undertake the great adventures that could lead them to fame and fortune:

With a good large winde the twentieth of September, we came to Padstow in Cornewall, God be thanked in saftey, with a losse of twenty persons in all the voyage, and with great profit to the venturers of the said voyage, as also to the whole realm, in bringing home both golde, silver, pearles, and other jewels great store. His name therefore be praised for evermore. Amen'[14]

Without the necessary official documents to prove conclusively that they were on the Queen's bona fide business, these daring explorers ran a strong risk of being accused of piracy, subsequently to be executed, left to rot in some distant tropical dungeon or condemned to the life of a galley slave, never to be seen again. Wily seafarers such as Drake and Hawkins, invariably sailing close to the wind in pursuit of profit by any appropriate means, were always careful to carry the Queen's authorization when voyaging out of their home port of Plymouth to the coast of Africa or the Spanish Main. In return, Elizabeth expected to collect a share of the proceeds on their safe return to port. It was an excellent arrangement for both Elizabeth and her explorers, one which the Queen was to exploit to the full throughout her reign: 'The 8 day being Friday, about 12 of the clocke we wayed at Detford, and set saile all three of us, and bare downe by the Court, where we shotte off our ordinance . . . Her Majestie beholding the same commended it, and bade us farewell, with shaking her hand at us out of the window.'[15]

Life was extremely cheap in the sixteenth century; it came and went with little cause for comment. No one embarked on an ocean voyage for the good of their health and death was an occupational hazard that was accepted as a routine event: 'William Pickman, a souldier was shot in the thigh, who plucked the arrowe out, broke it and left the head behinde. Whereupon the poison wrought so that night, that hee was marvellously swollen, and all his belly and privey parts were as blacke as ynke, and the next morning he died.'[16]

Drake was struck by an Indian arrow just below his eye on his epic three-year voyage around the world and was fortunate to escape with his life. Lesser mortals who were wounded far away from home were often regarded as an unwelcome inconvenience who were expendable and certainly not wanted on voyage: 'And all the sicke men in the Galeon were most uncharitably put ashore, into the woods, in the snows, raine and cold, when men of good health could skarcely endure it, where they ended their lives in the highest degree of misery.'[17] There was no room for passengers on the ships of the Elizabethan explorers. Those seamen who were fortunate enough to survive to tell the tale were equally laconic about those of their comrades who had been left behind: 'In this voyage we lost two men, one in the way by God's visitation, and the other homeward lost overboard with a surge of the sea.'[18] There was never any shortage of volunteers to man the ships that were being prepared for long voyages overseas, particularly those belonging to renowned seafarers such as Drake or Hawkins. Enthusiastic jack-the-lads filled the cobbled quays and crowded taverns of Plymouth's Barbican area, eager for a chance to get aboard. Drake commanded fanatical loyalty from crews devoted enough to follow him to the ends of the earth. In fact, this was where he often took them, sailing literally off the map into uncharted waters, where a navigator such as Nuno de Silva, who knew the local waters, could be hijacked to take them a stage further until his knowledge ran out and he was replaced. Most seamen were eager to risk all for the chance of adventure and a small share of the rich pickings that might come their way after a successful voyage to the Spanish Main: 'We found in her great riches, as jewels and precious stones, thirteen chestes full of royals of plate, foure score pound weight of gold, and sixe and twentie tunne of silver.'[19]

To a simple seaman from the back streets of Plymouth, Bristol or Southampton, there were marvellous sights to be seen along the way in these faraway exotic places: 'the nineteen day at twelve of the clock we had sight of the Canaries. Teneriffa is a high land, with a great high pike like a sugar loafe, and upon the said pike is snow throughout the whole year.'[20] Extraordinary creatures were encountered, the like of which they had never experienced before, wondrous to behold: 'the elephant . . . is the biggest of all foure footed beasts, his fore legs are longer then his hinder, he hath ankles in the lower part of his hinder legges, and five toes on his feete undivided, his snout or tronke is so long and in such forme that it is to him in the stead of a hand', though not everything was quite so favourably inclined towards this mighty tropical beast – 'they have continual warre against Dragons which desire their blood because it is very cold.'[21] Not surprisingly charts of this period contain fearsome drawings together with a warning 'here be dragons'.

New species of plants, fruit and vegetables, including the potato and tobacco, were discovered in foreign parts and brought back to England by Drake and Hawkins. Jean Nicot had introduced tobacco to France in 1560 and Catherine de Medici used to take snuff to cure her migraines, an affliction she had shared with Queen Elizabeth.

The legendary Hawkins family from Plymouth had been among the earliest of Tudor explorers to venture offshore:

Old Mr William Hawkins of Plimmouth, a man for his wisdome, valure, experience, and skill in sea caurses much esteemed . . . being one of the principall Sea-captaines in the West parts of England in his time, not contented with the short voyages commonly then made onely to the knowne coasts of Europe, armed out a tall and goodly shippe of his owne of the burthen of 250 tonnes, called the Paule of Plimmouth, where with he made three long and famous voyages unto the coast of Brasil, a thing in those dayes very rare, especially to our nation.[22]

On one particular occasion Hawkins was to return bringing with him a Brazilian native king whom he presented to the Royal Court at Whitehall Palace and whose exotic appearance caused a mild sensation. William's son, John Hawkins, followed his father to sea, initially trading on the West African coast. It was not long before he became involved in the highly profitable slave trade, financed by two of Elizabeth's Privy Councillors, Lord Robert Dudley and the Earl of Pembroke, using a ship provided by the Queen: 'they brought with them certaine blacke slaves. . . . The colde and moyst aire doth somewhat offend them. Yet doubtless men that are borne in hot Regions may better abide colde, than men that are born in colde regions may abide heat.'[23] Human rights was not an item to be found on the agenda of Tudor England.

Hawkins took his young cousin Francis Drake under his wing and together they started to trade with the Caribbean, challenging the Spanish monopoly in the New World. This led to disaster at San Juan de Ulua, where Spanish treachery cost Hawkins dear in terms of lost treasure and instilled in Drake a relentless hatred of all Spaniards that remained with him for the rest of his life. The Spanish view of this incident was more relaxed, 'an affair of foxes and not of lions'.[24]

Then came a seminal event in the unfolding story of Elizabethan exploration, as a small, storm-battered ship dropped anchor in Plymouth Sound, behind a little rocky outcrop, close to the shore, now known as Drake's Island:

> At Mighelmasse this yeare came Mr Fraunces Drake home to Plymouthe from the Southe Seay and mollocus and wasse roundabout the world and wasse Lacke towe years and thre quarters and brought home great stoore of golde and sylver in blockes. And was afterward in the same yere for his good seruice in thatt behalf done kneighted.[25]

This extraordinary feat of seamanship resulted in England becoming a major sea power, introducing a long maritime tradition maintained to the present day. Drake's achievement is recorded in the 'Black Book', 360 pages of thick paper bound in oaken boards covered in leather. So called on account of its dark colour, it was originally known as 'the town ligger', a contemporary account of Plymouth in the sixteenth century and kept in the West Devon Records Office in the city.

The momentous voyage of 'Francis Drake About the Whole Globe', had originated some three years earlier in 1577 with the Queen desiring that an expedition be mounted 'to the great southe sea',[26] the southern ocean where cartographers confidently believed lay a mysterious undiscovered continent. 'Terra Australis Incognita', hopefully contained treasure beyond their wildest dreams. In reality, this venture was to be a far-flung fund-raising trip to the lightly defended Spanish colonies on the Pacific coast of South America. Naturally, all the best-known sea captains worth their salt were eager to undertake this unique opportunity on behalf of the Queen and she carefully considered their individual merits before passing over the more obvious choices in favour of Francis Drake. Elizabeth felt that John Hawkins was too old for such a long, arduous voyage and could not be spared from the vital task he was about to undertake as her newly appointed Navy Treasurer. Ralegh had been equally keen, but Elizabeth did not consider him to be sufficiently reliable, while at the same time she thought that the fiery Grenville might prove too provocative for the Spanish in whose territory the expedition would be sailing. Likewise Elizabeth sensed that to give command to Frobisher might equally antagonize Spain, thereby jeopardizing the success of a venture for which she had such high hopes of favourable financial returns. She judged Drake to be the most determined of her seafarers, the one most hungry for success while possessing the ability to ensure its fulfilment.

The Queen would deploy the commander of this mission as a long-range political and military weapon, to be launched against Spain with little risk to herself. If all went wrong and Drake was captured by the Spanish, she could easily dissociate herself from the venture, as it seemed unlikely that he would have had any official written authorization. Yet again Elizabeth was manipulating one man's ambition to suit her own aims. Her sentiments were shared by the majority of the key members of the Privy Council: Sir Christopher Hatton, the Earl of Leicester, Sir Francis Walsingham and Lord Admiral Lincoln were all enthusiastic investors in the venture. Only the cautious Lord Burghley declined to participate, thoroughly disapproving of the whole concept, considering it tantamount to piracy as England was not at war with Spain at the time. Thus Drake was controversially chosen ahead of his more senior seafaring colleagues, much to their acute disappointment and irritation, as it was widely realized that this was a unique opportunity to become hugely rich and famous. Although Drake enjoyed the Queen's confidence, he was distrusted by many of his maritime colleagues and widely regarded by most of the more prominent royal courtiers as a bumptious upstart and far too big for his sea boots. In the end, the results of his voyages would totally vindicate Elizabeth's controversial judgement.

Drake was thirty-four years of age at the beginning of the voyage; his jaunty appearance appealed to the Queen, who greatly enjoyed his company, as he made a refreshing change from her sycophantic courtiers, bringing a welcome breath of salt air into the somewhat artificial atmosphere of the Court. Drake was the Queen's kindred spirit, her alter ego whenever she was in an aggressive mood, the warrior queen determined to take on the world. They suited each other's purpose, and Elizabeth realized that she could exploit that ego to her own personal benefit.

Drake's ship was three-masted, displacing around 140 tons, carrying a crew of around 150 including his young brother, Thomas, and John Hawkins's nephew, William. Originally the vessel had been named the *Pelican* but this was changed to *Golden Hind*, a beast that featured on the coat of arms of his patron Sir Christopher Hatton:

The famous voyage of Sir Francis Drake into the South Sea and there hence about the Whole Globe of the earth begun in the yeere of our Lord 1577. . . . This 15 day of November in the yeere of our Lord 1577. M. Francis Drake with a fleete of five ships and barques, and to the number of 164 men, gentlemen and sailers departed from Plimmouth.[27]

They sailed westwards down the English Channel and out into the Atlantic Ocean which they crossed without incident to make landfall on the coast of Brazil. Shortly afterwards there occurred a curious incident involving one of the members of the crew, Thomas Doughty, who, it has been alleged, was placed on the *Golden Hind* by Burghley for the specific purpose of spying on Drake. Although a long-standing friend and colleague of Drake, Doughty was accused of mutiny and heresy. He was tried and found guilty. Before his execution, Doughty dined with Drake and the two of them took communion together from the ship's chaplain Francis Fletcher: 'Whereupon done, the place of execution made ready, he having embraced our Generall and taken his leave of all the company, with prayers for the Queene's Majestie and our realme, in quiet sort of way laid his head to the blocke, where he ended his life.'[28] Drake was later to excommunicate Francis Fletcher merely for preaching a sermon that did not meet with his approval. After the voyage, the Spanish tried to bribe John Doughty, the brother of the executed man, to assassinate Drake.

Just over a month later, Drake's small fleet entered the Straits of Magellan, named after the great Portuguese navigator who had sailed around the world some fifty years earlier: 'The land on both sides is very huge and mountainous . . . covered with snow. This strait is extremely cold, with frost and snow continually. The trees seem to stoope with the burden of the weather.'[29] Shortly afterwards, Drake and his company were hit by a ferocious storm and blown off course well to the south. This mishap had some benefit for it established that South America and Antarctica were not joined together as had previously been supposed, but separated by many miles of empty ocean. Nearly forty years were to pass before the Dutch explorer, Willem Schouten, sailed around the most southerly tip of South America and named the cape Hoorn, after the place where he was born.

When the gale finally abated, Drake was able to resume his trip northwards into the Pacific, the first Englishman to sail this ocean. This manoeuvre caught the Spaniards completely by surprise and wholly unprepared, their territory along the west coast of South America being virtually unprotected. The fox had appeared among the golden geese: Drake was able to sail slowly northwards along the west coast of America, completely unmolested, free to attack and loot Spanish towns and shipping at will. He discovered his crock of gold when he encountered the *Nuestra Señora de la Concepciòn*, off the northern coast of Peru, out of Lima bound for Panama. This giant galleon proved to be a veritable floating treasure house, heavily burdened with gold, silver, jewels and precious gems, there being more than 20 tons of silver aboard. It took Drake and his crew almost a week to transfer this hoard of treasure from the Spanish galleon into the *Golden Hind*.

Continuing northwards, Drake landed on the Californian coast at a place thought to be near the location of the modern city of San Francisco: 'Our Generall called this country Nova Albion and that for two causes. The one in respect of the white bankes and cliffes, which lie towards the sea: and the other because it might have some affinite with our Country in name which sometime so was called.'[30] Just prior to their departure a huge wooden post was erected upon which was fixed a metal plate together with a sixpenny coin featuring the Queen's portrait and coat of arms. Upon the plate was prominently written:

> Be it known unto all men by those present June 17 1579 by the grace of God in the name of Her Majesty Queen Elizabeth of England and her successors for ever, I take possession of this kingdom whose king and people freely resign their right and title in the whole land unto her majestys keeping now named by me and to be known unto all men as Nova Albion. Francis Drake.[31]

Drake and the *Golden Hind* continued eastwards across the Pacific and disaster loomed when his ship hit a submerged rock off the island of Celebes in Indonesia and became firmly stuck. They were aground for almost twenty hours, 'but our generall as hee had always hitherto showed himself courageous, and of a good confidence in the mercie and protection of God . . . and we did our best indevour to save ourselves which it pleased God so to blesse, that in the ende we cleared ourselves most happily of the danger'.[32] This was more by luck than good judgement, for having unavailingly lightened the ship in an attempt to float clear, the *Golden Hind* was finally blown off the rock by a sudden storm. Once more, Drake's legendary good fortune had come to his aid when all seemed lost and he was able to voyage on across the Indian Ocean and around the Cape of Good Hope: 'This cape is a most stately thing. The fairest cape we saw in the whole circumference of the earth and we passed by it the 18 of June.'[33] From there, they journeyed via Sierra Leone to arrive back in England in the autumn of 1580, the entire voyage having taken two years, nine months and thirteen days. Of the five ships that had left Plymouth nearly three years earlier, only the *Golden Hind* returned at that time, and only half the original crew of Drake's ship remained with him at the end of the voyage.

As Drake turned into Plymouth Sound, past Rame Head, he hailed a fishing boat to enquire if the Queen was still alive. England would not be a safe place for him without her protection from irate Spaniards now demanding his head. He anchored offshore and Drake's first wife, Mary Newman, whom he had married in 1569, was brought out in a rowing boat by John Blytheman, the Mayor of Plymouth, to be reunited with her husband, whom she had not seen for three long years. Shortly, he was summoned to London to meet Elizabeth. 'He passes much time with the Queen, by whom he is highly favoured and told how great is the service he has rewarded her',[34] the angry Spanish ambassador, Don Bernardino de Mendoza, reported to an equally irate King Philip of Spain. At the New Year celebrations at Richmond, the Queen flaunted a glittering new crown of emeralds which Drake had presented to her to further taunt the seething ambassador. There followed a series of stormy meetings between Elizabeth and Mendoza during which the Spaniard threatened her with war. Elizabeth was totally unmoved and in April dined with Drake on board the *Golden Hind* which by that time was lying at Deptford; afterwards he was knighted on deck before a large and enthusiastic crowd. This was Drake's finest hour.

Sir Francis Drake's voyage around the world remains one of the greatest journeys ever undertaken. In the Prince's Chamber at the House of Lords, there is a bronze which contains the inscription, 'Sir Francis Drake, Knight, has circumnavigated the globe from east to west and has discovered in the south part of the world many unknown places.' It was a venture which reaped handsome rewards for the Queen and the other investors and at the same time made Drake a legend. Yet again, Elizabeth's keen judgement of human nature and her choice of a man to carry out an important mission was more than justified by subsequent events. None of the original contenders for command of the expedition ever accomplished anything remotely comparable to Drake's dazzling achievement. Frobisher's three voyages to find the Northwest Passage led to nothing of significance. Ralegh's search for the elusive El Dorado proved equally disappointing, while Grenville's hot-blooded and impulsive nature resulted in a heroic yet futile death. The Queen's assessment of Drake's unique qualities of a seamanship coupled with his ruthless and opportunistic nature enabled her to achieve the aim she most desired: profit and prestige on a massive scale. Meanwhile, Spain had been humiliated before the entire world, its maritime supremacy brought into question in brutal fashion. The English Queen basked in Drake's glory as she counted her new-found wealth. Drake had also become extremely rich and, in 1580, he bought Buckland Abbey in

South Devon from the impoverished Sir Richard Grenville. This former Cistercian Abbey had been converted into a splendid private residence subsequent to the dissolution of the monasteries and was located quite close to where Drake had been born, in far more humble circumstances, some thirty-five years prior to his acquisition of the property. The local boy had indeed made good.

Nothing quite like Drake's three-year journey around the world was to occur again for a very considerable time. Another English navigator, Thomas Cavendish, who had been involved in establishing Ralegh's colony in Virginia, circumnavigated the globe between 1586 and 1588, but without such acclaim or material reward. He attempted a similar voyage five years later but perished in the storm-tossed waters of the South Atlantic. John Davis, yet another West Country explorer, penetrated further into the Arctic wastelands than Frobisher, reaching Baffin Bay off north-east Canada, yet still failed to find the elusive Northwest Passage. Davis discovered the Falklands and also gave his name to the strait lying between Canada and Greenland. The most northerly group of Canadian islands are today known as Queen Elizabeth's Islands.

These great maritime journeys into the unknown were truly remarkable feats of navigation, achieved despite very limited technology, in an alien and often hostile environment. Today any amateur sailor aided by satellite navigation can pinpoint their position down to the last yard – in the sixteenth century, there was no reliable method for calculating longitude, while latitude could only be determined using a primitive form of sextant in good visibility. Unlike a modern yacht, a sixteenth-century sailing vessel was square-rigged and could only sail upwind with difficulty. These vessels were small, fragile and unwieldy, oars providing the only alternative form of power to the wind. Although Drake is said to have travelled in considerable style, even reported to have taken a group of musicians with him, the conditions for the crews would be spartan to say the least. These seamen were poorly fed and badly paid, disease was rife, death ever present in a variety of violent forms. Despite all these difficulties and disadvantages, the European explorers progressively broadened the horizons of the known world and established the great colonial empires that were to last for many centuries.

The majority of Elizabethan explorers were in awe of their monarch, even worldly courtiers like Walter Ralegh or grizzled veterans such as Sir Humphrey Gilbert. The Queen was also exceedingly skilled at contriving gestures calculated to ensure their continued admiration and gratitude, as instanced in a letter from Ralegh to Gilbert written in 1583:

Brother, I have sent you a token from Her Majesty, an anchor guided by a lady as you see; and further, Her Highness willed me to send you word that she wished you as great good-hap and safety to your ship as if she herself were there in person; desiring you to have care for yourself as of that which she tendereth; and therefore for her sake you must provide for it accordingly. Further, she commandeth me that you leave your picture with me. . . . So I commit you to the will and protection of God, Who sends us such life or death as He shall please or hath appointed. – Your true Brother, W. Raleigh.[35]

The Queen's message would doubtless have launched Gilbert out across the ocean thinking kindly of his sovereign, exactly as Elizabeth had intended.

Exploration in the second half of the sixteenth century was considerably assisted by progressively greater number of detailed maps becoming available. Two men from the Netherlands, Gerardus Mercator and Abraham Ortelius, were the most influential cartographers of the time. Mercator lived between 1512 and 1594, his most useful contribution to navigation was the atlas which bears his name, which enabled a mariner to plot a course as a straight line, making the same angle on all the meridians. It remains in use to this day. Ortelius's greatest masterpiece was his magnificent *Theatrum Orbis Terrarum*, an atlas containing seventy uniform maps, published in 1567, two years after Mercator's definitive work. However, these world maps produced by Ortelius and Mercator relied on a degree of inspired theoretical guesswork which required updating by the reports of travellers who had actually visited the regions shown on their maps. Mercator acknowledged this in a letter to a colleague after receiving an intrepid Englishman's account of a trip to the Arctic Circle; Mercator amended his maps accordingly, in particular correcting the location of the city of Moscow, which was some distance away from where he had originally placed it.

Lord Burghley was one of Elizabeth's Privy Councillors quick to appreciate the importance of good, reliable maps and was constantly acquiring or commissioning new ones from any source that he could find; many fine examples of these can now be seen at the British Library in London. Cartographers were very highly regarded and could command considerable sums for their services, which were such a vital contribution to the success of any great voyage of discovery.

By the end of Elizabeth's reign, England had become a major maritime nation, largely thanks to the exertions of numerous fearless explorers. The seeds of the British Empire were sown and the foundations of future prosperity of a highly successful trading nation established during the time she was sovereign. Towards the end of her life, the Queen was instrumental in founding the East India Company when she granted a charter to a group of London merchants and City traders in 1600.

'There must be a beginning of any great matter, but the continuing unto the end until it be thoroughly finished yields the true glory',[36] declared Drake to Sir Francis Walsingham. The Queen's explorers valiantly tried to make Drake's words come true and often succeeded.

7

THE SUITORS

As soon as Elizabeth had inherited the English throne, both Privy Council and Parliament began urging their new young Queen to marry, not out of any romantic desire to see her happily settled in marital bliss, but to satisfy the more prosaic requirement of a healthy male heir to secure the succession and maintain the Tudor line. Succession had been a major preoccupation in England ever since the Wars of the Roses when a combination of mainly weak rulers, coupled with heirs who were either disputed, murdered or killed in battle, resulted in a protracted conflict within the nation which nobody wished to see ever again.

The Queen, therefore, soon found herself under considerable pressure to seek a suitable husband. The Privy Council agitated, Parliament petitioned, preachers lectured from the pulpit. Certainly there was no shortage of suitors: Elizabeth was young and desirable, far more attractive than her half-sister Mary had been when she became queen, and the possibility of becoming her consort was a glittering prize either for a member of the English aristocracy or for foreign royalty, even as far away as Russia, from where the Tsar of All the Russias, Ivan the Terrible, ardently sought her favours. Closer to home, there was King Eric XIV of Sweden, as well as King Philip II of Spain, recently widowed from Elizabeth's half-sister, and Archduke Charles of Austria. Even the Pope is reputed to have murmured, 'our children would have ruled the whole world'.[1] Among the English nobility the ageing 12th Earl of Arundel, together with the good-looking yet conceited Sir William Pickering, were early contenders who soon fell by the wayside. Sir William Cecil, the Queen's newly appointed Principal Secretary, assured her that God would find her a husband and in due course the obligatory son.

Elizabeth was in no hurry to oblige. After the isolation she had endured at Hatfield, the new young Queen was revelling in all the attention. It was a hugely enjoyable experience which she wished to continue for as long as possible. She loved the spirit of the chase – it was fun to keep men guessing as to her intentions. She was also aware that actually agreeing to marry might lead to some considerable problems at home or abroad, opening up the unwelcome prospect of entering a political minefield as well as the nuptial chamber. Far too many of the foreign suitors were Catholic, and Elizabeth had vivid memories of how Mary's popularity had quickly waned following the announcement of her intention to marry Prince Philip of Spain. Now Philip had become King and Roman Catholicism had grown even more unpopular in England – Elizabeth had no desire to cause an uprising early in her reign in the manner that Mary had done.

The Queen also found the prospect of marrying the ex-husband of her dead half-sister somewhat bizarre. It had disturbing echoes of her father marrying Catherine of Aragon, his elder brother's widow. Catherine had also been Spanish and the marriage had begun to falter when there was no sign of a male heir. Yet when Elizabeth came to the English throne, Spain was still a major ally and England was at war with France. Therefore, Philip's opportunistic proposal had to be turned down gracefully, with as much tact as could be mustered, in order not to cause offence and generate a Franco-Spanish alliance against England. Much to his secret relief, Philip learnt that Elizabeth would not marry him as she considered herself to be a heretic in his eyes. Shortly afterwards the Spanish King married the French King Henry II's daughter instead. If Elizabeth was surprised at the speed that her supposedly ardent suitor had been able to find an alternative bride, then it was a painless introduction into the international marriage game, wherein politics mixed with pleasure with smoothly practised assurance.

The royal marriage game was like a giant version of chess whereby the map of Europe became an enormous board for knights, kings, queens, the occasional bishop, princes and dukes to be moved around cleverly and endlessly. Like chess, the marriage game was an activity which required vision, patience and consummate skill. Anticipation of moves contemplated by other participants was another key factor – these could be devious, cunning and breathtakingly unorthodox. On one occasion, Elizabeth even proposed Lord Robert Dudley as a suitable husband for Mary, Queen of Scots, thereby enhancing her reputation for a mischievous sense of humour. Other Grand Masters of the game included Catherine de Medici, widow of the French King Henry II. Catherine had produced six children by a husband who still had plenty of time for a mistress, the beauteous Diane de Poitiers. Considerably older than Henry and permanently in mourning for her dead husband, Diane always dressed in black and white. Henry was so entranced by her that he also wore the same colour clothes, giving the amorous couple the appearance of a pair of chess pieces.

Shortly after marriage negotiations with Philip of Spain were halted, an ambassador from Philip's uncle, Ferdinand I, Emperor of the Holy Roman Empire, arrived at the English Court singing the praises of Ferdinand's younger son, the Archduke Charles. This was to prove a more protracted courtship lasting several years, involving envoys and Privy Councillors, such as the Earl of Sussex, shuttling energetically between London and Vienna, together with extensive meetings of the Privy Council to discuss the merits of the potential marriage. Eventually negotiations floundered as Charles was also a Catholic and declined to make the necessary compromises in practising his faith that would prove acceptable in Protestant England. Again, Elizabeth was not unduly concerned, she had merely been going through the motions in order to please her Council.

Eric XIV of Sweden was at least a Protestant, being a keen Lutheran. The Queen dispatched the Flemish artist Steven van der Muelen to Stockholm to have the royal Swede's portrait painted in order to establish what he looked like. The Swedish King was so pleased with the finished result that he rewarded the artist handsomely. Yet beauty is in the eye of the beholder, and Elizabeth was less impressed – Eric's advances were quickly rebuffed despite sending his brother, Duke John of Finland, over to England to plead his cause. This was to prove most unfortunate for Eric, as he was not to last overlong on the Swedish throne, being deposed some seven years later and subsequently poisoned – by his brother Duke John. Eric had first sought Elizabeth's hand some years earlier in 1554 when she was still a princess. Turning down his proposal, Elizabeth wrote to her sister Queen Mary asking, 'for leave to remain in that state I was, which best pleases me. I am at present of the same mind, and intend to continue with Her Majesty's favour. There is no life comparable to it . . . though I was offered the greatest prince in Europe.'[2] And so it was to prove, as the greatest princes in Europe came and went in ever-increasing numbers, continually seeking to claim her hand only to face rejection. The problem appeared to be either a lack of passion or of politically acceptable suitors. In either case, the chemistry never seemed quite right.

Equally irreconcilable considerations inhibited a choice of husband from the ranks of nobility, for to satisfy one was to upset considerably more, thereby causing dangerous divisions within the Royal Court. Elizabeth was mindful of the risk involved in selecting a consort from her own aristocracy following the salutary experience of her cousin, Mary, Queen of Scots. She had been married to the French King François II, who had died barely a year after succeeding to the French throne, leaving Mary to return to her native Scotland. Here she made two short-lived and disastrous marriages with husbands drawn from the nobility. The first was to Elizabeth's young cousin Lord Henry Stuart Darnley, who had been considered by some as a suitable husband for Elizabeth. The marriage was not to last long before Darnley was assassinated, supposedly on the orders of the arrogant James Hepburn, the 4th Earl of Bothwell, who went on to marry Mary and was also suspected of being implicated in her previous husband's murder. This gruesome, Macbeth-like scenario ended with them both in exile, Mary fleeing to England, Bothwell imprisoned in Denmark. These traumatic events hardly encouraged Elizabeth to choose a husband from the ranks of her own nobility. By this time she had fallen in love with Lord Robert Dudley, but he was already married.

The Queen had created the handsome young Lord Dudley her Master of Horse when she first came to the throne in November 1558. He had previously held the post of Master of the Buckhounds when Elizabeth's half-brother, Edward, had been on the throne, and was widely acknowledged as one of the most accomplished riders in the kingdom. The Queen was well aware that he already had a wife, the former Amy Robsart, daughter of a wealthy Norfolk squire, whom Dudley had married when still in his teens; Elizabeth had been a guest at the wedding. When Lord Robert came to Court, Amy was left behind in the country, not an unusual state of affairs for an important royal courtier. However, it was rumoured that their initial loving relationship had already cooled and that Dudley was seeking romance elsewhere.

By the following spring, it had become perfectly obvious that Dudley had become much more to the Queen than merely her Master of Horse; the entire Court was shocked at the intimacy of their passionate relationship and the way in which it was so openly flaunted. Very soon, news of the scandal had spread throughout Europe and scoffing remarks were being made that the English Queen had intentions of marrying her 'horse keeper'. Elizabeth cared not what people thought. After all those tedious years, interspersed with moments of tension and acute terror, prior to ascending the throne, she was having the time of her life. She was deliciously conscious of the sensation she was creating, and gleefully sensed that many members of the Court were envious of Robert Dudley's increasingly close relationship with her. Meanwhile, the besotted young Queen showered Dudley with gifts and honours, making him a Knight of the Garter and Constable of Windsor

Castle, endowing him with extensive country estates and large sums of money. The dispassionate observer would not have found it difficult to see exactly why Elizabeth found Dudley so utterly irresistible. He was physically very attractive, nearly six foot tall, with skin so dark that he was nicknamed 'the gypsy'. He had the athletic figure of a horseman with the long lanky legs and tight buttocks of a modern-day polo player. Lord Robert Dudley and the young Queen were virtually the same age and had much in common – both were fluent in French and Italian, and enjoyed similar cultural interests such as drama and poetry along with a love of the outdoor pursuits of hunting and hawking. Dancing was one of their favourite pastimes – the entire Court was held spellbound by the intensity of their relationship as their expert and emotionally charged interpretation of the *Gaillard* or the *Volta* elevated mere dance to the heights of the ballet.

The less dispassionate spectator, watching the evolution of this royal romance, was far from pleased. Those such as the conscientious William Cecil regarded it as an unmitigated disaster. Whenever he needed the Queen to discuss important matters of state, she was all too often riding out with Lord Robert. Even when the earnest Principal Secretary was finally successful in gaining an audience with Elizabeth, her mind seemed to be elsewhere. It was all very distasteful and distressing to the anxious Cecil, who pondered where this unwelcome romance would lead. He regarded the dashing Dudley in a far less favourable light than Elizabeth, seeing only an insolent and highly dangerous distraction to a young and impressionable Queen during the all-important early period of her rule, when her attention needed to be firmly focused on the tasks in hand. Wasn't he already married, with a dreadful reputation for chasing every pretty girl in sight? Had not both his father and grandfather been executed as traitors and Dudley himself been a prisoner in the Tower for plotting against Queen Mary? No wonder Cecil considered him to be such a thoroughly undesirable individual from a highly disreputable family. This view was shared by many other senior members of the Royal Court, those who represented the opinion-formers and the decision-makers within the kingdom. To William Cecil and his colleagues, Dudley represented an irrelevant yet highly unwelcome distraction to the important task of ruling the nation, particularly one with so many problems at that particular moment in time.

Dudley appears to have been extremely conceited. The large number of flattering portraits commissioned by him from the leading artists of the day, depicting him in a variety of flamboyant poses, demonstrates either a passionate interest in the visual arts or an obsessive concern for himself. In Steven van der Muelen's portrayal of him, painted around 1565, and now part of the Wallace Collection in London, Dudley stares insolently out of the canvas, hand on hip, expensively attired, madly in love with both the Queen and himself.

Precisely what Dudley ultimately hoped to achieve in this headlong pursuit of the Queen is difficult to imagine. Quite where Elizabeth thought this highly indiscreet romantic and dangerous liaison with a married man was going to end is equally a matter of pure speculation, as tongues wagged furiously across the length and breadth of Europe. Perhaps Elizabeth had given it little thought or did not really care. For a young woman of twenty-five years of age, with a normal healthy sexual appetite, Elizabeth had hitherto led an almost nun-like existence; now all this pent-up emotion had exploded into the relationship with Dudley, and as so often the case, the romance was with a person considered by the majority of the Court to be thoroughly unsuitable.

These considerations were overtaken by events when the body of Lord Dudley's wife was discovered at an isolated house in the Oxfordshire countryside, lying at the bottom of a flight of stairs with a broken neck. There were no witnesses to the cause of Amy's fall; the precise reason for her death was never established and remains a mystery. In the autumn of 1560, the Court buzzed with wild rumours of foul play. These unsubstantiated accusations were to continue despite an inquest reaching a conclusion that Amy's death had been accidental. This tragic situation proved to be a disaster for Dudley and at the same time posed a dilemma for the Queen: although now free to marry should she so desire, the circumstances that made this possible placed a question mark over the wisdom of becoming his wife and probably incurring a huge stain on her character. Sir Nicholas Throckmorton, the English ambassador at the French Court, glumly warned the Queen that if she went ahead and married Dudley she would be discredited throughout the whole of Europe. Although this was conceivably true, it was not what Elizabeth wished to hear. It was therefore not surprising that she became deeply enraged a few years later when discovering that Sir Nicholas's daughter, Beth, had fallen in love with Sir Walter Ralegh, by then another of the Queen's favourite young men.

Publicly, the Queen continued to support Dudley but privately gave up any thoughts she might have secretly harboured of becoming his wife. She valued her reputation with the world at large far too highly to risk it in order to satisfy any romantic inclinations. Once again, the Queen's acute grasp of reality was to overrule her personal considerations; she was also acutely aware that Dudley was hugely unpopular in her Court and that marriage to such a controversial character could well alienate the support of her citizens and prejudice her position as Queen at a crucial stage in her reign. By then she was enjoying the power and privilege of being the sovereign far too much to endanger her position – not for Elizabeth any romantic nonsense of 'giving up the throne for the person I love'. Her career was far more important than love and marriage. Much to everyone's relief, the torrid affair between Elizabeth and Dudley gradually cooled into the warm friendship that was to last until Robert Dudley, by then Earl of Leicester, died in the autumn of 1588, nearly thirty years later, probably from malaria contracted when campaigning in Flanders. The stricken Earl wrote to the Queen from his deathbed, and when she died some fifteen years later his letter was discovered lying in a jewel box beside her bed; written on the letter, in the Queen's own handwriting, the simple phrase 'his last letter'.[3]

Dudley had been the great love of Elizabeth's life, an unfulfilled romance that was to remain with her and influence her actions for as long as she lived. Their friendship was to survive Dudley's secret marriage in 1578 to Lettice Knollys, following an intermittent affair with this lively red-haired daughter of Privy Councillor, Sir Francis Knollys, the Queen's cousin. Dudley had first started the relationship with Lettice purely to make Elizabeth jealous – George Gower's portrait of her shows a face that bears more than a passing resemblance to Queen Elizabeth. Lettice was the widow of the 1st Earl of Essex, who had died of dysentery while campaigning in Ireland. Many years later her son, Robert Devereux, the 2nd Earl of Essex, was to become the last of the Queen's great favourites. When Elizabeth found out about Dudley's secret marriage to Lettice Knollys, she was incandescent with rage, feeling totally betrayed and humiliated by the only man she had really loved. It was with considerable difficulty that her Lord Chamberlain, the Earl of Sussex, no friend of Dudley's, was able to persuade the Queen not to consign him to the Tower of London. Some considerable time was to elapse before he was able to regain royal favour and Lettice was never allowed to return to Court. She outlived them all, dying in 1634 at the age of ninety-five, a remarkable age for those days.

In the years that followed the very public affair with Dudley, the Queen was to have a succession of particular court favourites, all equally handsome, attentive and effortlessly charming at all times, all dazzling smiles and witty repartee. These superstar courtiers included Sir Christopher Hatton, Sir Thomas Heneage, Edward de Vere, the 17th Earl of Oxford, and towards the end of her reign, Robert Devereux, the 2nd Earl of Essex and stepson of Robert Dudley.

Although Elizabeth undoubtedly found them all both attractive and amusing, none was regarded as a serious suitor or attempted to be so, nor did they delude themselves that they were likely marriage material. In all probability, only Christopher Hatton was seriously in love with his sovereign and like Elizabeth was destined never to marry. Hatton was intensely jealous of any other handsome courtiers whom Elizabeth showed an interest in, those such as the Earl of Oxford who was every bit as good at dancing and horseriding as Hatton, and at the same time considerably younger. When Hatton was away from Court and separated from his beloved Queen, he bombarded her with passionate love letters, lengthy and sometimes a little ludicrous, hoping for 'longer life so that his faith and love may be found enviable and spotless towards so royal and fearless a princess', [4] as he was to declare in the autumn of 1586. Meanwhile, a stream of suitors from abroad continued unabated. This activity intensified when the formidable Catherine de Medici, Queen Mother and Regent of France, successively offered her three sons for Elizabeth's inspection and possible approval, like prize bulls at auction. First was her eldest son, Charles, who had inherited the French crown at the age of ten after his elder brother, François II died suddenly after less than a year on the throne. Charles was now fourteen, less than half the age of the English Queen, who worried that people might sneer that Charles appeared to be marrying his mother! It was hardly surprising that negotiations soon collapsed amid bitter recriminations between England and France, as a tearful Elizabeth screamed at her Privy Councillors. Undeterred, Catherine de Medici later advanced her next son, the effeminate Prince Henry of Anjou. Once more there was a wide age gap, this time nearly twenty years. The tactless Lady Frances Cobham, one of the Queen's attendants, informed Elizabeth that in her view marriages worked best when the happy couple were of a similar age. There were further problems prejudicing a successful union between the English Queen and the young Frenchman, as in addition to being a well-known transvestite, notorious for his promiscuity with either sex, the French Duke was a devout Catholic, 'obstinately papistical', as the English ambassador, Sir Thomas Smith, was to pompously declare. None of these characteristics indicated an ideal husband for a Protestant English Queen. Yet again, proceedings were terminated, this time without tears.

After a suitable interval, the indefatigable Catherine de Medici, matchmaker extraordinaire, brought forth yet another son, François, the Duke of Alençon. The initial reports of this latest cross-Channel suitor received at the English Court appeared singularly unpromising. It was said that the Duke was both exceedingly small and extremely ugly, with a face heavily pock-marked through smallpox and a nose of Cyrano de Bergerac proportions, comic beyond belief. Elizabeth was by now in her mid-forties, her diminutive suitor but half her age. However, the Duke was apparently extremely eager to marry Elizabeth and, unlike his elder brothers, was willing to come to England to plight his troth.

Much to everybody's amazement when Alençon arrived at Court in the summer of 1579, the Queen seemed enchanted and immediately nicknamed him 'my little frog', finding him amusing, articulate, highly intelligent and politically astute. To a bemused Privy Council, this situation appeared to indicate a meeting of minds. Not all her courtiers or citizens were quite so enthusiastic about the prospect of the Queen marrying a French duke, particularly one who was Catholic, albeit not as devout as his brothers. Sir Philip Sidney, one of the Queen's favoured courtiers, wrote her a long letter in which he strongly voiced his disapproval of the match with a Frenchman and 'a Papist', while John Stubbs, a Norfolk squire, wrote and published a pamphlet violently condemning the prospect of the Queen taking a French husband. Elizabeth was deeply enraged and Stubbs had his right hand publicly chopped off with a meat cleaver outside Whitehall Palace. Thereupon, according to William Camden, who witnessed the event, Stubbs doffed his hat with his left hand, shouted 'God Save the Queen' and promptly collapsed.[5] He was then taken away to the Tower.

The Privy Council met in secret to debate the prospect of the union, an all-day session which ended with the majority of the Councillors opposed to the idea of their Queen marrying the French Duke. A small deputation of the Council, led by Lord Burghley and the Earl of Leicester, condescendingly informed the Queen that they would endorse the marriage if it would please her and was what she truly wanted. Later they advised that she should decline the Duke's proposal as there was such strong opposition to the marriage right across the kingdom. Elizabeth found Leicester's rigid opposition to the thought of her marrying Alençon particularly upsetting, having recently discovered his secret marriage to Lettice Knollys, and feeling badly let down by the man to whom she had given so much love, so many titles and choice possessions. She was extremely bitter that someone who had lacked the courage to tell her about his own wedding would so openly oppose her own desire to marry. Ever sensitive to public opinion, Elizabeth reluctantly agreed to bow to the Privy Council's recommendation. Yet again, public duty was to override private happiness.

In the autumn of 1581, a changing political climate caused nuptial

Henry VIII by Hans Eworth, after Hans Holbein.

Queen Mary by Hans Eworth.

The Ditchley Portrait by Marcus Gheeraerts the Younger, one of relatively few pictures of the Queen using *chiaroscuqro*.

The Armada Portrait by George Gower.

The Earl of Essex, by Marcus Gheeraerts the Younger.

Sir Francis Drake, statue on Plymouth Hoe.

Philip of Spain by Alonso Sanchez Coello.

Robert Dudley, Earl of Leicester, by Steven van der Muelen.

The Boyhood of Ralegh by John Millais.

English ships engaging the Spanish Armada, 1588.

Archbishop Thomas Cranmer by Gerlach Flicke.

Francis Bacon by Paul van Somer.

William and Robert Cecil, artist unknown.

Longleat House, Wiltshire, classic Elizabethan architecture.

Shakespeare statue by Sheemakers (1743).

Drake's game of bowls on Plymouth Hoe.

negotiations to be reopened again as progressively worsening relations between England and Spain led to the greater desirability for an Anglo-French alliance, symbolically sealed by a royal marriage. The Duke of Alençon journeyed to London once more and romance was in the air. It was reported 'there is no talk of any weighty matters of the realm and the Queen doth not attend unto other matters but only to be with the Duke from morning to noon and afterwards to two to three hours before sunset. I cannot tell what the devil they do.'[6] The Court awaited developments with breathless anticipation.

Matters escalated further when Elizabeth took Alençon to a service at St Paul's Cathedral and publicly kissed the Duke in front of the entire congregation. Later, when the French ambassador encountered the couple walking together in the Long Gallery at Whitehall Palace, he enquired of their intentions. The Queen warmly kissed the Duke again, took a ring from her finger and placed it on his, informing the delighted ambassador that he may tell the King of France that his brother would be marrying her. An anxious Spanish ambassador, Bernardino de Mendoza, reported to Philip of Spain:

. . . on the 22nd however, at eleven in the morning, the Queen and Alençon were walking together in a gallery, Leicester and Walsingham being present, when the French Ambassador entered and said that he wished to write to his master, from whom he had received orders to hear from the Queen's own lips, her intentions with regards to marrying his brother. She replied, 'you may write this to the King: that the Duke of Alençon shall be my husband', and at the same time she turned to Alençon and kissed him on the mouth, drawing a ring from her own hand and giving it to him as a pledge. Alençon gave her a ring of his in return and shortly afterwards the Queen summoned the ladies and gentlemen from the Presence Chamber to the gallery, repeating to them in a loud voice, in Alençon's presence what she had previously said. Alençon and the French are all extremely overjoyed by this. . . .[7]

It was a moment of high drama. This sensational announcement inevitably caused great consternation at the Royal Court. The Privy Council was appalled, the courtiers confused, and Sir Christopher Hatton reduced to tears. The Queen's Ladies of the Bedchamber and her Maids of Honour become so hysterical that their cries of anguish kept Elizabeth awake throughout the night. It was as if the whole Court had conspired to orchestrate an anti-marriage campaign. Mendoza, the cynical Spanish ambassador, was less impressed, 'Notwithstanding all this, I cannot avoid saying that, according to my poor understanding, I am unable to look upon this matter as by any means concluded.'[8] Sir Christopher Hatton visited the Queen privately in order to make a passionate appeal to her to give up the French Duke for the good of her kingdom. The English sovereign quickly appreciated how her situation was publicly perceived and began to bombard the King of France with additional terms for the marriage which she knew would be totally unacceptable. This time it was Alençon's turn to burst into uncontrollable sobs. It was to be of no avail; armed with a large amount of money to fight the Spanish in the Netherlands, the 'little frog' left the Court. Elizabeth bade a fond farewell to François, Duke of Alençon as he sailed away to war. There was no fairytale ending and the Queen never saw him again.

Had the prospect of this particular wedding proposition been more favourably received by the Privy Council, with less opposition from the Court and the nation as a whole, it seemed perfectly conceivable that Elizabeth may finally have married and taken her 'little frog' as her lawfully wedded husband. This would have been as much for political reasons as any other: England's relationships with Spain were always fragile and Spanish military muscle was considerably enhanced when Portugal was annexed and its powerful ocean-going fleet became available to the Spanish cause. Meanwhile, the military situation between the Flemish rebels and the Spanish occupational forces in the Netherlands was worsening daily, prompting the possibility of direct English intervention to support the rebels.

Elizabeth was now well into middle age and past child-bearing age, making her a progressively less attractive marriage proposition and ultimately ending her Privy Council's desire to find for her a husband and father for her child. Whether by luck or judgement, subsequent events were to cast serious doubt over the wisdom of a marriage between the Queen and her 'little frog'. Alençon proved to be an extremely inept military commander and died barely three years later, some say of syphilis, the form of venereal disease so prevalent at the time. If true, it would appear that both the Queen and country had a lucky escape.

The wily Mendoza's clinical analysis of this protracted romance casts an interesting light on the Queen's character and her precise motives, pointing a finger at her devious and cunning manipulation of events to suit her own purposes. Elizabeth was now able to regretfully indicate to Alençon that it was because of her Privy Council that they were unable to marry – his own brother, the French king, had also refused to accept the terms of the marriage, resulting in strained relationships between the two brothers. In turn, Elizabeth could indicate to her Council that while they repeatedly said they would like her to marry they had once again rejected a serious suitor and thereby damaged diplomatic relationships with France. Mendoza's opinion was that if Elizabeth ever seriously intended marrying Alençon she would have done so without further delay following her dramatic public announcement at Whitehall. The Spanish ambassador believed that the Queen never had any firm intention of becoming a bride; to her it was merely a game. Mendoza could well have been right.

How serious Elizabeth really was about marriage remains a matter of interesting speculation and in many respects the fact that she never took a husband is not particularly surprising. First, her choice was extremely limited to candidates either from her own aristocracy or the so-called cream of royalty from abroad. Unlike her father, Elizabeth was far too status-conscious to marry a commoner. Selection from overseas was further inhibited by the growing English antipathy towards Roman Catholicism, while very few of the foreign suitors were of her status – all too often they came from a motley bunch of dukes, princes and monarchs from minor kingdoms with major delusions of grandeur. Only King Philip of Spain equalled her as a mature ruler of a major nation, but his religion stood against him in England. Regardless of other considerations, Elizabeth needed someone of equal stature to sweep her off her feet and carry her to the altar. No such man existed in the whole of Europe throughout her reign – there was no Charlemagne, Peter the Great or Charles the Bold in the sixteenth century.

Elizabeth may always have been a reluctant bride: her father's experience of marriage, two wives divorced, two executed and one dying in childbirth was hardly a ringing endorsement of marital bliss. Henry's sixth wife, Katherine Parr, had survived him but died in childbirth shortly after remarrying. Elizabeth's half-sister Mary's husband quickly deserted her. Her cousin Mary, Queen of Scots, experienced three short-lived unsuccessful marriages. Almost everywhere Elizabeth looked conveyed an unhappy picture when it came to marriage. Neither experience nor observation encouraged Elizabeth to take a husband regardless of ardent suitors or the urging of her Privy Council and Parliament. As time progressed the necessity of marriage lessened, the number of serious suitors declined, and the Council's urging became a distant murmur. Elizabeth had become accustomed to being Queen of England and had no desire to share this intoxicating power with anyone else:

'God's death my lord, I will have here but one mistress and no master',[9] were the famous words she once used to berate Robert Dudley. Power was paramount to Elizabeth: she needed to be in control, and no one should prejudice her enjoyment in exercising her authority in any way or at any time, particularly a husband.

It remains undisputed that the Queen never married, but did the fact that she never shared the English throne mean that she never shared her bed? Much is made of Elizabeth dying as a 'Virgin Queen', but was this just another example of the Tudor propaganda machine making a virtue out of a necessity, turning an unwelcome fact into glorious fiction? Supporters of the Virgin Queen scenario largely hang their scholarly hats on Elizabeth's impassioned statement when she thought she was dying of smallpox in 1562, declaring that there had never been any impropriety between herself and Robert Dudley. It is pointed out that she would hardly perjure herself when death was thought to be so imminent. However, the Queen was delirious when she made that statement and contemporary documentation is from a prejudiced foreign source. So is this another Tudor cover-up of the true facts in order to perpetuate the fashionably shining image of the Virgin Queen, concocted some time later when the cult of 'Gloriana' overrode everything else, including the facts?

Certainly, at the height of the Queen's affair with Robert Dudley, rumours of sexual indiscretions ran riot through the Royal Court. Dudley's quarters were conveniently close to Elizabeth's own private apartments and he was reportedly seen with her at all hours of the day and night, prompting memories of Elizabeth's own mother, Anne Boleyn, and her supposedly wanton behaviour. At the time of the liaison with Dudley, the Queen was young, lusty and in love: might it be the case of like mother, like daughter? Was her undoubted love for Dudley fully consummated? 'Lord Robert Dudley hath had five children by the Queene',[10] was one of the more scurrilous stories in circulation. Inevitably much of the more strident rumour-mongering was put about by those who had a vested interest in discrediting the Queen. According to Count Feria, the one-time Spanish ambassador, Lord Robert was so much in the Queen's favour that he was able to do exactly as he pleased and that Her Majesty would visit his chambers day and night. This vicious gossip reached such a fever pitch that Kat Ashley, Elizabeth's long-time companion who was Chief Woman of the Bedchamber, felt compelled to voice her alarm to her beloved sovereign and urged her to distance herself from Dudley to avoid doing further damage to her reputation. The Queen remarked that a thousand eyes noted everything she did. Certainly, she was always surrounded by her lady attendants; even at night they were in close proximity, one of them often sleeping in the Queen's bedroom with her. Her lady attendants were known to be notoriously indiscreet, something that the Queen was well aware of and was constantly chastising them in no uncertain terms. Kat Ashley was 'the Queen of gossip' and Elizabeth would recall how her tittle-tattle had landed both of them in serious trouble once before when, as a young princess, she had indulged in unwise and questionable behaviour with Thomas Seymour, also a married man. Now that she was queen, she would have access to the state papers relating to these particular embarrassing incidents, documents that would provide a constant reminder of the perils of risky misconduct of a sexual nature.

There was also the decided risk of becoming pregnant, birth control being virtually non-existent in Tudor times. There is no proven indication of any illegitimate children belonging to Elizabeth, unlike her father Henry VIII who had an illegitimate son, Henry Fitzroy, conceived by his mistress Elizabeth Blount. Henry made his son Duke of Richmond in 1525 and had even considered him as his successor but the young Duke suffered from consumption and died in 1536, the year before Jane Seymour produced the future Edward VI, Elizabeth's half-brother. No factual record exists of Elizabeth ever conceiving, not even the vestige of a rumour in an age of decidedly double-standards, when a man fathering an illegitimate child caused little comment but a woman was universally damned. Furthermore, syphilis was rife in the sixteenth century, posing a grave risk in an undoubtedly highly promiscuous age. Dudley already had a high-profile reputation as a sexual athlete. Whether or not Elizabeth had sexual relations with him or indeed with anybody else is of no historical consequence and had no material subsequent effect on the Crown. Salacious speculation is considerably outweighed by the undoubted certainty that she never took a husband or produced an illegitimate heir to the throne with the consequences that would have ensued. The resultant effect of a childless queen was the demise of the Tudor dynasty and the enforced introduction of the Stuarts onto the English throne, permanently altering the authority of the monarchy and quickly plunging the nation back into a civil war far worse than the one which Elizabeth's grandfather Henry VII had rescued it from in 1485.

Had any one of Elizabeth's suitors proven to be successful there may have been no Gunpowder Plot, no Pilgrim Fathers, no Oliver Cromwell, no English republic, and Charles I might have kept his head. The longer-term implications are equally interesting: no

Dutch or German monarchs on the English throne, no Bonnie Prince Charlie, no Highland Clearances nor Orangemen still celebrating the Battle of the Boyne every year. Speculation is an entertaining, yet futile pastime – nevertheless, the failure of any of the Queen's suitors to persuade her to abandon her spinsterhood, undoubtedly had profound consequences for the English nation subsequent to her death. In the short term, it undid many of the achievements of her lifetime, as her Stuart successors failed to keep up the momentum that she had created during forty-five years of largely successful rule.

Elizabeth usually demonstrated a wonderful ability to choose men to perform important tasks, but this attribute deserted her when it came to picking a man for herself. She consistently proved to have a poor judgement in choosing her favourites. Robert Dudley was married and generally unpopular at Court. Hatton and Ralegh were considered upstart opportunists with inadequate social background. Heneage and the Earl of Oxford were never serious contenders, the latter squandering his fortune only to rely on a small pension from Elizabeth in order to eke out a meagre existence. As the Queen aged, the men who attracted her became progressively younger and Elizabeth's biggest mistake was the 2nd Earl of Essex, a classic example of someone for whom success had come too early and too easily, making him impetuous, spoilt, petulant and arrogant. Perhaps the ageing Queen was trying to turn back the clock in order to relive those carefree, earlier days with Robert Dudley. Once more tongues wagged around the Court: 'When she is abroad nobody is near her but my Lord of Essex. . . . He cometh not to his own lodgings until birds sing in the morning',[11] wrote the young courtier Anthony Bagot to his father.

In the last decade of the sixteenth century, Elizabeth was in her late fifties, her looks had faded along with the energy and vitality of earlier years. Her once auburn hair was now thin and grey, hidden under a very obvious and garish wig, her skin ravaged by time and concealed under heavy white make-up, so thick in appearance that it looked like plaster. An allegorical portrait, now in Corsham Court, that magnificent Wiltshire treasure house, shows a sad-faced old lady staring into space, not liking what she sees. The artist is unknown and the picture was probably painted after her death as a realistic portrayal of the Queen – such a portrait as this would never have been permitted during her lifetime.

For some considerable time, artists had been forbidden on orders of the Privy Council to paint Elizabeth as an ageing queen. Instead, they formulated the ingenious solution of showing her to be completely ageless, resulting in portraits which conveyed an almost Madonna-like image. One of the supreme ironies of the Elizabethan era is that the nation who had removed worship of the Virgin Mary from the religious service, had later replaced her with their own version: Elizabeth as a visionary, celestial figure, majestic, all powerful and immortal. By the 1580s Robert Dudley, Earl of Leicester had also aged, the once trim figure had thickened, the once finely chiselled face coarsened, his skin reddened. Leicester was unconcerned that his stepson Essex had assumed the position of Elizabeth's favourite; on the contrary, he positively welcomed it as it helped to weaken Sir Walter Ralegh's hold on the Queen's affections.

The besotted Elizabeth indulged young Essex outrageously, much to Lord Burghley's irritation – the veteran statesman must have felt an acute sense of *déjà vu*. It was as if a miraculously rejuvenated Robert Dudley had somehow contrived to return in order to once more distract the Queen and disrupt his plans. This time Burghley felt far less concerned than he had been at the time of Dudley's relationship with the Queen nearly thirty years earlier. So outrageous was Essex's conduct, so much did he upset the more powerful members of Court and Council, that Burghley felt quietly confident that Essex would somehow self-destruct. Thus it was to prove when his arrogance had totally outstripped his abilities, and he was sent to the scaffold. The relationship had, however, been a disastrous one for Elizabeth and one which considerably damaged the Queen's reputation late in her reign.

Traditionally, it is customary in marriage for the man to seek the bride, but because Elizabeth was the ruler of a major sovereign state, this precept did not apply and the initiative was therefore with Elizabeth to choose a suitable companion. However, a chronic inability to make decisions was essentially the Queen's greatest weakness. When she hesitated on other issues, the Privy Council was there to stiffen Elizabeth's resolve. On the question of marriage they were keen on the concept, yet lukewarm on the contenders, and never gave their wholehearted support to any of the serious suitors. Therefore, it was as much their fault as Elizabeth's that she never found a husband. Maybe both Elizabeth and her Privy Councillors were too stringent in their requirements or perhaps, secretly, in the final analysis when it became necessary to act, neither Queen nor Council really wanted a marriage. Whatever the motives, whatever the reasons, when it came to the decisive moment, none of the suitors proved suitable.

8

MEN OF GOD

At the time when Elizabeth became Queen, England was still
essentially a Catholic kingdom, practising the same faith
which had existed within the nation for many centuries,
except for a short period of Protestantism under her half-brother,
Edward VI, before this process was swiftly reversed by Elizabeth's
half-sister Mary. This rapid swing of the religious pendulum may
well have gone largely unheeded by the majority of England's
population, particularly those outside the towns and in northern
England. Out in the country, the ordinary folk continued to worship
in much the same manner as they had throughout the Middle Ages.
Elizabeth had inherited a predominately Catholic country, albeit a
very divided one, and she may well have been inclined to keep it
that way, for it would have been easier to continue a religious
practice that was reassuringly familiar to the majority of her
citizens. It was also the official faith of both Spain and France, the
two most significant nations in western Europe, at the time of her
succession to the throne in 1558.

Even when her father Henry VIII had ceased to recognize the Pope
in Rome as head of the English Church, the King was still regarded as
'His Most Catholic Majesty'. The bidding prayer of 1544 declares
Henry VIII as, 'being only immediately next unto God, the only and
supreme head of this Catholic Church, of England'. Elizabeth may
have been tempted to re-establish the official religion in England
precisely as it had been in the land of her father – it would have suited
her conservative inclinations, been much simpler, and avoided a
potential confrontation early in her reign with either France or Spain,
respectively controlled by the Catholic Catherine de Medici and Philip
II. On her northern frontier, her Catholic cousin, Mary, ruled Scotland
which was at that time at war with England. Retaining the religious
status quo was at first sight the easy option.

However, when Elizabeth became Queen, most of Europe was in
religious turmoil as the old Catholic order was threatened by new
religious doctrines; radical concepts questioned established
theological values, challenging fundamental thinking which had

existed almost since the dawn of Christianity. Men such as Martin Luther, Jean Calvin and Ulrich Zwingli had vigorously pioneered a new theology that was to have a profound impact on the traditional way in which the Christian faith had been practised for so many centuries. This trio of eminent theologians were active in the first half of the sixteenth century, the French-born Calvin in Geneva and Zwingli in Switzerland, while the German Luther, originally an Augustinian monk, lived in the university town of Wittenberg, where he had become both teacher and preacher. Luther was largely instrumental as the founder of Protestantism while Calvin's concepts led to Presbyterianism, which in turn exercised a lasting impression on the Scottish reformer John Knox, who was to found the Church of Scotland in the early part of Elizabeth's reign.

These new religious philosophies were to have an equally significant impact on English hearts and minds; in Tudor England, Cambridge University was the place destined to become the centre of the developing Protestant faith in the kingdom along with Puritanism, a more extreme form of this new theological thinking. Three of the best-known Protestant martyrs burnt at the stake during Mary's reign – Cranmer, Ridley and Latimer – had been at Cambridge. Parker, Grindal and Whitgift, the three clerics who Elizabeth was to successively choose to become her Archbishops of Canterbury, had also been exposed to the new Protestant thinking during their time at Cambridge, as had William Cecil while studying at St John's College. Thus the most prominent men surrounding the new young Queen when she came to the throne were virtually all Protestant in their convictions. Elizabeth was acutely conscious that they regarded her as the new champion of Protestantism and the saviour of their faith, dedicated to sweep away all traces of Catholicism from her new kingdom. Indeed, John Foxe, author of *Acts and Monuments*, better known as *The Book of Martyrs*, stated in that hugely influential publication that Elizabeth had been protected by God for that very purpose. Foxe's book did much to popularize Protestantism during Elizabeth's reign, particularly among the ordinary people, while stirring up anti-Catholic feeling across the nation.

Elizabeth had long been subject to strong Protestant influence. Her stepmother, Katherine Parr, had been a devout member of that faith, being a friend of Miles Coverdale, the English Protestant priest. Coverdale's complete translation of the Bible in 1535 was the first to be printed in English, thereby continuing the earlier work of Tyndale, while his translation of the Psalms still features in the Book of Common Prayer. The widespread availability of these religious works in the nation's own language was to have a considerable influence on the thinking of the Queen's citizens. Katherine Parr had ensured that the young princess was diligently brought up in the Protestant faith during the time that Elizabeth lived with her, a process continued by Roger Ascham, her principal tutor, also a devout Protestant. By the time Elizabeth had come to the throne she was firmly immersed in the 'New Religion', a devoted, if not particularly fervent member of that faith, 'an image of demure evangelicalism',[1] as one observer noted. She attended morning service daily in her private chapel and undoubtedly regarded herself as firmly Protestant. The new Queen, therefore, understandably came to the momentous conclusion that England should become a Protestant kingdom. It was her first major decision, one not entirely of her own choosing but nevertheless a hugely courageous one so early in her reign. It was a decision that was to have an enormous impact both on her personal life and the nation as a whole, governing the destiny of both Queen and country for the rest of her time on the throne and establishing the lasting nature of the Church of England right up to the present day.

Elizabeth instinctively sensed that the mood of the nation was to become Protestant. Unlike her half-sister Mary, she responded to this feeling rather than superimposing her own beliefs regardless of the best interests of her subjects. However, she wanted to be Queen of the whole of England, not just the Protestants and this desire governed her initial attitude towards the many Catholics residing within her kingdom. Elizabeth was no fanatic – indeed, she was just as conservative in her religious outlook as in other important issues. She did not wish to alienate a large number of Catholics within England at the beginning of her reign or risk antagonizing Spain in the initial phase of her rule. Conversely, she needed to distance herself from her half-sister's unpopular reign together with the religious extremism that had prevailed during those unhappy years. It was important that Elizabeth should retain the loyalty and justify the expectations of powerful Protestants such as William Cecil, who had enabled her to become Queen of England. Thus she gave out strong and very public signals as to her intentions from the beginning of her reign, in order to clearly indicate that she was a Protestant Queen but one who was tolerant towards Catholics, without approving of their customs if they should deviate from the principles of Protestantism. When Bishop Ogelthorpe attempted to celebrate Mass in the traditional way by elevating the Host, the Queen ostentatiously rose to her feet and left the service. 'Away with those torches, for we see very well,'[2] Elizabeth declared as she swept past a group of monks carrying tapers when she entered

Westminster Abbey for her first opening of Parliament in January 1559, amid clouds of incense and much sprinkling of holy water.

The Queen was equally determined that any changes in the nation's religious procedures should be of a moderate nature. She did not wish any significant innovations carried out during her reign to be considered in any way harsh or unjust. At all times, she wanted her citizens' private and personal beliefs to be respected: 'Not liking to make windows into men's souls and secret thoughts',[3] as Francis Bacon so memorably murmured. The Queen was not prepared to allow extremism in any direction, even though this might dismay her Protestant supporters. Elizabeth was ultra keen for England to be a nation of moderate religious practices with all her citizens living together in harmony. This somewhat idealistic attitude enabled England to successfully avoid the disruptive religious wars that occurred in other European nations such as France, and, when Philip II of Spain finally launched his Armada against England in 1588 in an attempt to restore Roman Catholicism within her nation, the majority of the Queen's citizens who were still Catholic remained loyal to the Crown.

Elizabeth had also displayed her open-minded attitude towards Catholics by retaining the Marquess of Winchester as well as the Earls of Arundel, Derby and Shrewsbury on her Privy Council, all of whom were of Catholic persuasion and had served on Queen Mary's Council. Later, she was to appoint Sir James Croft to her Council, regardless of the fact that he was a practising Catholic, while she favoured a number of prominent courtiers such as the Earl of Oxford who were also openly Catholic. Across the country, recusants – those who declined to attend Protestant services in their local church – initially went unpunished, as did the continuing practice of Mass within the private chapels of large country houses in the first half of the Queen's reign. Elizabeth herself displayed a crucifix and candles on the altar of her own private chapel, where her organist William Byrd was staunchly Roman Catholic.

The Queen was fortunate that Queen Mary's Archbishop of Canterbury, Cardinal Reginald Pole, had conveniently died of a fever very shortly after Mary's death, leaving the way clear for Elizabeth to appoint a new archbishop of her own choosing to this key clerical appointment, someone of her thinking who would establish the Church of England in precisely the manner she had in mind. She selected a man who had been known to her since her early childhood, Matthew Parker, who had been made Vice-Chancellor of Cambridge University during the reign of Edward VI, and was then defrocked during Mary's reign because he was married. Unlike many Protestants, Parker had not gone into exile abroad during Mary's reign and thus had not been subject to the radically reforming religious zeal prevalent in places such as Geneva. He therefore retained the moderate outlook favoured by the Queen.

Parker had been chaplain to Anne Boleyn, the Queen's mother; indeed, it was primarily on account of this that he accepted the post of archbishop, having promised Anne Boleyn that he would look after her daughter's spiritual needs. The prospect of becoming Archbishop of Canterbury filled Parker with deep foreboding: he was a shy, scholarly man from a relatively humble background, his father having been a weaver in Norfolk. Matthew Parker had been a student at Corpus Christi, a college where he later became Master, and he was happiest mulling over his books amid the cloistered calm of Cambridge. He dreaded having to be Elizabeth's Church leader, head of a spiritual task force dedicated to converting the English nation to the path of Protestant righteousness. 'Onward Christian Soldiers' was definitely not Parker's style, but the Queen could be extremely persuasive when she wanted someone for such an important task as becoming her first Archbishop of Canterbury. Nevertheless, more than six months were to elapse between Parker first being approached and his consecration as archbishop. Among those witnessing the ceremony was Miles Coverdale.

As a student, Parker had attended the White Horse Inn, the Cambridge meeting place for Protestant debate where Coverdale, Latimer, Ridley and other reformers had been regular attenders. At this time he became friends with William Cecil and Nicholas Bacon, by now prominent members of Elizabeth's Privy Council, and both strongly supportive of Parker becoming archbishop. He was probably the best available choice in the circumstances: the majority of the existing bishops appointed during Mary's time were of strong Catholic persuasion, while the priests now flooding back into England from exile abroad were invariably far too radical for Elizabeth's tastes. It was noticeable that relatively few of those returning were consecrated as bishops, as together the Queen and Parker began restructuring the clerical hierarchy across the nation.

Parker may have had a shy and retiring nature, but he possessed a sound judgement and was gentle but firm in his approach to the task that Elizabeth had given him, one far more difficult than the Queen had envisaged and one which would require a particularly delicate balance of tact and determination. Fortunately for Elizabeth her first archbishop, a wise and saintly man, proved equal to the immense task that she had thrust upon him.

The Queen's first major initiative in re-establishing the Protestant faith as the official religion in her kingdom was to persuade Parliament to pass an Act of Supremacy, thereby confirming her as head of the Church of England, as her father Henry had been. In this issue, Elizabeth was to experience the first setback of her reign. While the bill passed easily through the Puritan-dominated House of Commons, it ran into considerable opposition from the House of Lords, being vetoed *en bloc* by the Catholic bishops and by a considerable number of the nobility, many of them also being Catholics. A distinctive feature of Protestantism in England compared with France was that the strength of the English movement was among the intellectuals and in the growing middle classes, whereas across the Channel it was the aristocracy who favoured the movement. The bill was finally passed by the Upper House only after the Queen agreed to a change of title from 'Supreme Head of the Faith' to that of 'Governor of the Faith'.

The Act of Uniformity, the next major piece of legislation put before Parliament by Queen and Council, met with even more opposition. The Act of Uniformity contained modifications to the church service, in particular the wording in the prayer book involving the communion service and the taking of the sacrament. Herein lies one of the fundamental distinctions between the Catholic and Protestant faiths: the Catholic concept of transubstantiation, the belief that bread and wine actually becomes the body and blood of Christ, as opposed to the Protestant doctrine that it is purely symbolic. Again the Queen was fortunate that the late Archbishop Pole had neglected to fill a number of vacant sees, and as a result, the total number of bishops was rather less than it should have been. Their numbers were further reduced as a pair of bishops had been conveniently imprisoned on a charge of disobedience to common authority. When the vital vote came, the Bishop of Lincoln and the Bishop of Winchester were languishing in the Tower of London, while another was unaccountably absent; this proved to be highly convenient for, despite a number of peers voting against the proposal, including three Privy Councillors, the Act of Uniformity was passed by the slim margin of three votes. Elizabeth had been successful in an issue that was vital to the establishment of the Church of England. It was, however, a narrow victory, raising contentious issues and causing the young and inexperienced Queen considerable anxiety. The majority of the recalcitrant bishops subsequently refused to take the Oath of Supremacy required by the Act, and were subsequently deprived of office and dispatched to prison. Archbishop Parker gradually replaced them with Protestant priests, while most of the rest of the clergy, being all for a quiet life, were willing to conform to the new theology. The well-known Vicar of Bray was a cleric in the diocese of Salisbury throughout this period.

By this time John Knox, one of the most fanatical flag-bearers of the Protestant cause, had returned to his native Scotland after living in exile in Geneva throughout Mary's reign, having been a royal chaplain in the Court of Edward VI. While in Geneva, Knox was to meet Jean Calvin. Back in his homeland, Knox lost no time in preaching a series of characteristically fiery sermons which steadily undermined both the position of the Scottish Queen and the Catholic faith in Scotland. It might be thought that Elizabeth would have welcomed this threat to her Scottish cousin and the possibility of the Catholic faith being replaced north of the border, but she thoroughly disapproved of anyone attempting to overthrow the legitimate ruler of a nation, Catholic or otherwise, even one hostile to her own kingdom. Furthermore, Elizabeth felt that Knox's inflammatory publication, *The First Blast of the Trumpet Against the Monstrous Regiment of Women*, was directed as much against her as Mary, Queen of Scots, and considered its publication the very year she came to the throne to be particularly significant.

Sir William Cecil had been watching events in Scotland with considerable interest. Elizabeth's new Principal Secretary had been keen for the Queen to meet Knox and had already had a number of meetings with Knox himself with a view of bringing him to Court. However, Elizabeth's animosity toward this Scottish firebrand who had written that being ruled by women was 'repugnant to nature and contrary to God',[4] grew to such an extent that Cecil's resolve weakened and Knox went back to Scotland without a meeting between himself and the feisty English sovereign. It would have been a memorable encounter but by that time alarm bells were ringing across her kingdom: 'God keep us from such a visitation as Knox has attempted in Scotland,'[5] muttered Parker to Sir William Cecil. John Knox's continual agitation against the Scottish Queen assisted her downfall and flight to England in 1568. He died four years later, having successfully established Presbyterianism in Scotland, together with the foundation of the Church of Scotland, a faith that has endured there until the present day.

Knox had little time for Elizabeth's efforts to establish Protestantism in her own kingdom, thundering, 'Among many sins that have moved God to plague England . . . slackness to reform religion when time and place was granted was one.' The Queen had embarked on a difficult course of action in the manner she chose to adopt in order to establish the Church of England in the Protestant faith. Knox's stinging rebuke highlights the nature of her problem, for in deciding to steer a middle course between the old belief and the new theological thinking, the Queen risked considerable criticism from both sides. In positioning her Church between the heavy scent of Catholicism and the raw undercurrent of more radical doctrines, Elizabeth could well end up antagonizing many while pleasing few. Thus her archbishop was branded the 'Pope of Lambeth' by disgruntled Protestants, while the Spanish ambassador sneered, '. . . what can be expected from a country governed by a Queen'.[6]

Traditionalists were alarmed by the changes, particularly when zealous Protestant commissioners toured the parishes demanding that altars and ornaments be removed. Statues, banners and roods were torn down in a frenzy of iconoclasm, much of which was later unfairly blamed on Cromwell's rampaging soldiers during the Civil War. This religious vandalism was all very sad and particularly pointless, as a great deal of fine medieval craftsmanship was deliberately destroyed in pursuit of theological correctness. A depressing feature of the sixteenth century was the amount of death and destruction which was instigated in the name of God.

Reformers, on the other hand, were concerned that the pace of change was insufficient. Priests were still required to be properly attired in vestments considered by some to be an outmoded Catholic relic. Due reverence and ritual had still to be observed at all times during the course of services. The old order changed, but not quickly enough to satisfy those of more extreme religious persuasion, particularly the Puritans, 'those diligent barkers', as they were sometimes derisorily called – the very term 'Puritan' had originated as a term of insult.

Arguably, Elizabethan reform was squeezing both majesty and mystery out of religious worship. Many of her citizens preferred the orderly ritual and the sheer theatre of the old medieval service, finding earnest Bible-reading rather boring and the tedious preaching of bumbling parsons not at all to their liking. Country folk in particular enjoyed the drama and reassuring mystique of the traditional service; in their eyes the liturgy was becoming far too serious, much too intellectual. Sixteenth-century Protestantism could well be described as appealing more to the head than the heart. Perhaps the Church was beginning to lose touch with its congregation, as the clergy stood in their newly installed pulpits six foot above contradiction. Attendances began to decline, in spite of the Act of Uniformity making church-going compulsory on the Sabbath and holy days. Questions were asked in Parliament but it was of no use, for at the same time Elizabethan society was becoming progressively more materialistic. Leisure activities, such as archery, dancing and football, were sometimes considered preferable to church-going, particularly by the younger generation.

Elizabeth had chosen Matthew Parker to be her archbishop despite the fact that he was married. The Queen preferred her clergy to be single and celibate. Married clerics were one of her pet aversions, a view which possibly resulted from her own chosen lifestyle. When she visited her archbishop's home at Lambeth Palace, where he lived in considerable style, she encountered Parker's wife, Margaret. When it was time for the Queen to take her leave she was for once uncharacteristically lost for words, finally blurting out, 'Madam, I may not call you; mistress I am ashamed to call you so I know not what to call you but yet I thank you.'[7] Margaret Parker sensibly maintained a low profile yet was nevertheless a strong and beneficial influence on her archbishop husband; when she died in 1570, Parker sorely missed her, and was never quite the same man again.

In 1561, Elizabeth's dislike of married clergy had led her to ban all women from residing within the colleges or cathedral closes. She would like to have banned married clergy completely, but was dissuaded from this controversial proposal by Cecil and Parker, albeit with considerable difficulty. At this time, the hapless archbishop experienced one of the Queen's notorious tongue-lashings, during which he was deeply shocked by her choice of language. Despite such stormy moments the relationship between Elizabeth and Archbishop Parker was essentially a productive partnership, as he strove to maintain the authority of the Church and firmly establish the Anglican faith while struggling against a rising tide of Puritanism whose followers firmly intended to push England far further along a path of reform than either the Queen or her archbishop wished to happen. *The Thirty Nine Articles of Religion*, introduced in the mid-1560s, to which all clergy were required to conform, outlined the precise nature of Church doctrine, while the *Book of Homilies* defined their manner of preaching.

When Parker died in 1575, Elizabeth turned to Edmund Grindal as his replacement, largely as a result of the recommendation of her trusted Lord Treasurer Burghley, who was an enthusiastic supporter along with most other moderate Protestants. Grindal had studied at Pembroke College, Cambridge, where Nicholas Ridley had been his tutor. When Mary became Queen of England, Grindal went into exile, first to Strasbourg and then to Frankfurt. This resulted in Grindal being far more radical in his religious outlook than Parker, at the same time displaying a more sympathetic attitude towards the Puritans than his predecessor. After Grindal returned to England, following Elizabeth's succession to the throne, he had first been appointed Bishop of London and then created Archbishop of York in 1570. Grindal was a deeply devout and pious man with a far more positive attitude towards the role of archbishop than Parker had shown. He had a clear vision of how the Anglican Church should evolve, together with the role of the clergy within it – furthermore, he was unmarried. Unfortunately, Grindal's grand design did not coincide with that of the Queen and it was not long before serious disagreement arose between them. Essentially, there were two fundamental reasons for discord between the Queen and her new archbishop: his leniency towards the Puritans and his enthusiastic support of the concept of prophesying, a form of religious seminar designed to develop theological thinking and assist in advancing the technical ability of the parish clergy In the performance of their duties. Grindal had been accused of being soft on Puritans during his tenure as Bishop of London, a city where there was a relatively high concentration of this more extreme Protestant faction, whose increasingly strident actions were causing the Queen progressively more concern. Thus she required her Archbishop of Canterbury to adopt a strong line with them and not sympathize with their beliefs as Grindal was doing.

The issue of prophesying caused a far more serious rift between the increasingly irate Elizabeth and the obdurate Grindal. Not that this was a new concept that he had introduced: prophesying had been around for some time, but as the Queen was never particularly interested in mere mundane ecclesiastical routine, it took some time for her to become aware of its existence. Prophesying had originated from good intentions coupled with sound reason, an attempt to improve the quality of the clergy, school them in the art of preaching and generally advance the cause of the Reformation in an orderly and constructive manner. This was to be achieved in group sessions, calling on the instructional abilities of better-quality clerics, a period of intense activity followed by a good dinner – an excellent and innovative procedure it might have been thought. The Queen, however, saw it differently, regarding activities such as these with grave misgivings, suspicious that they might degenerate into potential hotbeds of evangelicalism and missionary mayhem which could undermine the orthodox, well-regulated uniformity that she preferred. Nothing should be allowed to take place that might threaten the carefully orchestrated practice that the Queen and her Privy Council desired.

Grindal was ordered to ensure that the practice of prophesying ceased forthwith. When he refused, he was summoned to Court to be confronted by an angry Queen in the spring of 1576. Grindal presented her with an extremely detailed and well-reasoned argument as to why this concept should be allowed to continue. The defiant archbishop then overreached himself when loftily informing Elizabeth that while she was indeed a mighty Prince, there was One in heaven that was even mightier and as a mere mortal she would be answerable to Him on Judgement Day. The Queen was not accustomed to such blunt speaking from one of her subjects, even one as august as an archbishop. Grindal's criticism of her, together with the hectoring manner in which it was delivered, caused Elizabeth to become incandescent with rage and fully determined to remove him from office forthwith, raising echoes of Henry II's religious power struggle with Thomas à Becket. Only the combined efforts of Burghley and Walsingham managed to dissuade the Queen from this course of action, being concerned that his dismissal would considerably weaken the Protestant cause in England and send unfavourable signals to Spain at a time of worsening relationships between the two nations. They reasoned that, '. . . if the Bishop of Canterbury shall be deprived then upstarts the pride and practice of papists.'[8] Elizabeth permitted the wretched Grindal to continue in office but completely forbade him to fulfil any further meaningful part in Church activities. In effect, she had consigned her stubborn archbishop to a spiritual limbo, one in which he was unhappily destined to remain until his death six years later. Nobody was permitted to challenge the Queen's authority, not even the Archbishop of Canterbury, and if he would not do as requested, Elizabeth was quite prepared to do without the services of an archbishop until she found somebody more to her liking.

Grindal's demise meant the end of further reformation in England during Elizabeth's lifetime. The evangelical movement had come to an abrupt halt in her kingdom and further reform of ecclesiastical procedures was firmly rejected. The Puritans realized it was futile to continue their attempts to change the Church from within; this would have to be achieved by mounting an external challenge. Elizabeth's firm line with Grindal would produce some considerable problems for her successors but that moment lay firmly in the future – for the time being, the Church of England would remain precisely as she wished it to be. A Frenchman visiting England towards the end of the sixteenth century considered, 'there is little difference between their ceremonies and those of the Church of Rome'.[9]

Elizabeth was always ready to learn from experience, particularly one that had not gone according to plan. Grindal had not been a bad archbishop or even a poor choice, but he had failed to conduct the

Church in the manner that Elizabeth required. Grindal had strayed from her ecclesiastical agenda while developing a dangerously independent attitude in a religious world where there was already far too much free-thinking for the Queen's liking. Elizabeth was determined to find an archbishop more sympathetic to her way of thinking and more ready to put her thoughts into practice. In John Whitgift, Bishop of Worcester, the Queen discovered a fellow soulmate. It was a marriage made in heaven; she even called her diminutive new archbishop, 'my little black husband'. Whitgift was an administrator rather than a theologian – he had been at Pembroke College during Nicholas Ridley's time as Master, subsequently becoming Master at Trinity College, Cambridge. Here his encounter with Thomas Cartwright, a Fellow of the college and religious hard-liner, on the extreme edge of radical reform, fully demonstrated Whitgift's ability to take a tough line with anyone daring to challenge the authority of the Church. Cartwright's desire to abolish the bishops was the mere tip of the ecclesiastical iceberg in his enthusiasm for religious reform. Yet Cartwright was a skilled debator whose preaching drew enormous crowds whenever he appeared and he was considered to have one of the finest minds of all the Puritans. It was a tussle of theological titans: Whitgift's skilled exposition of orthodox Anglican philosophy was both cogent and masterly, marking him out as a man destined for greater things. His subsequent speedy dismissal of Cartwright demonstrated that his practice was every bit as incisive as his theory. This man-to-man contest between orthodox and nonconformist thinking did not go unheeded in the corridors of power and Whitgift was singled out for high office, becoming successively Vice-Chancellor of the University, Bishop of Worcester, and finally Archbishop of Canterbury in 1583.

At the time when Whitgift was consecrated as Elizabeth's third archbishop, the Puritan challenge to the established Church was reaching a crescendo, while the Privy Council contained a nucleus of hardline Protestants such as Leicester, Knollys, Walsingham and Hatton who were not wholly unsympathetic to the Puritan cause. The Puritan party dominated a Parliament where the fanatical Peter Wentworth was particularly vocal, only to be silenced when thrown in the Tower. Whitgift faced formidable opposition, yet had the full and unqualified support of the Queen, something conspicuously lacking with her two previous archbishops, whenever unpopular measures were required. Whitgift endured a sustained and vicious propaganda campaign from the Puritans aided by their underground press, in particular the amusingly scurrilous Martin Marprelate tracts which viciously lampooned him at every conceivable opportunity. At the same time, Whitgift was constantly obstructed and opposed by the more militant Protestant members of the Privy Council. The archbishop was totally unmoved. He was both tough and resourceful – the Puritan press was silenced, the Council outflanked, and Whitgift managed to push through the measures he desired. He was even conciliatory towards his old adversary Thomas Cartwright, gaining him an academic position in Warwick. Whitgift had triumphed and was secure for the rest of Elizabeth's lifetime. There were periods of turbulence throughout the rule of the Stuarts, but Protestantism survived to be England's official religion to the present day. Elizabeth had cause to be grateful to Archbishop Whitgift, he had served her faithfully and well. He outlived her by barely a year.

When the Act of Supremacy and Act of Uniformity were successfully passed at the beginning of Elizabeth's reign thereby establishing the Church of England in the Anglican faith, both the Queen and her Privy Council had hoped that Catholicism would gradually die out in England of its own accord, as both priests and congregation either defected to Protestantism or grew old and died. It was reasoned that without any bishops, and faced with a diminishing number of priests, Catholicism would wither and die like a neglected plant. This turned out to be sheer wishful thinking by Elizabeth and her Council: Catholicism in the mid-sixteenth century was an extremely well-established, enduring and deeply held faith. It had already suffered a period of persecution during the reign of Edward VI, but survived relatively unscathed. It was not about to obligingly disappear in Elizabeth's reign. Catholicism was surprisingly resilient in the north and the far west of her kingdom and in the middle period of Elizabeth's long reign, seminary priests who had been educated on the continent in religious establishments, such as Douai and the English College in Rome, were discreetly infiltrated back into England like so many religious secret agents. In turn, these were followed by the more fanatical Jesuits, members of the Society of Jesus, men like Robert Southwell, Robert Parsons, John Gerard and Edmund Campion, who were fearlessly prepared, even eager, to die for their cause. They were encouraged by Cardinal Allen, the Englishman who would have become the Archbishop of Canterbury and Lord Chancellor had the Armada succeeded and England been conquered by Spain.

Parsons came to England with Campion but eventually returned to Rome to die there in 1610 and was buried alongside Cardinal Allen. The extremely handsome Robert Southwell possessed a passionate faith coupled with an equally passionate longing for martyrdom, a wish which was fulfilled when he was arrested and executed at the age of thirty-four, following particularly hideous torture. Gerard was also captured but made a spectacular night-time escape from the Tower where he had been imprisoned with Southwell.

Campion was the best known of all the Jesuit martyrs, dying at the age of forty-one in 1581. The young Campion had been a precocious orator who had made an eloquent welcoming oration to Queen Mary when she entered London for her coronation in 1553. He was subsequently to deliver an equally fine speech to Queen Elizabeth when she visited Oxford in 1566. Elizabeth was hugely impressed and became his patron. Campion was ordained in the Anglican Church but later defected to Rome to enrol in the Society of Jesus, returning to London in 1580. When apprehended, he was consigned to the Tower of London and subsequently questioned in the presence of the Queen who offered him a full pardon providing he return to the Anglican faith. When Campion graciously declined the Queen's offer, he was put on trial, endured the rack on three separate occasions and then publicly hung at Tyburn in front of a huge crowd. Campion is considered the noblest of all the Catholic martyrs – scholarly, courageous, honourable in all his actions, which were entirely to preserve the Catholic faith in England and did not involve any political motives. The fact that he was well known and highly regarded by the Queen makes Campion's martyrdom particularly poignant. His story also gives an interesting insight into the activities of the Jesuits, whose actions are all too easily dismissed as those of misguided and fanatical conspirators who were traitors to the country at the time when it was facing great danger from potential Spanish invasion.

Many of the Jesuit martyrs fell foul of the odious Richard Topcliffe, self-appointed persecutor and torturer of Roman Catholics, who approached his ghoulish task like a vengeful angel. Topcliffe kept a rack, together with a formidable array of torture equipment, at his own home; the latter were rumoured to be more horrific than those kept in the Tower. Topcliffe was to die only a year after the Queen, who must have been fully aware of activities belonging to the darker side of her reign.

More than one hundred Catholic martyrs were to die for their cause in the second half of Elizabeth's reign, by which time religion had become hopelessly embroiled with politics. The hostilities with Spain had caused all Catholics in England to be regarded as potential traitors to their country, rather than merely individuals with a different religious persuasion. The fact that they did not turn against England during the Spanish invasion was most worthy and that they continued to flourish in such numbers in the face of continual persecution was truly remarkable. The traditional doctrine of Roman Catholicism remains largely unchanged to the present day.

The efforts of the seminary priests and the Jesuits to keep the flickering flame of Catholicism burning in England was a brave feat, yet because circumstances led them to concentrate their efforts in the more welcoming North Country and to conduct Mass in the private chapels of the landed gentry, meant that the grass roots of the population became neglected along with most of southern England. This was particularly true of London, which had a significant bearing on Catholicism in England in the due course of time and was only restored by Irish immigration many years later.

The essential ethos of Elizabethan religion is embodied in the writing of two outstanding religious personalities: John Jewel, Bishop of Salisbury, and Richard Hooker, a leading theologian of the day, who like Jewel had studied at Oxford University. Jewel was an early champion of Protestant reform and was particularly anti-Catholic, branding clerical vestments as 'theatrical habits' and composing a long diatribe against the perils of idolatry which he considered to be 'spiritual fornification'. Jewel combined deep piety with profound learning, and was so dedicated to the service of God that he exhausted himself by continually preaching around his diocese. *An Apology of the Church of England*, written by Jewel in Latin in 1562 and translated two years later into English by Lady Bacon, mother of Francis Bacon, was a detailed justification of the Anglican faith, setting out the religious agenda in the early part of Elizabeth's reign. 'Questionless, there can nothing be more spitefully spoken against the religion of God than to accuse it of novelty, as a new-come-up matter: for, as there can be no change in God himself, so ought there to be no change in his religion,'[10] declaimed Jewel.

There was a heartfelt desire for the Church of England to reflect the early days of Christianity, in essence a religious renaissance which returned Elizabeth's Church to the spirit of the first centuries following the teaching of Christ and His apostles, before the purity of their message had been corrupted by dogma and irrelevant ritual: 'The call was for a return to the sources of the Christian religion, the Bible, the apostolic teaching and the writing of the early fathers.'[11]

John Jewel had been born the son of a yeoman farmer in North Devon in the early summer of 1522; at the age of thirteen, he went to Merton College, Oxford, completing his education at the adjacent Corpus Christi College. Because he was skilful at shorthand, in 1554 Jewel was employed as a notary at the trials of Cranmer,

Latimer and Ridley, the three Oxford martyrs later burnt at the stake. Jewel fled into exile abroad, initially to Frankfurt and then Strasbourg, where he lived at the home of the Italian reformer Peter Martyr. Following the accession of Elizabeth, Jewel returned to England and was appointed Bishop of Salisbury in 1560 by the new Queen; at thirty-eight years of age, he was her youngest bishop.

Jewel had accepted the appointment with some misgivings, being uncertain as to the precise nature of the Queen's reformation programme for her Church. He subsequently became a fearless and vocal critic of her progress whenever he felt that her reform was not going in the direction he desired. Jewel was the conscience of Elizabeth's Church – on one occasion when preaching before the Queen, 'Jewel pointedly but respectfully informed the Queen that he and his fellow ministers had hoped for changes on her accession, but the problem remained "as miserable as it did before". He reminded her that she was the governor and "nurse of God's church", and only she could redress the calamitous state of the clergy.'[12] This was not the only time that the bishop publicly upbraided the sovereign but fortunately for Jewel and the developing Church of England the Queen did not take umbrage in the manner she was to do when chastised by Archbishop Grindal. Therefore, Bishop Jewel survived to write his definitive *Apology* during 1562:

> It was not only a defence (which is the meaning of 'apology') of the doctrines and practices of the English Church, but it was a scathing attack on the Church of Rome. It received the approval of the Queen and Archbishop Parker and was to become the official definitive work on the beliefs of the Elizabethan Church influencing the development of the Church for at least the next fifty years.[13]

The dedicated Jewel literally wore himself out in pursuit of his calling – arriving at the exquisite St Cyrica's Church in the pretty Wiltshire village of Lacock, the church wardens advised him that he was not well enough to preach. 'It well became a bishop to die preaching,' replied Jewel.[14] A few days later, he was dead. Jewel was not yet fifty years of age. He is buried within Salisbury Cathedral. The Bishop of Salisbury in the last years of the twentieth century commented, 'It is for his *Apology* that he is best known. This classic defence of the "catholic" Church – catholic in the sense of deriving from the years of the early undivided Church – became a foundation document for the Elizabethan church.'[15]

Towards the end of the Queen's lifetime, the first volumes of Richard Hooker's masterly *The Laws of Ecclesiastical Polity* were published, an eloquent, deceptively simple, yet highly persuasive work. His was a quiet voice of reason to silence the strident sound of Puritanism and firmly establish the Anglican faith beyond doubt or debate:

> He that goeth about to persuade a multitude that they are not so well governed as they ought to be shall never want attentive and favourable hearers, because they know the manifold defects whereunto every kind of regiment is subject, but the secret lets and difficulties which in public proceedings are innumerable and inevitable, they have not ordinarily the judgement to consider. . . .[16]

Richard Hooker was also born in Devon, in 1554, and like Jewel went to Corpus Christi, Oxford, where he became a Fellow and then ordained in 1582. He was befriended by Jewel and became Rector of Boscombe in the diocese of Salisbury. It was at this small Wiltshire village that Hooker began his great religious masterpiece, *The Laws of Ecclesiastical Polity*, firmly mapping out the territory which the Church of England was destined to occupy until the present day, claiming that the Church is an organic, living institution, not to be governed by its past, but to thrive and grow in response to continual changing circumstances. The majestic tones of the initial statement also place Hooker among the masters of Elizabethan literature: 'Under this fair and plausible cover whatsoever they utter passes for good and current, that which wanteth in the weight of their speech is supplied by the atlas of men's minds to accept and believe it. . . .'[17]

The permanent foundation of the Church of England was conceivably Elizabeth's finest and most enduring achievement, one for which the entire Anglican world should be profoundly grateful. In turn, Elizabeth owed a considerable debt of gratitude to Whitgift, Hooker, Coverdale, Jewel, Parker and the other great men of God throughout her reign.

9

THE SCHOLARS

Elizabeth's reverence for scholarship had been inherited from her father and, like Henry VIII, she had acquired a thorough education, especially in the field of languages for which she displayed a ready aptitude, being possessed with a particularly retentive memory. She was fluent in French and Spanish and had a good knowledge of Flemish and Italian, with an excellent grounding in Latin and Greek. The great Tudor antiquary, John Leland, had been much impressed with Elizabeth's knowledge of Latin when he met her as a young girl in the company of her half-brother Edward. Elizabeth could even speak some Welsh, presumably acquired from her long-serving Welsh attendant Blanche Parry. The young princess's enthusiasm for learning was so intense that her one-time tutor, the eminent Cambridge scholar Roger Ascham, became alarmed that she might be overdoing her studies.

Elizabeth had cause to be grateful for all these attributes, first to her father, and then to Henry's sixth wife, Katherine Parr. Henry VIII had founded Trinity College at Cambridge in 1546 by the simple expedient of combining two far older colleges, Michaelhouse and King's Hall, both originally established in the fourteenth century, the latter by Edward III. His statue still stands on the clock tower above one of the entrances to Trinity, while Henry's statue graces the Great Gate, clasping an orb in one hand, the sceptre from the other replaced by a chair leg as a result of some long-forgotten student prank. Both the clock tower and the Great Gate are remains of the original King's Hall, as is the range of buildings which front onto the Fellow's Lawn behind the college chapel, which was created by Elizabeth's half-sister Queen Mary when she inherited the throne after Henry VIII had died in 1547.

Displaying uncharacteristic modesty, Henry did not name the college after himself but dedicated it to 'The Holy and Undivided Trinity', at the same time endowing it with considerable revenues that had flowed from the dissolution of the monasteries. He died the year after he had founded Trinity College. Hans Eworth's magnificent full-length portrait of the King is today displayed at the far end of the Great Hall; the painting is a sixteenth-century copy of the work by Hans Holbein, which was lost when most of Whitehall Palace was destroyed by fire in the late seventeenth century.

Henry's last wife, Katherine Parr, was also very well educated, uncharacteristically so in an age when a daughter's education was usually considered far less important than a son's. Katherine was one of the few women in her time to have published a book, *The Lamentation or Complaint of a Sinner*. More importantly, Katherine was able to persuade Henry not to allow the universities to suffer a similar fate to that of the monasteries, after Thomas Cromwell had begun to cast a covetous glance at the huge amount of property and land owned by the colleges.

Under Katherine's supervision, Princess Elizabeth's schooling was undertaken by some of the nation's most gifted scholars, commencing with William Grindal, a Fellow of St John's College, Cambridge. Grindal was an outstanding Latin scholar who was equally proficient in ancient Greek, a language enjoying a considerable revival of interest as a result of the Renaissance placing a renewed emphasis on classical studies. When Grindal was suddenly struck down by bubonic plague in the year after Henry VIII's death, his place as tutor to the young princess was taken by another brilliant young scholar, Roger Ascham, a former pupil of Sir John Cheke, a Fellow of St John's College. Cheke had taught Elizabeth's most prominent Privy Councillor, William Cecil, while he was at Cambridge, Cecil later marrying his tutor's sister Mary, much against his father's wishes. Cheke had held strong Protestant views and had therefore fled abroad when Mary became Queen and restored Catholicism to England. However, he had been kidnapped on the orders of Prince Philip of Spain and brought back to England where he had been forced to publicly and ignominiously renounce his faith, an act of weakness of which Cheke was greatly ashamed and he died shortly afterwards.

Ascham read both the Greek testament and Sophocles with Elizabeth each morning, and during the initial two years as her tutor the pair completed virtually all the works of Cicero, together with most of those by Livy. Ascham subsequently boasted that the princess spoke more Latin than most of the clergy at the time. After Elizabeth had become queen, he continued to read Greek regularly with her up to the time of his death in 1568.

Roger Ascham was an extraordinary man and a first-class scholar, who displayed many other talents together with an eclectic range of interests not normally associated with the academic mind. He was a compulsive gambler with a lifetime enthusiasm for playing dice and the delights of cockfighting, thereby ensuring he always remained poor. He was equally keen on archery and wrote a book entitled *Toxophilus* which explained the theory and practice of a sport in which he indulged virtually every day. He had also firmly intended to write a definitive work on cockfighting, but it was Ascham's authoritative work on the principles of education entitled *The School Master*, which fully established his reputation as an author. This enlightened work had arisen out of a discussion over dinner with William Cecil, which had also involved the Privy Councillors Sir Walter Mildmay, Sir Richard Sackville, Sir John Mason and Sir William Petre, the latter pair being Fellows of All Soul's College, Oxford. After dinner, Sir Richard visited the Queen's private quarters where she was reading Greek with Ascham in order to urge him to write *The School Master*.

Like so many Cambridge scholars of the day, Roger Ascham held extremist Protestant views, deploring anyone who was even contemplating taking the 'Grand Tour' to Italy, worried about its seductive powers and uttering dire warnings that 'More Papists be made by your merry books of Italy than your earnest books of Louvain.'[1] Previously Ascham had warned, 'Those enchantments of sirens brought out of Italy mar most men's attitudes in England.'[2] It was this sort of bigoted stance that had considerably hindered the introduction of the Renaissance into England and reflected a growing Puritan distaste for the visual arts which was eventually to lead to the closures of theatres throughout the nation after Cromwell had established a republic in England. Religious extremism can indeed inhibit cultural progress.

Ascham possessed beautiful handwriting, so elegant that he was employed by Cambridge University to produce their official correspondence. He was able to pass on to Elizabeth his talent in the art of calligraphy, an ability that is manifestly evident in the documents depicting her handwriting that can be seen today in places such as Hatfield House, the British Library in London and the Bodleian Library at Oxford. He was also a passionate advocate of the English language. *The School Master*, to which he devoted the last years of his life, is an excellent example of Ascham's belief in the merits of 'The Englyshe Tonge', and he did a considerable amount to advance its cause; *Toxophilis* portrays a remarkable contemporary example of Elizabethan English prose, a passionate plea for its more extensive usage which eventually was fulfilled as a result of Shakespeare's literary genius.

In addition to always being short of money, Ascham invariably suffered poor health. He contracted a bad chill in the winter of 1568 while staying up late at night in order to compose a special poem for the Queen. He never recovered. Elizabeth was greatly saddened to learn of the death of someone who had taught her so much and had been one of the great English scholars of her lifetime.

Another leading intellectual who had a profound influence on Elizabeth was Dr John Dee, who had also been a Fellow of St John's College, Cambridge, and one of the inaugural Fellows at Trinity College when Henry VIII founded it in 1546. Dee was a remarkable scholar who miraculously managed to combine mathematics, astrology and alchemy, while also finding time to dabble in the mysteries of the occult. He was widely travelled and at various times had visited Antwerp, Venice and Hungary, where he had met and greatly impressed Maximilian, Emperor of the Holy Roman Empire. Dee found favour with many of the European rulers of the day, and it is said that the Tsar of Russia had offered him a post, but this had been graciously declined. While travelling in Europe Dee had encountered three of the most outstanding continental scholars of the day: Abraham Ortelius, Gemma Frisius, the Court Astrologer to Charles V, and most importantly, the illustrious Flemish cartographer, Gerardus Mercator, who was to become a great personal friend of Dee. Mercator had devised the first truly modern atlas, one that was to prove invaluable in compiling navigational charts. Dee was able to return to England with the first astronomer's staff and ring, a gift from Frisius, together with two globes that had been constructed by Mercator. These were the first astronomical instruments to be seen in England and were to prove invaluable in the advancement of the knowledge and practice of navigation by the early Elizabethan mariners. Dee is reputed to have taught this art to some of the first English explorers such as Chancellor, Jenkinson, Frobisher and Humphrey Gilbert. His eclectic circle of friends also included the chronicler John Stow, antiquary William Camden, and Richard Hakluyt, the author of *Principal Navigations, Voyages, Traffiques and Discoveries of the English Nation*.

John Dee could well have provided the inspiration for Christopher Marlowe's *Dr Faustus*, and during the reign of Queen Mary had been imprisoned on the suspicion of heresy and attempting to poison the Queen. Miraculously, the intrepid doctor was able to escape indictment of both of these grave charges. In the sixteenth century, the borderline between science and sorcery was often perilously narrow. Sir Walter Ralegh and his circle of friends practised sorcery at his infamous 'School of the Night', at his home at Sherborne in Dorset.

Lord Robert Dudley and the Earl of Pembroke introduced Dee to Elizabeth, and he was able to find favour with the new sovereign when he selected a propitious date for her coronation, as a result of which she made him her official Court Astrologer. Dee was destined to have a powerful influence over the impressionable monarch for the rest of her reign and was summoned into her presence many times. On one particular occasion, Elizabeth is said to have listened to him in rapt concentration for the best part of three days while he eloquently held forth on the significance of a new comet whose sudden appearance over England had terrified the Court. Elizabeth was also in the habit of visiting Dee at his house in Mortlake beside the River Thames in London.

John Aubrey, the early seventeenth-century antiquary, described Elizabeth's Court Astrologer as having 'a very fair clear rosy complexion, a long beard as white as milke . . . a gown like an artists with hanging sleeves and a slit. A mighty good man was he.'[3] While Aubrey's graphic description is borne out by Dee's portrait which can now be seen in the Ashmolean Museum at Oxford, not everyone viewed him in such a favourable light. In 1584, while he was travelling in Europe, an angry mob, believing Dee to be a sorcerer, ransacked his house, destroying many of his valuable books and papers in the process. Dee claimed to have the power to turn base metal into gold; he was also a hugely prolific writer and is reputed to have been the first person to use the term 'British Empire'.

In the 1580s, most of Europe decided to adopt the Gregorian calendar. Dee was commanded by the Queen and her Council to examine the merits of adopting it in England. However, this alternative method of measuring the year had been originated by the Pope in Rome and therefore its introduction in England was violently opposed by the Church, the ultra-Protestant Edward Grindal being Archbishop of Canterbury at the time. This resulted in the nation continuing to use the Julian calendar until 1752, remaining ten days out of step with continental Europe, thereby demonstrating that there is nothing new in England's dislike of perceived interference from the European mainland: 'The French are wiser than they seem and the Spaniards seem wiser than they are,'[4] said that Elizabethan Eurosceptic, Francis Bacon. Although he was born in 1527, Dee was to outlive Elizabeth by more than five years, finally dying in 1608 aged eighty-one, a remarkable age for those days and a truly remarkable man.

John Dee's friend, Richard Hakluyt, came from a family with Flemish origins, his father a lawyer and businessman who was friendly with both William Cecil and Francis Walsingham. Hakluyt acquired his Bachelor and Master of Arts at Christchurch, Oxford, where he was a contemporary of Sir Philip Sidney, the hugely talented Elizabethan courtier who was later to be killed at the Battle of Zutphen in Flanders. After coming down from Oxford, Hakluyt took Holy Orders and became Chaplain to Sir Edward Stafford, Elizabeth's ambassador in Paris and brother-in-law to the Queen's relative, Lord Howard of Effingham, commander of the English fleet, who fought and defeated the Spanish Armada. It was the discovery of a map lying on a table that led Hakluyt to decide to devote the rest of his life to the study of geography – in the process he became a friend to the great cartographers Mercator and Ortelius. As Hakluyt recalled, '. . . it was my happe to visit the chamber of M. Richard Hakluyt, my cosin a Gentlemen of the Middle Temple, well known to you . . . at a time when I found lying open upon his boord certeine bookes of cosmographie with a universall mappe: He seeing me somewhat curious in the view thereof, began to instruct my ignorance. . . .'[5]

Hakluyt was a tremendous patriot, a prime voice in urging English expansion overseas beyond the blue horizon to Africa, the Orient and the New World. He translated the French explorer Jacques Cartier's stirring account of his discoveries in Canada and included these in his *Principal Navigations*. Today Hakluyt is regarded more as an editor and a researcher than an original writer: 'The silent man, seated in a dark corner, who is content to listen and remember', according to the nineteenth-century author Walter Ralegh, a descendant of the original Elizabethan courtier and Hakluyt's biographer. Richard Hakluyt's *magnum opus* was his magnificent *Principal Navigations, Voyages, Traffiques and Discoveries of the English Nation* which was first published towards the end of the sixteenth century and dedicated to his patron Sir Francis Walsingham, who had employed him in a variety of activities including that of secret agent. Some one and a half million words portray a vivid contemporary account of the pioneering voyages undertaken by illustrious Elizabethan sea captains, men like Drake, Hawkins, Gilbert and Frobisher as seen through the eyes of the actual seamen involved at the time, the words of those who took part in great adventures and survived to tell the tale: 'Upon Monday, the second of October 1567. The weather being reasonably faire, our Generall, M. John Hawkins, having commanded all his Captaines and Masters to be in readiness to make saile with him . . .'.[6]

Hakluyt was the archetypal Renaissance scholar, a man of vision, articulate, acutely inquisitive, passionate about everything he did. He was fluent in an impressive variety of languages and above all was a man who helped to put science into the ancient art of discovery and map-making, which had traditionally involved following a star or gazing at a map with vague terms like 'here be monsters', conveniently and artistically filling the gaps in the cartographers' knowledge. As that other eminent Elizabethan scholar, Francis Bacon, stated, 'this proficiency in navigation and discoveries may place also an expectation of the further proficiencies and argumentation of all sciences'.[7] Hakluyt's exploits ranged from lecturing in cartography at Oxford University to being appointed the expert geographical adviser to the newly formed East India Company. Most importantly, Hakluyt's brilliant writing superbly portrays the majesty of Elizabeth's reign and the exuberant vitality of her kingdom.

Francis Bacon, the younger son of Sir Nicholas Bacon, Elizabeth's venerable Lord Keeper of The Great Seal, was conceivably the greatest scholar of the age, his dazzling range of attributes undoubtedly make him the essential Renaissance man. His legal expertise enabled him to rival Sir Edward Coke, the most outstanding lawyer in sixteenth-century England, while his effortless command of language has subsequently led some academics to speculate that it was Bacon rather than Shakespeare who was responsible for the works attributed to the Stratford bard, an idea later advanced by the late eighteenth-century writer James Wilmot, in his book *The Baconian Theory*, first published in 1785. Though this idea may be rather fanciful, Francis Bacon was indeed a literary genius, his marvellous 'Essays' sparkle with wit and wisdom mixed with memorably waspish sentiments such as 'new nobility is but the act of power, but ancient nobility is the act of time'. This was possibly a not-too-subtle side swipe at his uncle, Lord Burghley, his one-time friend and mentor, who had turned against Bacon thereby thwarting his political ambitions and causing him to join forces with his elder brother Anthony and Robert Devereux, the 2nd Earl of Essex, arch-rival of both Lord Burghley and his ambitious son Robert Cecil.

Bacon was also to establish an enviable reputation as one of the foremost philosophers of Elizabethan England, while his pioneering concepts on the application of scientific knowledge are succinctly expressed in such seminal works as *The New Atlantis* which was first published in 1626, some time after his political career had been ruined. He had been heavily fined for taking bribes and had even endured a brief spell in the Tower of London, not something that the fastidious Bacon would have enjoyed very much.

Francis Bacon had originally been born in London in 1561 and had studied law at Trinity College, Cambridge, from the tender age of twelve. Today his marble bust can be seen in the college library together with other distinguished members such as fellow scientist Sir Isaac Newton and the poet Alfred Tennyson. Bacon continued his law studies at Gray's Inn in London, which in his day was bordered by green fields. He worked closely with Queen Elizabeth, both in a legal capacity as her learned counsel and as a political adviser. This work gave him an invaluable insight into the intricacies of the Elizabethan Court and its policies, providing valuable information that he was able to convey to his friend and patron, the Earl of Essex, who was seeking to boost his own influence with the Queen at the expense of his deadly rivals, William and Robert Cecil. Essex lobbied both the Queen and William Cecil ceaselessly yet unavailingly in an attempt to secure important political posts for Bacon. Bacon later defended his denouncement of Essex at the latter's treason trial in his book *Apologie, certain imputations concerning the late Earle of Essex*, written in 1604, the year after Elizabeth's death. Bacon's conscience was clear: he felt he had given the reckless Essex more than sufficient warning as to precisely where his foolhardy behaviour would eventually lead. However, the early eighteenth-century poet and satirist Alexander Pope was later to brand Bacon as 'the wisest, brightest and meanest of mankind'.[8]

It is perhaps unfortunate that Francis Bacon's political aspirations for high office were to come to nothing during Elizabeth's lifetime, largely because he had elected to hitch his wagon to a rising star destined to plunge so spectacularly back to earth. Bacon's hopes were only to be fulfilled later during the reign of James I and proved short-lived, yet political disgrace belatedly enabled him to parade the full dazzling array of his scholastic ability, achievements that outlive this hugely talented yet often mercurial individual.

Elizabethan scholarship reached new heights with the publication of William Camden's *Britannia*, in 1586, which together with his later *Annals of Queen Elizabeth*, are the impressive works of a man who became headmaster of Westminster School and lived throughout Elizabeth's long and glorious reign. *Britannia* is dedicated to William Cecil, later Lord Burghley, who greatly encouraged Camden's work and always made his extensive library available to him together with access to a wide range of official papers, Burghley being particularly keen that there should be a comprehensive, contemporary account of Elizabeth's reign. The *Annals* proved to be the first truly authoritative biography of Elizabeth, having been written in the early seventeenth century, thus very close to her lifetime. *Britannia* is a panoramic account of the nation as it appeared to Camden's perceptive eye in the second half of the sixteenth century, originally written in Latin as Camden hoped it would circulate widely elsewhere in Europe. *Britannia* is masterly, far-reaching, an academic overview redolent with evocative prose. Camden's obvious love of the English countryside shines out of *Britannia*, the fields of Bedfordshire 'smelling sweet in summer of the best beans'.[9]

Despite his intellectual prowess, William Camden remained a modest man and he declined the Queen's offer of a knighthood. Yet he inspired universal admiration coupled with great affection, and when he finally died at the age of seventy-two, Camden was honoured with an impressive funeral at Westminster Abbey. The Camden Society was formed in 1838 in order to commemorate and maintain his indisputable academic prowess.

Elsewhere in Europe, Galileo, the Italian mathematician, astronomer and physicist, had developed the astronomical telescope and extended the revolutionary theories that had been first advanced by the Polish astronomer Nicholaus Copernicus, which propounded that the earth revolved round the sun rather than vice versa as had been previously thought. Predictably, these radical concepts were regarded as heresy by the notoriously conservative Catholic Church: Galileo was brought before the Inquisition in Rome and forced to repent his visionary yet unwelcome ideas in order to avoid being burnt at the stake. When the English poet John Milton later undertook the Grand Tour to Italy and met Galileo, he found him to be a broken man. Galileo was, however, more fortunate than the Italian philosopher Giordano Bruno, who was burnt at the stake in Rome because of his heretical views at the end of the sixteenth century. Bruno had lived in England between 1583 and 1585 during which time he had written some of his most influential work. His presence in the country had benefited English scholarship in the same manner as Erasmus when the Dutch scholar and humanist had come to England on a number of occasions earlier in the sixteenth century, during which time he had become friendly with Sir Thomas More, Henry VIII's one-time Lord Chancellor.

Ironically, one of the few positive side-effects of Queen Mary's disastrous reign had been that a considerable number of English intellectuals had fled the country in order to avoid religious persecution and gone into exile in continental Europe. Here they had become directly involved with the 'New Learning'. When Elizabeth came to the throne in 1558 and restored the Protestant faith, they were able to introduce this 'New Learning' into England after returning from such places as Hamburg, Basle and Geneva, places that were brimming with radical new concepts and stimulating new ideas.

Had Protestantism not been restored, these exiles would have been unable to return and it would have been doubtful that England would have benefited from their newly acquired knowledge. Elizabeth's arrival on the throne did much to stimulate the nation's intellectual vigour, accelerating the progress of science, law, philosophy, theology and medicine. Conversely, the Catholic faith elsewhere in Europe was usually far more conservative in outlook, where challenging perceived wisdom could quickly be branded as heresy. Indeed, the final period of the High Renaissance in Italy was severely curtailed by the Counter-Reformation that was gathering pace in the second half of the sixteenth century, when most of the new thinking was developing in Germany, Scandinavia and other Protestant areas.

In England, the two long-standing universities, Oxford and Cambridge, had been in slow yet relentless decline. Oxford had once been one of the foremost universities in Europe but had progressively lost its ascendancy to continental rivals such as Paris and Padua, as the Renaissance gathered momentum in Europe while England was slow to respond to the winds of intellectual change. Initially the nation had been preoccupied with the Wars of the Roses, followed by two decades of internal rebuilding during the reign of Henry VII, after which his successor Henry VIII did little to encourage a movement that was perceived to centre on Rome.

Fortunately, in the wake of the Queen's enthusiasm for scholarship and her belief in a religion that was not only tolerant of intellectual advancement but positively encouraged it, Elizabethan England witnessed a considerable acceleration of academic skills. During the Queen's time on the throne, Jesus College was founded in 1591, the first Protestant college at Oxford, while other colleges such as Queen's greatly increased their student numbers. Thomas Bodley, a wealthy retired diplomat and scholar, was to restore the derelict Duke Humphrey's Library in 1599. By the last years of Elizabeth's reign it housed more than two thousand books and manuscripts, including the original of Bacon's 'Essays' annotated by the Queen, together with her own translation of Cicero. It was renamed the Bodleian Library in 1602, the penultimate year of her reign.

At Cambridge University, three new colleges came into existence in Queen Elizabeth's lifetime. Sir Walter Mildmay, her long-serving Privy Councillor and able Chancellor of the Exchequer, founded Emmanuel College in 1584, primarily for the specific training of a better calibre of clergy; '. . . it should be a seed-plot of learned men for the supply of the Church', Sir Walter wrote at the time, the study of theology at university having been in serious decline in the mid-sixteenth century. The Queen accused her philanthropic Councillor of potentially instigating a hotbed of Puritanism and as so often proved the case, Elizabeth was not far wrong. When Archbishop Laud attacked the college for religious irregularities in the reign of Charles I, some three dozen former students of Emmanuel, who all held strong Puritan beliefs, departed England for the New World. Among them was John Harvard, whose generous endowment on his death in 1638 led to the foundation of Harvard University, destined to be the first American university in a town which is today also called Cambridge. Emmanuel College was built on the former site of a religious house once occupied by Dominican friars which had ceased to function after Elizabeth's father had dissolved the monasteries, the original friar's chapel being converted into the student hall.

Magdalene College had been established in 1542 on a one-time monastic site that had been acquired by Lord Thomas Audley, Henry VIII's Lord Chancellor at the time of the dissolution of the monasteries. The mellow red brickwork of Magdalene's First Court remains virtually as it appeared in Elizabeth's lifetime. To this day, the Master is elected not by the Fellows of Magdalene, but by the descendants of its founder, whose coat of arms is displayed above the doorway leading to the college hall, still lit only by candlelight at night.

Sidney Sussex was the third Cambridge college whose foundation dates back to the Elizabethan era. It is also built on a site that had become available as a result of Henry's dissolution of the monasteries, in this particular instance a thirteenth-century Franciscan establishment, the student hall being in the monk's former chapel. Lady Frances Sidney, the Countess of Sussex and the wealthy widow of one of Elizabeth's prominent Privy Councillors, Thomas Radcliffe, the Earl of Sussex, had bequeathed a substantial sum of money derived from her estate to found Sidney Sussex College. Building began towards the end of Elizabeth's reign after the site had been acquired from its previous owner, Trinity College, to whom it had been given by Henry VIII. The Fellows of Trinity had used much of the stone from the friary in order to extend their own college and it was at this time that the colleges either side of Trinity were being radically extended. At St John's, a second court was under construction while Dr Caius, who had founded Gonville and Caius College the year before Elizabeth came to the throne, was building a court whose imposing Gate of Honour is an early example of Renaissance architecture in England, doubtless introduced as a result of the learned Dr Caius's earlier visit to Italy. It was not very long before Sidney Sussex was to house a young student who never did take his degree but was destined to become one of the most famous figures in English history – Oliver Cromwell.

It was in the late sixteenth century that some of the most important developments within the whole of Cambridge University were to take place at Trinity, entirely due to the arrival of a dynamic new Master, Thomas Nevile, appointed by Queen Elizabeth in 1593. This was to prove to be one of Elizabeth's many characteristically shrewd and significant appointments. Formally Dean of Canterbury, Nevile was a favourite of the Queen and had originally been a student at Pembroke College, Cambridge, and later Master at Magdalene, before becoming Vice-Chancellor of Cambridge University in the year of the defeat of the Armada. Nevile was a confirmed bachelor, dedicated to the university and extremely wealthy. The new Master, therefore, combined two very useful attributes, a reverence of scholarship and considerable riches, to put his altruistic ideas into practice. Nevile immediately set about the immense task of pulling down the muddle of medieval buildings that still remained after Henry had founded Trinity by amalgamating the ancient King's Hall and Michaelhouse nearly fifty years earlier. In the words of G.M. Trevelyan, a twentieth-century Master of Trinity, 'If Henry VIII founded Trinity, Nevile built it.'[10] He constructed the Great Court virtually as it appears today, the largest court in either Oxford or Cambridge. Its huge central fountain was also introduced by Nevile. The Great Court features a tower, created by Nevile, bearing a statue of Elizabeth I. In the twentieth century, while a student at Trinity, HRH the Prince of Wales, the eldest son of Queen Elizabeth II, occupied rooms adjacent to the tower. Nevile went on to build a second court that was to be named after him which features an elegant semi-classical cloister in the Renaissance tradition; the court was originally three-sided, being open to the river at the far end until Sir Christopher Wren built the library which is widely considered to be one of England's great architectural masterpieces. A considerable amount of this massive extension to Trinity, which remains Cambridge's largest college, was financed by Thomas Nevile out of his own pocket. No wonder that Bishop Hacket who had been at the college with this highly energetic and generous man was to write, 'He never had his like for a splendid, courteous and bountiful gentleman.'[11] It was a highly significant moment for Trinity, Cambridge University and English scholarship as a whole, when the Queen appointed Thomas Nevile as Master. To this day the sovereign still appoints the Master of Trinity, one of the world's most outstanding centres of learning, whose members have collectively won more than twenty Nobel prizes. One of the college's distinguished Fellows was the renowned twentieth-century philosopher, Bertrand Russell, a descendant of Francis Russell, the 2nd Earl of Bedford, a distinguished Privy Councillor during Elizabeth's reign.

Elizabeth took a keen personal interest in both universities and visited them on a number of occasions, the most notable time being her visit to Cambridge in 1564. When invited to say a few words, Elizabeth, without hesitation, delivered an eloquent 600-word oration in Latin to the assembled throng at King's College Chapel, a building that had been completed previously by her father. Several of Elizabeth's leading Privy Councillors were university chancellors at different times, Sir John Mason, the Earl of Leicester and Sir Christopher Hatton at Oxford, and Lord Burghley at Cambridge, where Archbishop Whitgift had once been vice-chancellor. Characteristically, Burghley was to take his appointment at Cambridge particularly seriously. Overall both the universities benefited greatly from the attentions of the Queen and those of her Privy Council, many of whom had attended university.

However, it was by no means necessary that students at either Oxford or Cambridge should necessarily be drawn from the ranks of the nobility, or even the rapidly increasing number of gentry that were coming into existence as a result of growing prosperity across Elizabethan England. A considerable number of student places at the universities were taken up by members of the poorer classes, often in a category known as sizars or sub-sizars, students who paid no fees but undertook various menial tasks such as waiting at table in exchange for tuition, but in all other respects enjoyed the same privileges as other more wealthy students. One of Trinity College's most eminent members, Isaac Newton, had first entered the college as a sizar. Undergraduates normally went to university at a far earlier age than today; both the Earl of Essex and Francis Bacon were not even in their teens when they joined Trinity. However, attendance at the university was often for a far longer period than in modern times, a length of seven or eight years prior to taking a degree not being uncommon. No women were to attend either university for many centuries to come.

The multi-talented and idealistic courtier Sir Humphrey Gilbert, half-brother to Sir Walter Ralegh, had conceived the idea of an academy in London, an embryonic London University for the teaching of ancient and modern languages, philosophy, astronomy, mathematics, physics, engineering and chemistry. Sir Humphrey was an eloquent man and attached particular importance to the development of the English Language, both written and spoken. 'The choice of words, the building of sentences, the garnishment of figures, and the other beauties of oratory,' Sir Humphrey enthused.[12] Unfortunately, like so many of Gilbert's innovative ideas, this visionary scheme never developed any further. The

Queen had expressed some initial enthusiasm but as usual was waiting for somebody else to provide the money for its development. Then Gilbert was tragically drowned at sea and the whole concept sank out of sight.

In London, a new seat of learning was established during Elizabeth's reign with the creation of Gresham College, which resulted from the generosity of Sir Thomas Gresham, the greatest financial expert of the Elizabethan age, who had previously established the Royal Exchange. Gresham had originally considered founding a college at either Oxford or Cambridge but in the end decided to provide a splendid house in Bishopsgate, together with sufficient revenue to maintain a number of professors drawn from Oxford and Cambridge, three from each university, the most eminent of which were later to be Robert Hooke and Christopher Wren. The subjects to be taught at Gresham were astronomy, divinity, law, rhetoric, geometry, physics and music. The last post was filled at the Queen's own personal recommendation by her chapel organist Dr John Bull. As Bull spoke no Latin, he was given permission to conduct his classes in English. Founded towards the end of the sixteenth century, initially the college flourished and might well have developed into a full-scale university given more favourable circumstances. However, in the reign of George III, the City of London inexplicably took the decision to hand the site over to the Crown, which resulted in Gresham College becoming sadly neglected and run down. Today a limited number of lectures are the only events to take place in this once enlightened and much utilized institution which seemed to have so much potential when it was originally founded by Sir Thomas.

Another centre of learning in London that did flourish greatly during Elizabeth's reign were the four Inns of Court together with the nine Inns of Chancery located in an area between Temple Bar and the River Thames. Gray's Inn, Lincoln's Inn, the Middle and Inner Temples all thrived in a period of greatly expanding requirement for legal expertise in the extremely litigious Tudor world. Christopher Hatton, Walter Ralegh, Anthony and Francis Bacon, Philip Sidney and John Donne were just some of the eminent Elizabethans who acquired their scholarship here. These illustrious legal establishments were much more than merely a place of study: considerable extramural activity took place. It was at a masque conducted at the Inner Temple that the Queen first encountered Christopher Hatton in 1561, the year *Gorboduc*, the first blank-verse English tragedy, was introduced there. Shakespeare's plays were performed in the Middle Temple during the last years of her reign, Elizabeth being an avid supporter of the theatre. These events normally took place during the joyful period of celebration that ran between Christmas Eve and Twelfth Night, carefully orchestrated by the Master of Revels appointed by the Queen. It was her custom to attend these festivities with leading members of the Royal Court and the legal profession, who were seated around the highly impressive newly constructed hall of the Middle Temple in a carefully arranged order of precedence.

Throughout Elizabeth's kingdom, education was becoming more accessible and broad-based. Long gone were the days when the only way that most men could acquire an education was to enter a monastery. Indeed, the dissolution of the monasteries was to have little detrimental effect on education in England, for by then monastic establishments were no longer the eminent seats of learning that they had been in the Middle Ages. On the contrary, the closure of these medieval foundations were positively beneficial as the university colleges in particular inherited their sites, the buildings and in some cases even the revenues. In turn, the Renaissance and Reformation both gave a massive boost to scholastic activity in England. The Queen was as well educated as most in her kingdom; this factor, coupled with the intellectual qualities of so many of her Privy Councillors and other members of her Court, meant that scholarship and education were highly respected activities, ones to be actively and energetically pursued.

The Queen's acknowledged enthusiasm for education, coupled with the growing realization by her subjects of the necessity for more widespread schooling to meet the growing demands of an increasingly more sophisticated and enlightened nation, led to an explosion in educational facilities, as both the gentry and an expanding middle class required better schooling for their children. Eton, St Paul's, Shrewsbury and Westminster were all well-established schools by the time Elizabeth ascended the throne; they were to be joined by public schools such as Harrow, Tonbridge, Merchant Taylors, Charterhouse and Uppingham, all were founded in the Elizabethan era. There were also more than 350 grammar schools in existence throughout England by the end of the sixteenth century. Elizabeth did not found a university college or even a single school herself, but she did give a considerable number of scholarships to both schools and universities while the majority of her courtiers were very well aware that they were much more likely to gain royal approval by being seen to actively support scholarship in a meaningful way. Most importantly the Queen created a climate in which scholarship was an important strand in the fabric of the Elizabethan society, thereby encouraging intelligent people to acquire an education, and others of lesser academic ability to give material support. Elizabeth made education fashionable and scholarship a status symbol so her reign represented an age of scholastic achievement of the highest order. Elizabeth's constant encouragement and approval of intellectual excellence ensured that England no longer remained a cultural backwater on the edge of Europe.

10

CAMBRIDGE CONNECTIONS

In the drawing room of the Master's Lodge at Cambridge's largest and most powerful college, Trinity College, hangs a portrait of Elizabeth I, thought to have been painted towards the end of the sixteenth century by Marcus Gheeraerts the Younger. This painting portrays a full-length, life-size figure standing on a red-covered step before a throne and is said to derive from the *Armada Portrait* by George Gower which currently hangs in Woburn Abbey. This fine portrayal of Elizabeth symbolizes a long and continuing connection between Cambridge and the Queen that had profound implications for this ancient seat of learning. Cambridge was to consequently benefit very considerably from the interest in its fortunes displayed by Elizabeth and the many powerful members of her Court who previously had been educated at the university.

Cambridge's connection with the Tudor Court had begun well before the reign of Elizabeth, when Erasmus had paid a number of visits to the university during the reign of her father, Henry VIII. The great Flemish humanist, whose reputation had spread throughout Europe, resided at Queen's College while he fulfilled the posts of Lady Margaret Reader in Greek and Professor of Divinity. The tower in the south-west corner of Old Court, where he is said to have lived, is traditionally known as Erasmus Tower, while the nearby President's Lodge is an excellent example of early sixteenth-century architecture. Erasmus much approved of the pretty girls he found in the town, but complained bitterly about the poor quality of the college beer and the penetrating cold and damp of the East Anglian climate. He became friendly with Sir Thomas More, Henry VIII's Lord Chancellor, and the presence of someone with such a distinctive reputation in theological studies helped to set in motion the rise of the Protestant faith in England. The seeds of the Reformation germinated at Cambridge in places such as the White Horse Inn, an unlikely meeting place which became a hotbed of Protestant debate, where enthusiastic students such as Nicholas Ridley and Thomas Cranmer came to listen and learn about the new doctrine. In time, the fortunes of the university prospered considerably amid the rigorous climate of the

Reformation, whereas Oxford was to go into relative decline as numerous Catholic scholars scurried abroad into self-induced exile, subsequently finding employment in such Catholic centres of learning as Louvain, Douai, and the English College at Rome. Many of these former scholars from Oxford were destined to become Jesuits; some, such as Edmund Campion, eventually returned to England and became martyrs, dying for their cause at Tyburn.

Today, Cambridge contains a considerable amount of Tudor architecture while Oxford remains predominately medieval in appearance. Erasmus noted that the 'New Learning' flourished at Cambridge, a fresh approach to scholarship born of the Renaissance, wherein medieval concepts were replaced by more modern thinking, a discipline which was wholeheartedly embraced by Elizabeth while still a young princess. The 'New Learning' centred on St John's College, Cambridge, where there resided a particularly brilliant group of intellectuals, among them Sir John Cheke, the leading Greek scholar of the day, Roger Ascham and William Grindal, both destined to become tutors to the impressionable young Princess Elizabeth. This was the time 'when the great scholars of St John's taught Cambridge and King Edward, Greek'. Cheke also had William Cecil as a pupil who was later to marry Cheke's sister, Mary. As a young student Cecil had been so keen on his studies that he paid a college servant to wake him every morning at four o'clock, even in the darkest depths of winter. William Cecil sent his son Robert to St John's, and his three young wards, the Earls of Oxford, Essex and Southampton, were enrolled next door at Trinity College, where Nicholas Bacon had once studied and where he in turn sent his two sons, Anthony and Francis, to study law.

The majority of the key members of the Queen's Privy Council, such as Sir William Cecil, Sir Nicholas Bacon, Sir Walter Mildmay, Sir Francis Walsingham and Sir Thomas Smith, had all studied at Cambridge, as had her major financial adviser, Sir Thomas Gresham, a former undergraduate at Gonville and Caius College, while the two greatest Elizabethan lawyers, Edward Coke and Francis Bacon, had been at Trinity at the same time as the Earl of Essex, who was also a member of Elizabeth's Privy Council. No wonder the eminent twentieth-century Elizabethan historian A.L. Rowse was to comment that the Queen could be regarded as a 'Cambridge figure'[1] – and Rowse was a Fellow of All Souls, Oxford!

Nearly all the most prominent figures in the Church throughout Elizabeth's reign eminated from Cambridge University rather than Oxford. This influence had originally begun with John Fisher, Bishop of Rochester, who was later to be executed by Elizabeth's father for speaking out against Henry's divorce from Catherine of Aragon and his traumatic break from Rome. Fisher had previously been Master of Michaelhouse, a college which Henry was to combine with King's Hall in order to form Trinity College. Fisher had been instrumental in persuading Lady Margaret Beaufort, Henry's grandmother, to found St John's College and later Christ's College as well. Her distinctive coat of arms with their dramatic mythical beasts remain above the main entrance of both colleges today. Fisher's presence at Cambridge had begun a trend of leading clerics occupying key posts at this university; Bishop Nicholas Ridley had been an undergraduate at Pembroke and was later to be elected a Fellow of that College. Thomas Cranmer studied at Jesus College and John Whitgift was Master of Trinity as well as Regius Professor of Divinity and Vice-Chancellor of the University. Edward Grindal was Master of Pembroke. Thus all three men who the Queen successively appointed as Archbishops of Canterbury during her reign came from Cambridge: first Parker, then Grindal, who had previously been Bishop of London, and finally Whitgift, who was by the Queen's side when she died at Richmond in 1603.

Cambridge was at the very heart of the new religious doctrines sweeping across Europe, firstly Protestantism, then the more extreme beliefs of Presbyterianism and Puritanism. These radical theologies were to have a profound effect on all those Cambridge men who later occupied such influential positions on the Queen's Privy Council. They in turn influenced the political and religious thinking of the English Queen and were to have considerable effect on the development of the Church of England. Cambridge had also provided the initial battleground in the ideological war between Protestantism and Puritanism. Feelings often ran high between over-excited rival groups of students: all the windows of Trinity College Chapel, a place of worship originally founded by Elizabeth's half-sister Mary, were smashed by Puritans in 1565. At this time one of the most influential men at Cambridge concerning religious issues was Thomas Cartwright, a Fellow of Trinity College and a fanatical leader of the Presbyterians, who advocated the abolition of both the bishops and the prayer book service.

Thomas Cartwright was vigorously opposed in these extremist views by John Whitgift, at that time the Master of Trinity. Their intense debate became so ferocious that at times it represented a form of single-handed combat; their titanic struggle ended with Cartwright losing his Fellowship and Whitgift being summoned by the Queen to be appointed firstly Bishop of Worcester and subsequently Archbishop of Canterbury. Cartwright lost his position as a Fellow at Trinity because he refused to take Holy Orders, at that time a mandatory requirement for all Fellows of the college. Fellows were also not allowed to be married and were required to remain celibate, a condition that continued at Trinity until Victorian times, although Isaac Newton was permitted to marry by Elizabeth's successor James I. G.M. Trevelyan, Master of Trinity between 1940 and 1951, was later to say 'that the great struggle of Anglican and Puritan, in which a man from Sidney Sussex was one day to take a hand, may almost be said to have originated, certainly to have been rehearsed, in the chambers and the chapel of Trinity'.[2] The man from Sidney Sussex was of course Oliver Cromwell and a student at that college at the age of seventeen.

The next great Master of Trinity was Thomas Nevile, formerly Dean of Canterbury. He was appointed by an ageing Elizabeth to the Mastership in 1593. Nevile instigated the massive building programme that made the college into what it is today. His Great Court, begun towards the end of the sixteenth century, remains one of the most spectacular sights to be seen in the whole of the university.

Elizabeth selected Matthew Parker to be her first Archbishop of Canterbury and entrusted him with the vital task of putting into practice the religious principles that would establish the Anglican Church of England. To assist him in this venture Parker in turn appointed a considerable number of new bishops, most of whom came from Cambridge. Thus the twin pillars of Elizabeth's kingdom, her Council and her Church, were dominated by the men of Cambridge and policies and practices of the nation were heavily influenced by the current philosophies of that university. In Henry VIII's time, the two most powerful men in the kingdom, Cardinal Wolsey and Sir Thomas More, had both come from Oxford University, as indeed had Queen Mary's Archbishop of Canterbury, Cardinal Pole, who, conveniently for Elizabeth, died at the same time as the last Catholic monarch to occupy the English throne. In Elizabeth's time, Cambridge was firmly in the ascendancy and relatively few of the influential men of that era emanated from Oxford.

Cambridge's influence on the Queen and her kingdom multiplied as the power brokers who had once been members of the university tended to favour their own kind: Grindal succeeded Parker as Archbishop of Canterbury largely because he had been recommended to the Queen by William Cecil and it was Cecil who persuaded Elizabeth to appoint Francis Walsingham as her Principal Secretary in the Council. When Walsingham died, Cecil convinced the Queen that his son, Robert, like his father a former law student at St John's, should be Walsingham's replacement as Secretary of State.

The Cambridge influence also extended into the cultural activities of the nation. Marlowe, Spenser, Nashe and Greene, that formidable quartet of poets, had all previously been Cambridge students. Edmund Spenser was successful in attracting the Queen's patronage and introduced the cult of 'Gloriana' when he wrote *The Faerie Queene*, a theatrical work which greatly influenced the public perception of Elizabeth during the second half of her reign. These poets were soon to be followed by Milton, who received his education at Christ's College, Cambridge; his epic work *Paradise Lost* could be said to symbolize the passing of the Elizabethan age.

Cambridge's influence on Elizabethan England was all-embracing at Court, in Council, in Parliament and in the Church. It extended even into more unorthodox services, such as those provided by the Queen's official Court Astrologer, Dr John Dee, one of the initial Fellows at Trinity College who had previously been at St John's. The exceedingly witty courtier, Sir John Harington, the Queen's godson, had been at Christ's College, Cambridge, while another of the Queen's eminent courtiers, George Clifford, the 3rd Earl of Cumberland, who succeeded Sir Henry Lee as her Champion of the Tilt and became a prominent naval commander in the latter part of her reign, had previously been at Trinity College. Lord Henry Hunsdon, Elizabeth's Lord Chamberlain towards the end of the sixteenth century, had also resided at the college, taking his degree at the age of thirteen.

In turn, Cambridge was to considerably benefit from its high profile throughout Elizabeth's reign. In addition to Thomas Nevile's extensive work at Trinity, Sir Walter Mildmay, a highly effective Lord Chancellor, had studied at Christ's and founded the new Emmanuel College, while the widow of the long-serving Privy Councillor, the Earl of Sussex, endowed Sidney Sussex College. The Second Court at St John's was financed by Mary, Countess of Shrewsbury, the daughter of Bess Hardwick. The Second Court's Tudor Long Gallery, currently the Senior Common Room, remains one of Cambridge's most impressive interiors with an elaborate plastered ceiling nearly one hundred feet long and dating from 1600. Cloister Court at Jesus College dates from the sixteenth century, as does the First Court at Magdalene, constructed in that mellow red brick which became such a fashionable material during that period.

The impact that Cambridge had on Elizabeth and her kingdom and the powerful patronage it received in return had long-lasting benefits. Four hundred years later, Cambridge remains a centre of academic excellence with an undisputed reputation as a major international university. Trinity, founded by Henry VIII, is currently Cambridge's biggest and most prestigious college, universally regarded for the quality of its scholarship; thus, the Master of Trinity, Professor Amartya Sen, is a recent recipient of the Nobel Prize for Economics. The tradition for intellectual genius which began in Tudor times is very much maintained as Henry VIII's statue guards the Main Gate and Elizabeth's gazes out across the immaculate lawns of the Great Court, the largest in either Oxford or Cambridge.

The origins of the 'Establishment', that mysterious network of power and influence, can be traced to the Elizabethan age. This highly authoritative, yet invisible force, is formed from the aristocracy, the Church, judiciary, the military and academia. It could be said to have had its roots in the days of Cecil, Whitgift, Coke, Bacon and Cumberland. Then, as now, educational background is one of the key factors that creates a common bond, a meeting of minds, a unified sense of purpose binding its members together. Today the term 'old school tie' is a well-known phrase – in Elizabethan times there was no such item in a gentleman's wardrobe but eminent public schools such as Eton, Harrow, St Paul's and Winchester already existed. The major educational impetus was to be found at Cambridge and so many of the great men of Elizabeth's reign originated from that centre of learning set among the remote fens of eastern England.

In the second half of the sixteenth century, just as today, the Establishment was a complex, mysterious web, essentially a predominantly masculine society with a female monarch at its centre. In the late twentieth century, the heads of the Church, the armed forces, the judiciary and academia surprisingly still remain largely a male prerogative. Although club-like in nature, the Establishment has never been a place for which membership can be applied: there is no rule book, no list of members, not even any firm evidence that it even exists. Yet it remains a major force in English society, seemingly oblivious to political, historical or social change, just as it was in Elizabethan England, where personalities such as Sir Walter Ralegh tried exceedingly hard to gain entry into this exclusive inner world but never succeeded. Ralegh was an Oxford man. The Queen and the Elizabethan Establishment definitely appeared to be coloured light, Cambridge, blue.

11

THE CREATORS

The dynamic changes continually unfolding throughout England during Elizabeth's reign were to impact significantly on the cultural life of the nation. The Queen maintained a lively interest in the arts throughout her lifetime with a particular interest in music and the theatre. She was an excellent musician, exceedingly proficient on the virginals, a small keyboard instrument which had become popular during the sixteenth century and one on which she practised diligently almost every day. Tradition has it that the Queen was playing the virginals when news of the Earl of Essex's execution was brought to her. Elizabeth is said to have paused momentarily, and then, without making any comment, continued to play.

The composers Thomas Tallis and William Byrd flourished under her patronage; both were employed at the Royal Court, despite being Catholic. Byrd was devout in his religion, a fervour which comes through strongly in the church music which he composed, particularly the Masses, although he also created a wealth of both vocal and instrumental secular music, which has led to Byrd being called the father of the English keyboard. The richness of Byrd's work contrasts with the more austere compositions of Thomas Tallis, and the strong tradition of English choral music dates from this time. The Queen generously granted Tallis and Byrd the sole rights to print, publish and sell music throughout her nation. Both lived into their eighties, Byrd outlasting Elizabeth by some twenty years. Along with Dowland, Byrd and Tallis are the best remembered of the Elizabethan composers, although the best-known musical work of the period is *God Save the Queen*, composed by Dr John Bull many years before it was adopted as the National Anthem.

The Queen's enthusiasm for theatrical performances, one shared by a number of her Privy Councillors, was essential in protecting the embryonic theatre from the growing hostility of the Puritans, who would have liked to see all theatres closed on a permanent basis and every theatrical company banned. Both needed a licence from the Lord Chamberlain in order to remain in existence, so Elizabeth's keen interest, which was shared by a number of her most prominent courtiers such as the Earl of Leicester, Lord Strange and Lord Hunsdon, was extremely important. Without royal interest and prominent courtiers' direct involvement, there may not have been any actors or theatres to perform the works of such dramatists as Ben Jonson, Christopher Marlowe and William Shakespeare.

The visual arts also flourished during Elizabeth's reign, particularly painting. It has been said that while the Queen had no great interest in painting, she enjoyed being painted. Certainly she was exceedingly vain and loved being depicted in the best possible light, considering the official portrait to be an ideal medium for adding a distinctive gloss to the royal image. During the long period of time when the most eligible bachelors in Europe were courting her, a flattering portrait was a favourite device utilized in this elaborate ritual in order to show an ardent yet distant suitor the object of his desires. As Elizabeth's reign developed and the fame of her exploits spread throughout Europe, the growing demand to capture her on canvas created a constant requirement for the services of the best artists of the day. Eminent European painters, such as the Italian Federigo Zuccaro and the Flemish artist Steven van der Muelen, came to England. At the same time, it became more and more fashionable for Elizabeth's wealthy courtiers to have their portraits painted, the exceedingly vain Earl of Leicester virtually supporting the art industry single-handedly by having himself constantly portrayed in a variety of progressively more arrogant poses. Leading royal courtiers such as Sir Francis Walsingham, Sir Robert Cecil and Sir Henry Lee became enthusiastic patrons of the leading painters of the time. One of the best-known paintings of the Queen, the so-called Ditchley Portrait, by Marcus Gheeraerts the Younger, resulted from Lee's patronage of Gheeraerts and is now considered to be the best portrait of the Queen created during her lifetime. Gheeraerts became extremely fashionable after the Queen had sat for him in 1592, working in England for more than thirty years and marrying fellow artist John de Critz's sister, Magdelena, while Gheeraert's sister Sara, became the wife of the miniaturist Isaac Oliver. Gheeraert's style of painting was greatly influenced by the emerging Antwerp School in the Netherlands whose best-known members were the Breughels.

During this time, loyal courtiers began to wear a miniature of the Queen pinned to their chest like a badge of honour, a craze that greatly assisted the fortunes of the leading miniaturists of the day, such as Levina Teerlinc, Isaac Oliver and Nicholas Hilliard. The latter's first miniature of the Queen is thought to have been painted in the early 1570s. A dozen or so years later even gung-ho seafarers such as Sir Francis Drake were proudly besporting one of Hilliard's miniatures of their sovereign. Today, Hilliard is considered the most significant portrait painter of the Elizabethan era.

Elizabeth's firm establishment of Protestantism as England's official religion meant that the nation provided a safe haven from Catholic oppression. A number of prominent Protestant Flemish painters settled in England in order to escape persecution from the Duke of Alva in the Netherlands, thereby making Elizabeth's kingdom an artistic asylum and strengthening the advancement of painting in the nation. Among their number was Marcus Gheeraerts the Elder who brought his young son with him, while John de Critz was befriended by Walsingham; Isaac Oliver was a French Huguenot refugee who first became Hilliard's pupil and then his greatest rival as a miniaturist – he was to paint Elizabeth on a number of occasions. Gheeraerts the Younger's classic painting of the Queen, the Rainbow Portrait, was painted at the end of the sixteenth century; it is to be found at Hatfield House and is thought to have been commissioned by Sir Robert Cecil who was building Hatfield at the time.

The presence of so many leading European artists in Elizabethan England, either on a permanent or temporary basis, was in turn helpful in assisting the cause of English-born painters such as George Gower, William Segar, Robert Peake and, most illustrious of them all, Nicholas Hilliard. Hilliard was born in Exeter in 1547, thereby demonstrating that Devon was capable of providing famous men other than great seafarers during Elizabeth's reign. He had originally trained as a goldsmith and for two years was employed in France as a miniaturist by the Duke of Anjou. To some extent, he was influenced by French court portraiture, but rather more by the most outstanding portrait painter of the sixteenth century, Hans Holbein. Hilliard's technique, based on simplicity of line and use of bright colour, greatly appealed to the Queen and he was to paint her on a number of occasions. It might be difficult to imagine that the restless Queen would agree to remain in one place long enough to be painted, but her sittings for Hilliard are well recorded by the artist himself, as are their conversations when he instructed her in the mysteries of limning and *chiaroscuro*. Limning, the art of painting on a small scale, greatly appealed to the Queen, who kept a collection of miniatures in a small cabinet in her bedchamber, carefully wrapped with names inscribed in her own hand on the paper. One had written on it 'My Lord's picture'; inside was a likeness of the Earl of Leicester. The term *chiaroscuro*, derived from the Italian for light, *chiaro*, and dark, *oscuro*, refers to the then relatively new technique of building up thin layers of paint on canvas or oak board, then applying rich impasto pigment, in order to achieve dramatic highlights. This found far less favour with a Queen as conservative in her appreciation of art as most other matters; 'the Queen cares not for novelties', noted de Maisse.[1] To Elizabeth, *chiaroscuro* represented modern art and her taste in painting was positively medieval.

It may also seem remarkable that the haughty Queen would have had a lengthy conversation with a mere humble artist like Hilliard, for in the mid-sixteenth century, the artist did not enjoy the same status as was to be afforded by society in later years. Artists were seen more as craftsmen, indeed Hilliard complains of being regarded as merely 'a needy articer' and although George Gower had the grand title of Sergeant Painter while the official court painter, he was to spend much of his time in mundane activities such as supervising the redecoration of the interior of various royal palaces. Gower had been the most sought-after portrait painter at the Royal Court prior to the appearance of Marcus Gheeraerts the Younger, having risen to prominence by painting a series of aristocratic ladies of the Court decked out in all their finery. He portrayed women such as Lettice Knollys, wife of the Earl of Leicester, and Elizabeth Sydenham, Sir Francis Drake's second wife. His career culminated in the archetypal portrayal of the Queen – the Armada Portrait – considered to be Gower's most outstanding work, an icon-like neo-medieval painting, and one of the world's most important historical works of art.

Robert Peake was another prolific Elizabethan artist who maintained a considerable studio where he employed a large number of assistants; he was later to flourish under James I. It was Peake who was to produce the celebrated *Procession to Blackfriars*, which depicts Elizabeth being carried in splendour by a number of adoring courtiers, accompanied by Garter Knights including Lord Howard of Effingham, the Earl of Cumberland, Edmund Sheffield, later Earl of Mulgrave, and Gilbert Talbot, Earl of Shrewsbury carrying the Sword of State. William Segar was another Elizabethan artist who was later to benefit from the favours of King James, being made Garter King of Arms in 1603 and subsequently knighted by Elizabeth's Scottish successor. Segar's great masterpiece is the Ermine Portrait, a painting of the Queen created shortly after the epic defeat of the Spanish Armada, which can also now be found at Hatfield House.

An appreciation of Elizabethan art has always been inhibited by being sandwiched between the eras of Holbein and Van Dyck; it is only in recent years that it has gained the recognition it fully deserves as an outstanding period of English art, largely through the efforts of Sir Roy Strong.

The Queen's connection with architecture is more tangential as she declined to build any royal palaces during her reign or commission any great public buildings on account of the expense to the royal purse. Elizabeth was not to provide the nation with any English equivalent of Versailles or Fontainebleau. At the same time, the Church had also ceased to provide patronage for the visual arts as it had in medieval times, the reasons being a combination of economic and theological considerations. Elizabeth's father's actions in the dissolution of the monasteries had left Church revenues severely depleted, a state of affairs that Elizabeth was to maintain as she diverted funds away from the Church in order to reward favoured courtiers. At the same time, rigid Protestant intellectual thinking progressively came to associate the visual arts with idolatry, resulting in both Church and Court taking a far greater interest in music and literature than painting, sculpture or architecture.

Architecture did not have the same standing in Elizabethan society as it enjoys today, nor did it attract the same level of interest as in continental Europe. Instead, architecture was regarded more as a craft, though Elizabethan craftsmen enjoyed a far greater status than the present day. The term 'architect' was little used in the sixteenth century: it was the master mason who drew up the plans and supervised the construction of buildings under the eagle eye of an owner who invariably would constantly change his mind while construction was under way. In Tudor times, there was no formal training for becoming an architect – even a century later, Christopher Wren, who had been the Professor of Astronomy at Oxford University when Charles II appointed him to be Surveyor of the Royal Works, was effectively his chief architect but still using a title which dated from the Tudor era.

The Renaissance in the visual arts had been slow to arrive in England, again primarily because of the actions of King Henry VIII. After the break with Rome, it was no longer advisable either to journey to Italy or to be seen to be influenced by ideas from a Catholic country. Conversely, no major continental architect was likely to risk papal wrath by accepting commissions in England, thereby jeopardizing potential employment in his own country. So while King François I was able to entice the likes of Leonardo da Vinci and Serlio to France, no foreign architect of comparable note dared to venture across the English Channel. These factors continued during the reign of the Protestant Queen Elizabeth: it was left to a young set designer named Inigo Jones, working in the theatre at the end of her reign, finally to introduce Renaissance architecture permanently to England in the seventeenth century.

Though the prospects for architectural advancement in England did not therefore appear auspicious, significant building activity did occur in Elizabeth's kingdom for a completely different reason. A favourable combination of peaceful conditions and more broad-based wealth existed within England during the first half of the Queen's reign. This meant that wealthy inhabitants no longer needed to defend themselves in a castle or fortress and a considerable number of recently self-made men wished to demonstrate their newly acquired wealth and social standing to society in an appropriate and instantly recognizable manner. Consequently, magnificent new country houses came into existence, not so much as an expression of architectural reverence but as status symbols par excellence for all to see and admire, resulting in the creation of Burghley in Lincolnshire, Longleat and Corsham Court in Wiltshire, Derbyshire's Hardwick Hall and Wollaton Hall in Nottinghamshire. These splendid houses were financed by 'new money', acquired through prosperous Tudor times after a considerable amount of land and building material had become available subsequent to the dissolution of the monasteries. Elizabeth's prosperous courtiers continued to build these great houses out of the wealth which she had helped them acquire. They hoped that they might gain that ultimate social cachet, a visit from the Queen, so that they could entertain her in suitably sumptuous style. She liked to live well, particularly at somebody else's expense, and encouraged this egotistical line of thinking to her own advantage. Thus Sir Christopher Hatton built Holdenby in Northamptonshire, Lord Burghley constructed Theobolds in Hertfordshire and the Earl of Leicester updated Kenilworth Castle in Warwickshire, virtually as additional royal palaces where their beloved Queen could be royally entertained. The Earl once entertained Elizabeth at Kenilworth for nearly three weeks of continual feasting and pageantry; on another occasion the Queen spent almost two weeks at Theobolds as Lord Burghley unsuccessfully attempted to persuade the sovereign to appoint his son Robert to be her Secretary of State. The Queen visited Theobolds on more than a dozen occasions during her time on the throne.

Elizabeth became well accustomed to visiting her wealthy courtiers:

Her Highness hath done honour to my poor house by visiting me, and seemed much pleased at what we did to please her. My son made her a fair speech, to which she did give most gracious reply. The women did dance before her, while the cornets did salute from the gallery, and she did vouchsafe to eat two morsels of rich comfit-cake and drank a small cordial from a golden cup.'[2]

Thus wrote Sir Robert Sidney after one of Elizabeth's visits to Penshurst Place in Kent, his description fully conveying the pleasure and excitement of entertaining the monarch at home.

Elizabeth's successor, James I, was later to fall in love with Theobolds, which by then had been inherited by Sir Robert Cecil following the death of his father, the King acquiring it in exchange for Hatfield. Cecil replaced the old Tudor palace with the magnificent edifice seen today using the designs of Robert Lyminge and possibly Inigo Jones. Cecil never lived there himself as it was not completed during his lifetime.

Thus Renaissance architecture crept into England virtually by the back door, in a rather oblique yet nevertheless effective manner, the Queen having stimulated a widespread desire among her most prominent and wealthy courtiers to build in order to impress. Compared to earlier private residences, these new homes for the *nouveaux riches* were enormous, huge prestigious glittering palaces built out of faced stone or brick rather than the half-timbered domestic buildings of earlier times. Like their owners they were flamboyant, brimming with confidence, and marvellous expressions of the mood of the nation in the halcyon years of Elizabeth's time on the English throne. Three key examples – Longleat, Hardwick Hall and Wollaton Hall – are the work of one man, Robert Smythson, who has only recently achieved the recognition he so richly deserves. Longleat, now the home of the 7th Marquess of Bath, is widely regarded as an outstanding example of English Renaissance architecture, its exterior remaining virtually identical to the time the Queen visited its original owner Sir John Thynne in 1574. The magnificent tapestries in the Great High Chamber and Long Gallery at Hardwick were originally purchased the year before the defeat of the Armada. Elizabeth never visited Hardwick though a fine portrait of her, attributed to Nicholas Hilliard, hangs in the Long Gallery.

Smythson built across the English landscape between the early 1560s and 1614, the year of his death at nearly eighty. His work was then continued by his son John, and grandson Huntingdon, for a further three-dozen years. Smythson first achieved prominence when he came to Longleat after it had been devastated by fire in the spring of 1568. He had been recommended to Sir John Thynne by the Queen's master mason Humphrey Lovell: 'According to my promes I have sent unto yowe this bearer Robert Smythson, freemason, who of laytt was with Master Vice Chamberlaine, not doubting hem but to be a man fett for your worshipe.'[3] Smythson virtually single-handedly personified the development of Elizabethan architecture as he constructed Longleat, Hardwick and Wollaton, together with other masterpieces such as Worksop Manor for the Earl of Shrewsbury, whom the Queen had appointed the gaoler of Mary, Queen of Scots. He was also the fourth and last husband of the formidable Bess of Hardwick, the creator of Hardwick Hall.

During Smythson's lifetime, architecture in Elizabethan England evolved from a mere imitation of the continental Renaissance, 'after the Italian modell',[4] to a more robust style which established an essentially English identity, blending the classical concepts of the Renaissance with more traditional Late Perpendicular features dating from the end of the Middle Ages. Houses such as Burton Agnes in Yorkshire and Montacute in deepest Somerset reflected this more national expression of architectural endeavour and displayed the confidence and sense of patronism that Elizabeth had created in her kingdom towards the end of the sixteenth century. This revival in Gothic interest intensified in the last quarter of Elizabeth's reign, as instanced in the popularity of jousting tournaments, the publication of Spenser's *The Faerie Queene* and Sir Philip Sidney's *Arcadia* together with Gower's neo-medieval *Armada Portrait* of the Queen. This almost Hollywood-style fantasy, which embraced so enthusiastically the concepts of medieval chivalry, even led to the building of mock castles such as Lulworth Castle in Dorset and Bolsover in Derbyshire, finally climaxing in the extravagant style of the Jacobean period subsequent to Elizabeth's death in 1603.

England had sniffed the cool breeze of Renaissance architecture and then firmly shut the door again in order to retreat happily once more into a nostalgic past, something which in architectural matters the nation has tended to do ever since. It was left to Inigo Jones to revive Renaissance interest much later in the seventeenth century. Nevertheless, Robert Smythson made a decisive mark across the landscape by creating some of the greatest houses in England today – it could be said that English architecture came into its own in Elizabeth's time as it began to establish a truly distinctive national identity, instead of slavishly imitating continental trends.

The rapid rise in educational standards across England during Elizabeth's reign had a particularly significant impact on literature and drama. The Queen and her Council had made considerable efforts to improve standards of literacy across England in order to facilitate the reading of the Bible on a far wider scale. Both the Old and New Testaments had been published in English and their contents made readily available in every parish church throughout the nation. The translation of the Bible was itself a literary masterpiece, and its creation was the publishing sensation of Tudor England. At the same time, the Queen's determination to ensure that its contents reached the widest possible audience, coupled with her continuing actions to improve her citizens' learning abilities, made them anxious to read as much as possible. Technological advancement in printing facility created a print culture that had much the same impact on Elizabethan society as the Internet in the latter half of the twentieth century. Suddenly, a huge amount of European literature became available in England as both scholars and authors were able to read Italian drama and French poetry. This happy state of affairs considerably enriched English cultural life and had a profound influence on the creative minds of Elizabethan England, particularly poets and playwrights as they devoured the latest work of their continental counterparts. Shakespeare for one was to benefit considerably from this situation, being always on the lookout for raw material that he could rapidly recycle into yet another masterpiece. Virtually all Shakespeare's comedies and some of his tragedies were largely based on Italian material which had been translated into French and then become freely available in England. So *Romeo and Juliet, The Merchant of Venice* and *Othello* were all drawn from Italian novellas, while Petrarch inspired the Roman plays such as *Julius Caesar* and Holinshed provided material for the great historical dramas such as *Henry V* and *Richard III*: 'Now is the winter of our discontent made glorious summer by this sun of York. . . .'[5]

Elizabethan dramatists were not impeded by the laws of copyright and completely uninhibited by any thoughts of plagiarism. Rival versions of *Richard III* and *Henry V* ran happily at adjoining theatres and there was at least one version of both *Hamlet* and *Romeo and Juliet* in existence before those now associated with Shakespeare, who displayed no qualms in taking memorable phrases from other sources. Thus Antony and Cleopatra's '. . . barge she sat in, like a burnished throne . . .' is essentially Sir Thomas More's translation of Petrarch transposed into verse. Elizabethan audiences placed far less importance on originality than today – style and sheer entertainment value were the qualities they most appreciated.

The Queen had also been anxious to improve the intellectual quality of her clergy and considerable efforts had been made at university level to ensure that Protestant clerics should be far better educated than their Catholic predecessors. If anything, this well-intentioned stratagem proved over-successful, resulting in a surplus of potential clergy in the latter half of the sixteenth century with no church livings readily available. Happily, however, this state of affairs coincided with the growth of the theatre, so many university graduates decided to see whether they could make a living writing for the stage rather than taking Holy Orders, thereby creating an instant army of potential playwrights for whom there was fortunately a rapidly expanding market. Nashe, Greene and Peele were three such young graduates, who became playwrights and were known as 'University Wits'.

The growth of the Elizabethan theatre is a classic instance of the laws of supply and demand: a constant requirement for new plays was met by an inexhaustible procession of new young playwrights, intelligent, highly creative and hungry for success. The rapid growth of the theatre towards the end of the sixteenth century is as much due to a variety of socio-economic factors as purely cultural influences. The population of London rose rapidly during Elizabeth's reign, becoming large enough to support the major capital cost of the purpose-built theatres which had begun to replace the tiered courtyards of traditional coaching inns as suitable venues for theatrical performances. There was an increasing demand for a wider range of entertainment and leisure activities, coupled with a growing, more sophisticated middle class with more leisure time to enjoy who were looking for new activities which were rather more intellectually stimulating than traditional pursuits such as bear-baiting and cockfighting. Conveniently for the new playwrights, the old style of drama provided by the traditional morality plays was no longer available, having been banned by the authorities as being theologically incorrect – the Protestants disliked God being portrayed as simply an old man with white hair and a long beard. Yet the working classes also wished to be entertained and flocked to the new theatres to stand in front of the stage in an area which became known as 'the groundlings'.

Suddenly theatre builders, impresarios, playwrights and actors had an audience. Action, lights, music! Theatre became the new art form of the Elizabethan age. A handsome living could be made out of live theatre: there was no such thing as a long-running production, the theatre company would stage a different play each and every day, creating a continual requirement for fresh material from new writers. So great was the demand that plays were created by teams of dramatists, in much the same manner as modern-day television scriptwriters create a long-running serial or soap opera. Rival theatre owners and impresarios scrambled to outdo each other in a frantic desire to attract the largest audiences to their own particular production. Speed was of the essence, in order to effectively respond to a neighbouring theatre's successful production or to cash in on the latest popular theatrical trend. As a leading modern-day Oxford literary don amusingly explains:

> If you read the diary of Philip Henslowe, the owner of The Rose, the rival theatre to The Globe, you will find him saying, 'what are we going to put on next Wednesday? Here's a shilling, go down to the pub and share it out amongst half a dozen popular poets and tell them to come and see me. The place up the road has a play about Anthony and Cleopatra, we must have our own Anthony and Cleopatra. Here's the story, carve it up, an act each, come back on Monday with it finished. We'll rehearse for two days and perform it on Wednesday.'[6]

It was in this frenetic atmosphere, this seething cultural climate, in which playwrights such as William Shakespeare, Thomas Kyd, Christopher Marlowe, Edmund Spenser, Ben Jonson and Thomas Dekker found themselves in London during the last decade of the sixteenth century, where actors such as Ned Alleyn, Richard Burbage and William Kempe trod the boards in front of enthusiastic and totally classless audiences.

None of their activities would have been possible without the direct interest and support of the Queen and a number of her most prominent courtiers, men such as the Earl of Leicester, Lord Hunsdon, the Lord Chamberlain and Lord Strange. Without the authority of the Lord Chamberlain, it was illegal to form a company of actors or perform a play; furthermore the Puritan-dominated City of London frowned on theatrical performances and made great efforts to have them banned. This threat caused the major new playhouses such as The Globe, The Swan and The Rose to be clustered together on the South Bank of the Thames so as to be outside the jurisdiction of the City of London. Amid this sprawling area could be found every conceivable pleasure and vice – gambling dens, brothels, cockfighting and bear-baiting pits – all ironically located on land owned by the Bishop of Southwark!

While the Queen could be said to have been lukewarm about art and architecture, she certainly made up for this supposed lack of interest in her enthusiasm for the theatre, attending performances at the Middle and Inner Temples and other locations such as the residences of wealthy courtiers. She also summoned theatrical companies to perform at the Royal Court and even had her own company of actors, 'The Queen's Men'. Elizabeth's enthusiasm and patronage successfully kept the Puritans at bay throughout her lifetime and encouraged her leading courtiers to become involved in the theatre. Theatrical companies, including the Earl of Leicester's Men, Lord Strange's Men and the Lord Chamberlain's Men, came into existence, while her Master of Revels, responsible for organizing court entertainment, shrewdly realized that it was more economical to hire groups of players for important functions at Court rather than finance full-time in-house performers. Thus, theatre flourished under the protection of the sovereign and the patronage of rich courtiers with cultural inclinations or pretensions. The Queen cleverly realized that theatre was an excellent place for her citizens to be entertained and kept out of mischief that could otherwise interfere with the orderly conduct of her kingdom. Thus she permitted the leading impresario James Burbage, who employed both Shakespeare and Marlowe, to produce plays virtually wherever he desired: 'As well for the recreation of our loving subjects as for our solace and pleasure.'

Elizabeth's specific interest in the stage is impossible to evaluate as examples of her personal involvement tend to rely on amusing yet apocryphal stories. Her favourite Shakespearean play was supposedly *The Merry Wives of Windsor,* written so it is said after the Queen had seen Shakespeare's *Henry IV* and requested him to write another play wherein Falstaff falls in love.[7] If there is any truth in this entertaining anecdote it would be a splendid early example of a Royal Command Performance! The Queen is thought to have attended the initial performance of *Twelfth Night,* escorted by her favourite, the Earl of Essex. A hilarious tale of particularly doubtful authenticity involves Elizabeth appearing on the stage in one of Shakespeare's productions. In those days it was apparently customary for VIPs to sit or stand around the stage during a performance – on one such occasion, the Queen supposedly became bored and walked across the stage through a crowd of actors that included Shakespeare, who was performing in one of his own plays as he was often accustomed to do. When the Queen's walkabout was studiously ignored, she retraced her steps and pointedly dropped a glove at Shakespeare's feet. Without pausing, Shakespeare picked up the glove and returned it to Elizabeth with a flourish, extemporizing:

> And though now bent on this high embassy
> yet stoop we to take up our Cousin's glove.[8]

There was tremendous applause from the audience. In the context of an age where the law did not permit female performers, the concept of the Queen in a walk-on part is ingenious yet implausible. It is highly unlikely that Elizabeth, always conscious of her social standing, would have attended a public performance at a theatre such as The Globe or The Rose although she certainly watched many at private venues. *The Merry Wives of Windsor* was said to have been premiered at Windsor Castle while the Court was present.

The attendance of Elizabeth and the Earl of Essex at *Twelfth Night* at the Middle Temple had a greater degree of credibility, as the young Earl of Southampton, a close colleague of Essex, was one of Shakespeare's major patrons, along with both the 3rd and 4th Earls of Pembroke. Shakespeare may have been concerned when, as a result of Essex's abortive uprising against the Queen, Southampton was thrown into the Tower and not released until after the Queen's death in 1603. Essex's ill-conceived coup had been signalled by his supporters arranging for Shakespeare's company, the Lord Chamberlain's Men, to put on a special performance of *Richard II*, Shakespeare's powerful play about an unpopular monarch being deposed. Shakespeare may well have been fearful of being suspected of an involvement in the plot against the Queen and being suddenly drawn into a real-life scenario every bit as dramatic as one of his own plays.

In many respects, Elizabeth's entire reign resembled a long-running stage performance of epic proportions, full of love and lust, death or glory, triumph and tragedy, heroes and villains, all the classic ingredients for a successful drama series. Shakespeare did not have to look far for his inspiration, it was all around him. He had arrived in London around the time of the defeat of the Armada and lived there in the euphoric aftermath of this famous victory. He subsequently witnessed the steady slide into the sea of disillusion which arose in the final years of the Queen's life, when rhetoric finally began to outrun reality. His work fully captures the flavour of Elizabethan England. Plays such as *Henry V* portray the more upbeat moments, Henry's stirring speeches to his soldiers at Agincourt having much in common with Elizabeth's to her troops at Tilbury at the time of the Armada. Productions such as *Hamlet* and *Measure for Measure* brilliantly convey the brooding intensity of the Royal Court, everyone anxiously watching each other while meddling in each other's affairs.

It was a time of both high tension and frantic cultural endeavour as London thronged with all manner of aspiring playwrights and poets, drawn from all walks of life and all levels of social strata. Marlowe, Middleton, Jonson, Spenser, Fletcher and Shakespeare were the dominant playwrights of the day. Christopher Marlowe was the son of a cobbler in Canterbury while Ben Jonson's stepfather was a bricklayer, Marlowe, Spenser and Fletcher were all university educated, whereas Shakespeare had been to grammar school in Stratford. Marlowe's work displayed his marvellous gift with words: 'Was this the face that launch'd a thousand ships, And burnt the topless towers of Ilium?' from *Doctor Faustus*; or from *Tamburlaine*: 'Accurst be he that first invented war'; and in *The Massacre of Paris*: 'pale death may walk in furrows on my face'. Yet Marlowe lacked Shakespeare's ability to create believable characters, while his plots displayed no real coherence or continuity. Truly powerful passages in *Doctor Faustus* were bewilderingly interspersed with frivolous practical jokes in scenes more suitable for a knockabout farce, as Marlowe lost the plot in order to engage in the trivial pursuit of a cheap laugh from the groundlings. He did not possess the ferocious, intellectual calibre of Ben Jonson or the ability to conjure up the chilling sense of menace which John Webster was later able to conceive, most particularly in his two brilliant tragedies *The White Devil* and *The Duchess of Malfi*, both works full of death, despair and decay. Marlowe lacked discipline, and his life contained too many diversions in the twilight world he inhabited when engaged in espionage for Walsingham on the Queen's behalf. Eventually he was to be murdered in an East End tavern. Marlowe was not yet thirty.

John Fletcher is said to have collaborated with Shakespeare on *Two Noble Kinsmen* and Shakespeare's last work, *Henry VIII*, which is more a pageant than a play. When produced at The Globe, a spark from a cannon which was part of the special effects, set fire to the thatched roof of the tiered gallery and burnt the theatre to the ground. A deeply shocked Shakespeare retired to Stratford and wrote nothing further. *Henry VIII* is rarely performed today, while Fletcher's own work is now considered to be rather too flavourless for modern-day tastes.

Edmund Spenser created *The Faerie Queene* in order to ingratiate himself with Elizabeth and acquire royal patronage, yet he too could write a memorable line: 'Sweet Thames, run softly, till I end my song.'[9] Predictably, the mean-minded Lord Burghley disapproved, 'What! All this for a song?'[10] he grumbled when the Queen instructed him to pay one hundred pounds for a collection of Spenser's poems. Thomas Kyd was also a popular dramatist when Shakespeare first arrived in London, his best-known play being *The Spanish Tragedy* which was enormously popular in its time. Thomas Middleton was as much in demand as Shakespeare as a dramatist towards the end of the sixteenth century and was playwright in residence at the Globe when Shakespeare was involved with that theatre. Middleton's play, *A Game Of Chess*, once ran for nine successive days, an unusual occurrence at that time.

Other playwrights such as John Lyly and Thomas Dekker were very popular in Shakespeare's day, but are now almost forgotten.

Poetry was equally important during Elizabeth's reign. An aspiring young man made his mark by writing verse full of wit, elegance and intellectual brilliance. A law student at the Middle Temple or Lincoln's Inn needed to demonstrate more than a sound knowledge of legal issues so he engaged with his fellow students in rowdy 'wit contests', shouting out elegies, satires and epigrams amid a literary Tower of Babel in order to appear the wittiest, most cynical and cleverest young man about town. John Donne acquired his position as secretary to Sir Thomas Egerton, the Queen's last Lord Keeper, and later Lord Chancellor under James I, in this manner. Donne, like many ambitious young men of the time, was desperate to become a gentleman but never fully succeeded. After he had been dismissed from Egerton's service for marrying without informing his employer, he had to endure many years of poverty, a situation not helped by Donne's unerring ability to make his wife perpetually pregnant. The ingenious Donne had tried a variety of ways of achieving success and had sailed with Essex and Ralegh on the Islands Voyage in 1597 as a volunteer. Originally a Roman Catholic, he converted to Protestantism, later taking Holy Orders, and was Dean of St Paul's for the last years of his life, noted for his fine sermons. Donne's verses were not published until after his death in 1631 and it was some considerable time before his delicate touch and subtle use of language gained him the recognition which his work now commands:

> Go, and catch a falling star,
> Get with child a mandrake root,
> Tell me, where all past years are,
> Or who cleft the Devil's foot.[11]

Michael Drayton was another poet of some standing in the last years of the sixteenth century; his patron was Mary, Countess of Pembroke and Sir Philip Sidney's sister. Drayton's verse, 'Nor night doth hinder day, nor day the night doth wrong. The summer not too short, the winter not too long',[12] displays all the bright imagery and deft rhythm to be found centuries later in the works of Laurie Lee, another poet possessing a great love of landscape.

Writing poetry, like writing plays, was a classless activity. While Donne's father had been an ironmonger, Francis Bacon came from an altogether different social strata, yet he too had studied law and, with Donne and Sir Henry Wooton, engaged in poetry contests based on the relative values of Court, city and country, a familiar theme of the day. Sir Philip Sidney, a prominent member of the Queen's Court, also acquired a formidable reputation as a 'serious sonneteer', producing such creations as 'Thou my mind aspire to higher things', together with longer works, such as the prose romance *Arcadia*. Sidney's virtues had been evident from an early age: 'Nights and days in ceaseless and related studies, he worked upon the anvil of wit, reason and memory . . .'[13] noted an approving observer of a young Sidney. He was the apple of his father's eye, Sir Henry Sidney, the Queen's one-time Deputy in Ireland, who urged Philip's younger brother Robert to 'imitate his virtues, exercises and actions, he is a rare ornament of his age, the very formula of all well disposed young gentlemen of our court . . . in truth I speak it without flattery to him or myself he hath the most virtues that I ever found in any man'.[14] Sidney followed his father to Court and into the service of the Queen but was bitterly disappointed by Elizabeth's manner towards him, feeling that he had not been granted the recognition he deserved. Just as the early twentieth-century war poet, Wilfred Owen, he was destined to die disillusioned amid the mud of Flanders and, like Rupert Brooke and Keats, was cut down in his poetic prime.

The work of most of the Elizabethan poets pales into insignificance when compared to Shakespeare's sonnets, such as the celebrated *Sonnet Number 18*:

> Shall I compare thee to a summer's day?
> Thou art more lovely and more temperate:
> Rough winds do shake the darling buds of May,
> And summer's lease hath all too short a date.

Scholars have agonized endlessly as to the identity of the 'Dark Lady' in these sonnets. Was it Mary Fitton, mistress of William Herbert, the 3rd Earl of Pembroke and godson of the Queen? It has been claimed that the initials 'W.H.' in the dedication contained in the first folio of Shakespeare's plays published in 1623 refers to William Herbert. Like so many issues concerning Shakespeare, these claims remain tantalizingly unsubstantiated and it is incredible that so much is known about Shakespeare's work yet the man still remains shrouded in mystery. Today an impressive statue of Shakespeare by Sheemakers stands in the front hall at Wilton House near Salisbury, the home of the present Earl of Pembroke. The statue is a copy of William Kent's sculpture of Shakespeare which is to be found in Westminster Abbey.

Shakespeare alone had the ability to transform a stage open to the sky without the advantage of props, lighting or the special effects of twentieth-century theatre, using purely the power of words to effortlessly transport his audiences to Agincourt, Elsinore or the River Nile. He had an uncanny ability to convince the spectators that the callow young man on the stage really was Juliet, Cleopatra or Viola. Shakespeare held an audience spellbound in the reign of Elizabeth I and can do the same 400 years later, not merely in London but anywhere in the world from New York to Tokyo, translating easily into any language. None of his fellow Elizabethan playwrights possessed his enduring genius, that universal, timeless appeal.

The great prose writers who lived through Elizabeth's reign should not be ignored; for example, William Camden's magnificent *Britannia* and *Annals* are sweeping surveys of the period giving a detailed personal insight into both Elizabeth's reign and her kingdom. John Stow's chronicles, particularly his authoritative portrayal of London, a city in which he lived for more than eighty years, minutely examine virtually every nook and cranny of Elizabeth's capital as it appeared towards the end of the sixteenth century. At this time Richard Hakluyt was writing one of England's first outstanding travel books; his marvellous *Principal Navigations, Voyages, Traffiques and Discoveries of the English Nation* used the first-hand accounts of those who travelled to the furthest corners of the globe and returned to recount their experiences. Francis Bacon is one of many men alleged to have written everything attributed to William Shakespeare, some scholars finding it difficult to accept that a mere grammar school boy, who had not been to university, could possibly have produced works of such expertise. Much of Bacon's elegant prose was created in the time of James I, but he did pen his stylish 'Essays' in the last few years of Elizabeth's reign, composing with polished wit and a persuasive term of phrase. Bacon died in bizarre circumstances in 1626 when, conducting a scientific experiment involving the freezing of a chicken, he contracted a fatal chill and became terminally ill.

Great art and literature is said to mirror the mood of a nation and, while Nicholas Hilliard, Shakespeare, Marlowe and their compatriots were active in England, the interpretation of life in Spain was altogether different. Instead of the vitality of Shakespeare and Marlowe, there was the wry, often bitter satire of Cervantes, conveyed through his account of 'the Knight of the Doleful Countenance', Don Quixote and his faithful donkey-riding retainer, Sancho Panza. (Cervantes died on the same day as Shakespeare, 23 April 1616.) In place of the vibrant optimism displayed in the works of most Elizabethan artists, Spain had the distorted religious images of El Greco together with the sombre drama of Titian, one of the acknowledged masters of the High Renaissance.

To some extent, the creators of this period of history reflect the natures of their respective monarchs. Where Elizabeth was dazzlingly colourful in both appearance and manner, Philip of Spain was austere and remote, invariably attired entirely in black, a solitary figure living a life of privileged isolation in the private apartments of his palace, largely ignoring El Greco, who lived in Toledo; Philip favoured Titian as a painter, taking over his patronage from his father Emperor Charles V. He commissioned this Italian artist to paint a series of dramatic mythological works.

Philip had inherited an empire at its peak and he presided over its gradual decline, a process which began after the Armada's defeat in 1588. Nations normally demonstrate their greatest vitality in their period of growth, but Philip had found Spain already in full bloom, whereas Elizabeth had come to the English throne when the flowering had yet to begin. The cultural life of the respective nations tended to mirror that state of affairs in many respects.

Neither Titian nor El Greco were Spanish – Spain did produce internationally known artists such as Goya and Velazquez, but both were of a later generation. Elizabeth on the other hand fostered a sense of pride and patriotism within her nation that encouraged indigenous artists to flourish. In turn, their work fostered the country's sense of self-belief, further developing patriotic feeling. This sense of identity helped to develop artistic expression unique to Elizabeth's kingdom, thereby reducing the necessity of summoning continental genius at every conceivable opportunity.

Though it would be foolish to claim that the Queen was entirely responsible for the flowering of so much creative endeavour during her time on the English throne, nevertheless she was the ruler of the nation when it occurred. Elizabeth was herself a cultured person, and created a climate that encouraged this creative process to flourish in a manner that did not exist before or after her reign. Her father, Henry, had also been a cultured man but was quick to summon Holbein, Eworth or William Scrots from overseas to paint the major portraits of his reign rather than seeking local talent; no English writers or musicians of real note came to prominence during Henry's time on the English throne, nor was there any comparable great creative advance in the period subsequent to Elizabeth's death, though Milton was a poet of substance. True, Dryden might have been more sophisticated than Shakespeare, but he totally failed to match the latter's shimmering imagery or awesome creative power. Charles I quickly reintroduced foreign talent in the shape of the Flemish painter

Van Dyck, while the architectural achievements of Inigo Jones were sadly cut short by the Civil War.

During Elizabeth's forty-five years on the throne, peaceful conditions within her kingdom combined with favourable social and economic circumstances to greatly encourage cultural advancement within the nation, particularly in the literary field. It was during the Elizabethan period that English literature can be said to have come of age and England began to establish a literary reputation to be taken seriously by continental Europe, which had hitherto regarded the Tudor kingdom as a cultural desert island. The English language had expanded enormously, from some 4,000 words during the time of Chaucer to the more than 24,000 words available to Shakespeare and his fellow playwrights and poets. They certainly made the most of the material available, putting England at last on the creative map of Europe, establishing its tradition as a literary nation. The Queen was the catalyst which enabled this to happen, besides being a consummate performer in her own right. Her address given to a potentially hostile parliamentary delegation, incensed over further Crown monopolies, at the time of her last Parliament in 1601, represented a *tour de force* which any modern actress would have been proud to deliver: 'Though God hath raised me high, yet this I count the glory of my crown: that I have reigned with your loves.'[15] This poses the intriguing question – did Elizabeth also write her own material?

12

MEN AT WAR

The defeat of the Spanish Armada in the summer of 1588 gave Elizabeth celebrity status among all the nations of Europe, ensuring her lasting fame for posterity. Ironically, this happy state of affairs arose largely as a result of the spectacular failure of her foreign policy leading to something she dreaded most of all – war with Spain, the greatest military power throughout the whole of the civilized world.

When Elizabeth inherited the English throne thirty years earlier, her kingdom enjoyed excellent diplomatic relations with Spain, traditionally one of England's staunchest allies. The two royal families had consistently intermarried, prosperous trading links existed between the two nations and England appeared relaxed about Spanish expansionist policy in the New World. However, once Elizabeth became Queen, it was not long before relationships between the countries began to deteriorate. It was almost as if both nations had simultaneously decided on a policy of embarking on a series of manoeuvres calculated to antagonize each other, a slow yet remorseless process beginning when Elizabeth had gently but firmly declined King Philip's offer of marriage, a rather half-hearted proposal representing an attempt to maintain the Catholic faith in England and isolate France. Elizabeth's swift reintroduction of Protestantism as England's official religion, and her subsequent support of factions in Scotland and France, was deemed heretical by Spain, which further aggravated the situation. Philip resolved to attack England to restore Catholicism – but only when the time was right.

By the late 1560s Elizabeth's greatest seafarers, Drake and Hawkins, had begun to undertake a series of voyages to the Caribbean, thereby challenging the domination hitherto enjoyed by the Spaniards in the New World. This process intensified throughout the next decade, culminating in Drake's circumnavigation of the globe, an enterprise which had enjoyed the Queen's fullest support and greatly outraged both King Philip and his country. By that time, a considerable number of hawks had gained seats on Elizabeth's Privy Council, men like Leicester, Hatton and Walsingham, who collectively outnumbered the ever-cautious Burghley and his supporters, and who continually encouraged the Queen to adopt a more aggressive stance.

Meanwhile, closer to home, two completely unrelated yet highly significant events occurred that were to further jeopardize the strained relationship between England and Spain. First, Mary, Queen of Scots had been deposed and forced to flee across the border into England to seek refuge from her English cousin, a disastrous mistake for Mary and a grave source of embarrassment for Elizabeth, who could not afford to have a Catholic Queen, whom some regarded as the true heir to the English throne, free to become a focus of insurrection within her kingdom. Elizabeth was left with little alternative but to imprison Mary, thereby outraging the whole of the Catholic world. The Pope firstly excommunicated Elizabeth and then urged the Spanish King to attack England as part of a Holy War to restore Catholicism, an enterprise which he promised to help finance from the Vatican.

Meanwhile, across the North Sea the Duke of Alva, Philip's Governor General in the Netherlands, then a Spanish colony, had imprisoned a group of English seamen in Antwerp and impounded their ships, an action which resulted in all trade between England and the Netherlands ceasing for almost five years. Antwerp had provided a vital commercial outlet for the London-based Company of Merchant Adventurers, exporting and selling the bulk of English woollen cloths to continental buyers, while the resultant export tax represented a major revenue for the Queen.

It was the Netherlands that was later to become the initial battleground between the armed forces of England and Spain, after the Privy Council had persuaded the Queen to give military assistance to support Dutch rebels seeking to overthrow Spanish rule in the Low Countries. The Treaty of Nonsuch, signed at the Queen's palace in Surrey during August 1585, committed Elizabeth to provide combat troops in support of the beleaguered Dutch who had recently seen Antwerp and Ghent fall to the Spanish forces subsequent to the assassination of their leader, William of Orange. By this time, Philip's nephew, the exceptionally talented Alexander Farnese, Duke of Parma had taken over as the Spanish commander in the Netherlands. Elizabeth had reluctantly promised 5,000 foot soldiers supported by 1,000 cavalry under the command of Colonel 'Black John' Norris, a seasoned veteran of the Irish wars. However, the rebels wished to have a military commander of greater status, and accordingly, the Queen's long-time favourite, the Earl of Leicester, was dispatched for overseas duty as her Lieutenant-

General in the Low Countries. Leicester had not been involved in military matters for many years but it was not long before the so-called 'glories of war' went completely to his head – basking in the adulation he received from the Dutch, Leicester allowed them to create him their Governor General. Elizabeth had previously turned down the offer of sovereignty of the Netherlands and was understandably furious when she learnt of the Earl's latest bout of self-glorification. It took the combined efforts of her entire Privy Council to calm the Queen down and persuade her not to humiliate Leicester in front of the Dutch by forcing him to renounce the honour that they had so recently bestowed upon him.

Shortly after this unseemly row between the monarch and her Commander-in-Chief, Leicester began to besiege the Spanish-held town of Zutphen. It was here outside the town walls that his nephew, Sir Philip Sidney, one of the most notable Elizabethan courtiers of the day, was fatally struck down by the enemy. Sidney had not been wearing armour on the lower half of his body, some think out of sheer bravado, others because he had become disenchanted with the way Elizabeth's reign was progressing and had developed a death wish. Sir Philip was out of favour with the Queen at that particular moment, following the writing of a highly critical letter advising against her marriage to the Catholic Duke of Alençon. Nevertheless, Elizabeth was greatly distressed when she heard the news that he had been so seriously wounded: '. . . the Queen much troubled at the report of Sidney's hurt'.[1] Sidney was taken to nearby Arnhem where he died, at the age of thirty-two, after gangrene set in, the first notable English poet to die in Flanders fields. The Queen and all the nation mourned and Sidney was awarded the supreme accolade of a state funeral at St Paul's Cathedral, the first commoner to receive the unique honour subsequently given to Lawrence of Arabia and Sir Winston Churchill many centuries later.

The Earl of Leicester proved to be a disastrous military commander and resigned his commission to return to England shortly after Sidney's death. The Earl was also destined to die only two years later, possibly as a result of a recurring bout of malaria which he had first contracted in the cold, damp marshlands of the aptly named Low Countries; the war was to continue for another decade before the Dutch finally succeeded in gaining independence. The conflict also proved disastrous for the Spanish, being so costly that the nation went bankrupt three times during the course of the war. Effectively, all the wealth they had accumulated in the New World was squandered in a vain attempt to keep the region a Spanish colony. The English were to receive little thanks for their part in this protracted war: the major enemy which Elizabeth's successors encountered in the seventeenth century was to be the Dutch. England's involvement in the Low Countries further hardened Spanish animosity towards Elizabeth and her island kingdom. In the same week as Sir Philip Sidney's funeral in London, there occurred another dramatic event calculated to take the two nations further along the relentless road to all-out war: the execution at Fotheringhay Castle of Mary, Queen of Scots on 8 February 1587, the fall of the axe virtually a signal for the Armada to set sail.

Queen Elizabeth may have appeared a reluctant warrior but she was continually persuaded into belligerent acts by the more militant members of her Privy Council. By the time of Drake's famous 'singeing of the King's beard', in the same year as Mary's execution, the die was well and truly cast. Drake's raid on Cadiz was essentially a pre-emptive strike on elements of the King of Spain's suspected invasion fleet, undertaken in order to buy further time for the Queen and her Council to prepare for the anticipated assault on her kingdom – it was no longer a question of if, but when, the blow would fall.

Drake's surprise attack on one of Spain's major naval bases was precisely the type of operation for which he was best suited, an audacious commando-like raid requiring minimum planning and maximum speed, surprise and sheer raw courage, coupled with an easy ability to rapidly adapt the assault as events dictated. Drake had sailed from Plymouth at the head of some two dozen ships, including six belonging to the Queen, urbanely signalling Lord Burghley, 'The wind commands me away. Our ship is under sail. God grant we may so live in His fear as the enemy may have cause to say that God doth fight for her Majesty as well abroad as at home. . . .'[2] As so often proved to be the case, Elizabeth then quickly changed her mind and abruptly cancelled her previous directive to Drake to attack Spanish ports and shipping, forbidding him '. . . to enter forcibly into any of the said King's ports or havens, or to offer violence to any of his towns or shipping within harbouring, or do any act of hostility upon the land'.[3] A small sailing vessel was dispatched after Drake but conveniently failed to catch up with him to countermand his original orders.

Drake's sudden appearance at Cadiz caught the Spanish completely off guard and the English fleet was able to sail into the outer harbour, creating havoc among the tightly packed shipping at anchor: 'In this yeare Sr Fraunces Drake . . . wente here hence to the seas the thirde daie of Aprill. He arrivede at Cales, where he did greatlie annoye the king of Spaines fleete, & sett manye of fire. . . .'[4] By the time Drake departed from Cadiz, more than two dozen large Spanish ships had been set ablaze together with a massive amount of stores which had been stockpiled on the adjacent quays ready for the Armada. Drake returned to Plymouth in triumph at the end of June 1587, bringing with him the *San Felipe*, a huge merchant ship belonging to the King of Spain that had been intercepted off the Azores, carrying valuable cargo of spices, gold bullion and other treasure: 'A great carricke of 1000 tonnes or upwardes, belonging to the said Kinge laden with spices and other commodities and brought the same into England to the great comforte of her majesty and her subjects.'[5] The Queen was exceedingly pleased and Drake's position as one of the leaders of the English fleet destined to fight the Spanish was assured – the transformation from pirate king to respected naval officer was complete, in English eyes at any rate.

The Spanish view of Drake's unheralded and unprovoked assault on Cadiz at a time when war had not officially been declared between the two nations was similar to that of the Americans after the Japanese had attacked Pearl Harbor some three hundred and fifty years later – a criminal act of despicable treachery. To Philip this was the latest outrage in a long line of provocative actions deliberately instigated by the English Queen against Spain: replacing Catholicism in her country by a heretical faith, persecuting a religious minority within her kingdom, murdering her cousin Mary, Queen of Scots after she had sought asylum, treacherously supporting revolutionaries within his Dutch colony, continually encouraging English privateers to prey on lawful Spanish territories and shipping in the New World. Queen Elizabeth and her followers must be destroyed for the sake of the Catholic faith and the good of the civilized world. The Pope, God's representative on Earth demanded it. It was Philip of Spain's bounden duty to respond.

Elizabeth was fortunate to possess so many capable seafarers who could become swordbearers in her hour of need. They had been unofficially practising war games against the Spaniards for many years: Drake and Hawkins, Grenville, Frobisher, Fenner, Borrough and Fenton were all highly experienced seamen who had become well acquainted with Spanish fighting techniques and adept at combating them. They were completely familiar with the nature of their warships, how they sailed and how their crews performed. This was to prove invaluable in the coming conflict which would be conducted in home waters as opposed to far away on the Spanish Main. Elizabeth's kingdom stood firmly in the front line.

In many respects, the events that preceded the arrival of the Spanish Armada off the south coast of England in the summer of

1588 proved to be every bit as important as the ensuing conflict and had a vital bearing on its eventual outcome. The Queen and her Council took a number of key decisions which were to considerably influence the course of a mighty conflict in which Elizabeth was to play no personal part; unlike many previous monarchs, she was not destined to lead her troops into battle, and was therefore unable to exercise any direct control once hostilities had begun. Nevertheless, two particular appointments, which she personally initiated prior to the two fleets engaging, proved decisive in ensuring ultimate victory in one of the most famous sea battles in England's long and turbulent history.

The first of these had been the Queen's appointment in the autumn of 1577 of John Hawkins as her Navy Treasurer. Hawkins's subsequent redesigning and re-equipping of Her Majesty's ships, based on his own practical experiences of voyaging on the Spanish Main, often in combat conditions against Spanish ships, provided warships capable of outsailing the larger, more cumbersome, Spanish galleons. Hawkins utilized knowledge gained from sailing in the Caribbean to cut down the original fortress-like topsides of the English ships, while at the same time reducing weight and deepening their keels, thus enabling them to be sailed closer to the wind. The English warships proved far more manoeuvrable than lumbering Spanish galleons, which were ideal for transatlantic voyages but far less suited to the confined waters of the Channel, the battleground for the two fleets when they ultimately met. The English vessels were also narrower in the beam in relation to their overall length than was customary in maritime design of that period and considerably lower in the water, thereby providing an excellent gun platform. The Queen had invested in a number of new vessels including her flagship, the *Ark Royal*, which she had purchased from Sir Walter Ralegh and was scheduled as her admiral's command post. As a result of her directives, a dozen or so of her ships were of very recent construction, while many more had been substantially altered and updated, providing the nucleus of a thoroughly modern fleet.

Elizabeth's second crucial decision prior to the battle was her choice of overall naval commander. While it was customary to have a member of the aristocracy in control, the Queen might well have been influenced by public opinion and appointed the hugely popular Sir Francis Drake, who was by then a national hero. However, the Queen was shrewd enough to realize his limitations in controlling large and substantial fleets as well as recognizing that this mercurial man was regarded with suspicion and heartily disliked by many of his fellow sea captains. So Elizabeth selected

Charles, Lord Howard of Effingham, for the vital post of Commander-in-Chief of her fleet, with Drake as Vice-Admiral and Hawkins as Rear Admiral. She made an excellent choice. Howard had succeeded the Earl of Lincoln as Lord High Admiral in 1585, the fourth Howard to hold this post. He was an experienced seafarer who had commanded fleets in the past and more importantly was prepared to listen to those like Drake and Hawkins, whose knowledge of the sea considerably exceeded his own, saying, '. . . and will yield ever unto them of greater experience'.[6] Above all, Howard commanded the respect of the greatest of the Elizabethan seafarers: 'I finde my Lord Admirall so well affectede for all honourable services in this accion as it dothe assure all his followers of good successe and hope of victorie',[7] Drake wrote to Lord Burghley. The Queen had displayed her usual impeccable judgement in selecting the only man capable of welding a highly temperamental bunch of buccaneering individuals into an effective fighting force, able to challenge the Armada.

Unlike the Spaniards, the English seafarers of the Elizabethan era had no experience of large-scale sea actions and a substantial Royal Navy as such did not exist at that time. Whenever a venture was contemplated that required more than a single ship, a number of vessels would be gathered together piecemeal on a private enterprise basis; those that survived the subsequent action would be returned to their individual owners together with an appropriate share of the spoils. These temporary fleets would normally be used to attack enemy ports rather than engage rival squadrons on the high seas.

Prior to the arrival of the Armada off the Cornish coast, English seafarers had not experienced a major battle at sea. The Spaniards, on the other hand, had defeated a large Turkish fleet at the Battle of Lepanto in the Mediterranean during 1571. One of those taking part as a young staff officer had been the Duke of Parma, now Spanish Commander in the Netherlands, while an equally young naval officer named Miguel Cervantes was wounded there while taking part in the fighting. A large Spanish fleet had also decisively beaten the Portuguese in a savage encounter off the Azores at Terceira in 1582. Thus the Spanish had much better experience of deploying large groups of ships at sea and engaging hostile fleets of similar numbers. This supposed advantage ultimately proved to be of no particular benefit as these encounters had involved the usage of tactics that were to prove completely outdated when the Armada confronted the English fleet under Lord Howard of Effingham. The Spanish regarded cannon as 'an ignoble arm'[8] and were accustomed to using their galleons as floating castles crammed with soldiers, sailing alongside the enemy and capturing a ship by boarding. Conversely, the English deployed their warships largely as gun platforms to bombard the enemy at long range. When first engaging the tightly packed Armada, they shocked the Spaniards by adopting a line astern formation in order to fire a series of devastating broadsides, a revolutionary manoeuvre in naval warfare at that time, which introduced tactics to be subsequently used by Nelson, Jellicoe and every admiral afloat for as long as there were big-gun warships.

While the English Queen had made an excellent choice of naval commander, the King of Spain's decision to appoint Don Alonso Perez de Guzman, Duke of Medina Sidonia, Lord of San Lucar and Knight of the Golden Fleece, to spearhead the assault on England represented a serious error. Medina Sidonia, Captain General of the Ocean Seas, possessed no previous experience of command at sea, suffered acute seasickness, did not want the job and had no faith in the plan of attack. In this last issue, Medina Sidonia had more than a degree of justification: the concept of sending the Armada up the entire length of the Channel, while running the gauntlet of a hostile fleet in order to rendezvous with the Duke of Parma off the coast of Flanders was seriously flawed, particularly as there were no suitable sizeable ports to use when he reached his destination. Instead, there awaited an open shoreline with treacherous sandbanks and shallow water wherein lay strong currents, erratic crosswinds and small, shallow-draft Dutch warships waiting to pounce.

Philip had presented his reluctant commander with an incredibly detailed plan of attack, but with no indication of precisely how it should be executed, and no flexibility whatsoever to vary it should circumstance demand. In many respects, the battle could be said to be lost before the Armada had even set sail, yet this strategy might have worked if vigorously pressed home by a resolute commander. Medina Sidonia was no such man. In the event, inability to maintain effective communication with Parma proved a serious handicap; furthermore, Medina Sidonia lacked the determination, experience, skill and sheer luck to succeed in fulfilling the extraordinarily difficult task that he had been set. Ultimately, it was largely his lack of good fortune that was to prove his downfall.

Drake correctly guessed the nature of the Spanish strategy and how to successfully combat it; with the Queen's authority he persuaded Howard to concentrate the bulk of his forces at Plymouth, leaving only a small squadron of ships under Lord Henry Seymour in the Straits of Dover to keep an eye on Parma. The Duke was poised just across the Channel at the head of a huge army, awaiting the Armada's arrival to assist the invasion of Elizabeth's kingdom. It was a moment of supreme crisis for the Queen and her nation: 'This mighty enemy now knocking at our gates',[9] as Leicester dramatically put it. It was a time of maximum danger, a forerunner to 1805 when Napoleon was poised to launch his Grand Armée across the Channel. Napoleon was also to be thwarted by a supremely skilful naval commander and a determined English fleet. It was also comparable to 1940 when Hitler's Panzers waited to invade, but they too lacked command of the sea and were opposed by Winston Churchill. In that fateful summer of 1588 similar favourable circumstances were required for invasion, that is, suitable weather conditions, coupled with complete control of the sea. Only Elizabeth's fleet stood between the Spanish and their desired aim. 'If the navy had not been strong at sea what peril England would now have been in,'[10] the Earl of Leicester later remarked to Sir Francis Walsingham.

One of the worst times in a war, particularly for those in command, is awaiting an expected enemy attack when all suitable preparations have been made and nothing further can be done. Tensions mount, tempers become frayed. The atmosphere in 1588 is graphically illustrated by the series of dispatches between Lord Howard aboard the *Ark Royal* at Plymouth and the Queen and her Council in London. Howard was irritated that Elizabeth, prompted by Burghley, was still pursuing peace negotiations with Parma in the Netherlands, even as the Armada sailed towards her kingdom, in the forlorn hope that hostilities might be avoided at the eleventh hour. 'I am very sorry that her Majesty will not thoroughly awake in this perilous and most dangerous time . . .'[11] fumed Howard. The following day the commander of the Queen's fleet was even more agitated: 'For the love of Jesus Christ, Madam, awake thoroughly and see the villainous treason round about you,'[12] he thundered.

There was also a fundamental difference of opinion between the Queen and her Lord Admiral as to the best course of action in the prevailing circumstances. Drake had convinced Howard that he should seize the initiative and launch a pre-emptive strike against the Spanish, either in their home port or shortly after they had put to sea, when they were still many miles from the English shore. The Queen and her Privy Councillors were understandably nervous that the Armada might elude Howard's fleet and arrive off the English coast to find it undefended. Sir Francis Walsingham expressed the Queen's views in the following words: 'She thinketh it not convenient that your Lordship should go so far to the south as the said Isles of Bayona, but to ply up and down in some indifferent place between the coast of Spain and this realm, so as you may be able to answer any attempt that the said fleet shall make either against this realm, Ireland or Scotland.'[13] Nothing infuriates a commander more than politicians meddling in military matters, particularly when they appear to have little idea of the true situation. Howard's withering reply was masterful: 'I must and will obey; and am glad that there be such there, as are able to judge what is fitter for us to do than we here, but by my instructions which I had, I did think it otherwise.'[14] Howard's sarcasm caused the Queen to relent and the English fleet was authorized to make a sortie out into the Western Approaches, but was driven back to port by adverse winds. The fleet had only just returned from a second similar foray, one for which the Queen had very likely not given her permission and was probably wholly unaware. Having sailed almost as far south as the northern coast of Spain without encountering the enemy, the English were repairing and resupplying their vessels within the inner harbour at Plymouth when sensational news arrived that the Armada had been sighted off the Cornish coast. This caught Howard's fleet at a considerable disadvantage, for the westerly breeze wafting the Armada up the English Channel towards Plymouth was blowing straight into the Sound, making it impossible for Howard to sail out to meet them. An adverse tide made it equally impractical for ships to be towed or warped out either. This was a critical situation, and one which gave some credibility to the memorable tale of Drake's airy comment regarding his game of bowls, 'There's time for that and beat the Spaniards after.'[15] Fortunately for Howard, the Armada's commander made the fundamental error of spurning a wonderful opportunity to destroy the English fleet at anchor by rigidly following his orders to sail directly up channel and not exploit this unique chance. Later that night when the tide turned the English ships managed to creep out of harbour in two separate groups. The largest group under Howard sailed boldly across the Armada's bows under the cover of darkness towards the Eddystone reef before tacking down channel in order to gain the weather gauge, while Drake's smaller force used local knowledge to take the advantage of a back eddy inshore and tack slowly westwards. Thus at dawn Medina Sidonia woke to discover English ships both to windward and behind his fleet, thereby completely losing his initial tactical advantage: 'With great difficulty they worked out of the harbour and on Saturday got sight of them, consisting of above a hundred sail, many of great burden. . . . At nine o'clock gave them fight but did not venture among them, their fleet being so strong. The captains of her Majesty's ships behaved themselves most bravely and like men',[16] Howard reported to Walsingham. The English commander had every right to be cautious, the Armada was an awesome sight as it surged majestically up channel in a crescent-shaped formation more than two miles across, 'the ocean groaning under the weight of them',[17] being William Camden's characteristically colourful description. Hawkins's assessment was rather more sober: 'This is the greatest and strongest combination that was ever gathered in Christendom, and must be mightily and diligently looked into',[18] he reported to Walsingham.

Certainly the Armada appeared impressive and this was a battle that Lord Howard could not afford to lose – Elizabeth had committed her entire naval forces, and if Howard failed, then England was virtually defenceless against the might of Parma's army. The English land forces drawn up at Tilbury under the Earl of Leicester were of no real consequence and deployed in the wrong place north of the Thames, as the Spanish forces intended to land in Kent. Howard correctly judged that discretion was the better part of valour: 'All the world never saw such a force as theirs was',[19] he later confided to Walsingham. Hostilities commenced in a rather quaint fashion. War had not been formally declared between the two nations so Howard elected to revive the old medieval custom of issuing a challenge and ordered a small vessel, appropriately named the *Distain*, to charge towards the packed ranks of the Armada and fire off a symbolic opening shot. Let battle commence. 'Their force is wonderful great and strong, and yet we pluck their feathers by little and little',[20] wrote Howard to Walsingham. The opposing fleets regarded each other warily, Howard's ships cautiously circling around the Armada while carefully assessing their relative strengths and weaknesses. The English were undoubtedly inhibited by the sheer size and numbers of the Spanish fleet and were reluctant to come too close, and it took some time for them to realize that a large part of the Armada consisted of transport ships carrying troops and weapons to reinforce Parma. These momentous events were clearly visible from the shore where William Hawkins, Mayor of Plymouth and John Hawkins's brother, together with a large crowd of citizens, used the Hoe as a grandstand, like spectators at a football match: 'The Mayor of Plymouth to the Council. Intelligence that the Lord Admiral has engaged the Spanish fleet within sight of the town . . . he is to windward of the enemy.'[21] Today at the Royal Naval Barracks in Plymouth, fittingly named HMS *Drake*, huge paintings on the wall of the Officer's Mess portray 'The Battle of Plimouth'.

The defeat of the mighty Spanish fleet did not turn out to be a single decisive battle like Trafalgar, but a series of running skirmishes, as the two fleets slowly progressed towards the Straits of Dover, the English firing mainly from long range and causing relatively little damage. Thus, more by luck rather than judgement, the Armada arrived at its required destination virtually intact, but so was the English fleet which the Spaniards needed to neutralize for Parma's invasion force to safely set sail. Worse still, it appeared that the Duke would be unable to embark for at least another week. The confused Medina Sidonia then committed another unforced error by anchoring off Calais, enabling Howard to send in fireships. Many of the Spanish captains panicked, cut their cables and fled into the North Sea, a foolish act that was to subsequently have grave consequences for the Armada. The Spanish commander decided to continue northwards, following a brisk close-quarter encounter between the rival fleets at Gravelines off the coast of Flanders, after Howard had been reinforced by the arrival of Lord Henry Seymour's squadron which had been stationed off Dover. The Armada suffered significant losses in men and ships for the first time, while the severe pounding that so many galleons took was to have a significant bearing on their chances of survival during the months ahead.

Meanwhile, the Queen together with her Privy Councillors, her courtiers and all her countrymen could do little but await the outcome of a train of events that Elizabeth had set into motion but which was now largely beyond her control or influence. At this perilous time, when all the Channel and its coastline had become a war zone the Queen predictably rose to the occasion and was at her magnificent best. 'It is a comfort to see how great magnanimity Her Majesty shows who is not a whit dismayed,' commented a highly impressed Robert Cecil. Elizabeth had been keen to travel to the south coast for an opportunity of seeing her fleet in action but was dissuaded by her Council as too risky a course of action. Instead she rode astride a magnificent white horse to Tilbury where she reviewed her army encamped there, accompanied by the Earl of Leicester, her Captain General. Here the Queen made a famous and highly emotional speech to her adoring troops: '. . . I know I have the body of a weak and feeble woman but I have the heart and stomach of a King, and of a King of England too. . .'[22] Elizabeth was in her element; she was Boadicea, the Warrior Queen, astride a white charger at the head of an army ready to defend her kingdom to her last drop of blood. Her stirring words certainly had the desired effect on the scratch body of part-time militia which was virtually all that stood between Parma's crack regiments and London, should the Armada have succeeded and an invasion of England become feasible.

Medina Sidonia then made his last and most fatal mistake. Against all odds, he had reached his planned destination with the substantial part of his fleet intact, yet ignoring the advice of his senior officers, combat veterans such as Recalde, Leyva and Oquendo, he decided to abandon his mission and return to Spain via northern Scotland and the west coast of Ireland. 'The Spanish have taken their course towards Scotland followed by the Lord High Admiral. Although much distressed they are still of great force',[23] wrote a surprised and highly suspicious Hawkins. The Spanish had no charts of this area and the unseasonable weather combined with a savage coastline to imperil the Armada as it struggled to return home. Most of the Spanish ships were greatly weakened with the pounding they had taken from the English guns. Many were unable to moor up anywhere because their cables and anchors had been left behind after the fireships had put them to flight off Calais. Their crews were short of food and water, completely exhausted after so many days of continuous actions. The result was a catastrophe for the Spanish, as ship after ship was wrecked off the north coast of Scotland or the south-west shoreline of Ireland where bedraggled survivors were slaughtered as they staggered ashore: 'One man, Melaghin Mcabb, boasted he had killed eighty with his galoglas axe.'[24] Soon reports were being received by the Queen and her Council that half of the Spanish fleet had perished. English army officers' treatment of the captured Spaniards was equally as savage as that inflicted on Elizabeth's sailors when falling into the hands of the Spanish – an orgy of killing took place: '. . . and since it hath pleased God, by his hand, upon the rocks to drown the greater and better sort of them, I will, with his favour, be his soldier for the despaching of those rags which yet remain,'[25] boasted Sir William Fitzwilliam, the Queen's Lord Deputy in Ireland, in a letter to the sovereign written towards the end of 1588.

Ferocious gales completed what Howard's fleet had begun – only half the number of ships that had so proudly set forth from Spain managed to limp home, while two-thirds of their crews were either dead or captured. 'I sent my ships to fight against men and not against the winds and waves of God,'[26] lamented Philip of Spain as he contemplated the massive disaster that had befallen his nation.

The decisive victory that the English fleet had gained was not without sacrifice. Throughout the actual battle, not a single ship was lost and casualties had been light; however, once back in harbour, exhaustion and disease played havoc among the fleet. 'Sickness and mortality begins to grow wonderfully among them. It is most pitiful to see the men die in the streets of Margate',[27] a distressed Howard reported to a largely indifferent Privy Council. Supplies of food and water had run so low that the fleet was 'driven to such extremity that the Lord Admiral has been obliged to eat beans and many of the men to drink their own water',[28] Sir Francis Walsingham was informed. He was one of the few members of the Queen's Privy Council to appreciate that the fleet had been continually handicapped by a shortage of supplies and ammunition. The Queen's and Burghley's parsimonious nature had led to victory being less decisive than Howard would have wished. 'I am sorry the Lord Admiral was forced to leave the prosecution of the enemy through the wants he sustained. Our half-doings doth breed dishonour and leaveth the disease uncured,'[29] apologized the Queen's Principal Secretary. The part Walsingham had played in supporting the war effort was much appreciated by those who had taken part in the action. 'Walsyngham has fought more with his pen than many in the navy fought with their enemies',[30] wrote Lord Henry Seymour. Regrettably, the attitude of the Queen and her Council towards those who had provided England with such a glorious victory appeared to be one of callous indifference. There was even a cynical school of thought among some of the Council that the more who died, the less would have to be paid – in a realistic Elizabethan world, once they had completed their task they were expendable.

The Queen had been distracted by private sorrow following the death of her beloved Earl of Leicester in September 1588, while Burghley and the Council were wholly preoccupied in joyous celebration and waging a gleeful public relations campaign exploiting England's triumph along with Spain's acute distress and embarrassment at such a catastrophic military setback in the eyes of the entire civilized world. The loss of so many Spanish ships and lives to the forces of nature was particularly helpful to the English propaganda exercise, as it clearly demonstrated the justness of their Protestant cause. God having punished Catholic Spain, the Almighty was manifestly on England's side and Elizabeth was His chosen creature. Burghley was determined to win the propaganda war just as decisively as Howard had won the battle at sea. Elizabeth's shameful disregard of the crews of her victorious fleet was in marked contrast to the far more humane conduct shown by the King of Spain towards the wretched survivors of his supposedly invincible Armada when they finally struggled ashore in Santander, San Sebastian, Corunna and various other ports along the northern coast of Spain. The pitiable Medina Sidonia lamented:

> The hardships and sufferings which have been endured cannot be described to your Majesty, for they have been greater than have ever been seen in any voyage, and there is a ship among those arrived here whose people passed fourteen days without a

drop of water to drink. In my flagship 180 persons have died of the sickness, including three of the four pilots on board, and all the rest are ill, many of them of an infectious disease; and all those in my personal service, to the number of 60, are dead or so sick that only two of them remained with me.[31]

Philip was very sympathetic, attaching no blame whatsoever to his Captain General of the Ocean Seas for his part in the debacle. Instead, his chief naval adviser, Diego Flores de Valdes, was made the scapegoat and sent to prison on his return to Spain, while those back at home who were thought to have contributed to the Armada's downfall by poorly fitting out and victualling its ships were punished accordingly. Reports were received in England of victuallers being shot, while others were imprisoned. Among the latter was Cervantes, whose accounts as a supply officer to the Armada were so poorly recorded that the investigating authorities were unable to distinguish between corrupt behaviour and sheer incompetence and therefore sentenced him to a long term in prison. Cervantes used this period of enforced confinement to write his definitive novel *Don Quixote*, one of the world's greatest literary works.

'Thus the magnificent, huge, and mighty fleet of the Spaniards, such as sailed not upon the ocean seen many hundreds of years before, in the year 1588 vanished into smoke',[32] noted the contemporary Dutch historian Emanuel van Meteren. The downfall of the Spanish Armada confirmed England's position in the eyes of the world as the dominant maritime nation and heralded the subsequent decline and fall of the Spanish Empire, which at its peak had been larger than that of Rome. At the same time, the Armada's defeat removed the immediate threat of invasion and encouraged the Dutch to intensify their efforts to gain independence. When this was finally achieved, they conveniently overlooked the part Elizabeth's forces had played and replaced Spain as England's greatest enemy, humiliating Charles II by burning his fleet at anchor off Chatham less than a century after the defeat of the Armada.

While England may have won a famous battle in 1588, this did not mean it had won the war. The English lacked sufficient resources to successfully exploit the victory over the Armada; at the same time the Spaniards were quick to rebuild and regroup. Elizabeth was to be at war with Spain for the rest of her life, as a global conflict remorselessly raged on land and sea for the next fifteen years. This proved extremely costly to the nation and progressively more meaningless to its citizens, as the euphoria of the Armada's defeat slowly faded into a distant memory. The English victory meant little to a new younger generation, impatient to get on with their lives and indifferent to former glories, as Queen and country inexorably became prisoners of an illustrious past.

Drake and Norris jointly led an unsuccessful expedition to Lisbon and the Azores in the year following the Armada's destruction. To a large extent their failure was Elizabeth's fault in setting them over-ambitious objectives – attacking Lisbon, and placing the Portuguese Pretender Don Antonio on the throne of Portugal while capturing a Spanish treasure fleet off the Azores, proved too much, even for the resourceful Drake. Nevertheless, the Queen was most displeased and Drake in deep disgrace. His Armada exploits were completely forgotten and Elizabeth did not employ him in any further commissions for a considerable period of time.

In 1596, Howard, Ralegh and Essex led a more successful sortie to Cadiz. The town was captured, many large ships destroyed and significant amounts of treasure fell into English hands. The Queen was better pleased, particularly when learning that her latest favourite, the Earl of Essex, had displayed considerable valour. Yet these types of action merely goaded the Spanish bull and completely failed to administer a decisive *coup de grâce*. Philip was to build two more Armadas, one in 1596, and another the following year, only to see them beaten back by storms, causing severe losses. The King died not long afterwards, yet even the demise of the Queen's long-time adversary failed to end the war. A farcical situation now existed whereby although this prolonged conflict was extremely costly to England, it had to be continued in the hope of capturing a substantial treasure ship to produce much-needed revenue for Elizabeth's kingdom; for example, a vessel such as the *Madre de Dios* which conveniently fell into English hands with a very valuable cargo in 1592. This was a highly unorthodox and unsatisfactory way of improving the country's financial affairs, and it was not surprising that the tidy-minded Robert Cecil speedily concluded a peace treaty with Spain shortly after the Queen had died in 1603. The Spaniards had been equally anxious to conclude hostilities and relationships between the two countries soon improved to a point where James I's son, later Charles I, was able to journey to Madrid to woo the Spanish King's daughter.

War had also dragged on in both the Netherlands and France, where the Queen's forces under Lord Willoughby were supporting the Huguenot king Henry IV after his predecessor Henry III had been assassinated by a monk in 1589. English troops fought ineffectively against Spanish soldiers in Normandy and Brittany. Among their number was the Earl of Essex, who childishly saw war as a glorious game to be pursued energetically in all directions regardless of the real military objectives. This campaign ended abruptly when the French King converted to Catholicism and made peace with Spain. His airy comment, 'Paris is well worth a mass',[33] must go down as one of history's more cynical exit lines. The Queen then made one of her rare major mistakes in appointing Essex as her commander in the long-running war with Ireland. Military reputations disappeared in the Irish bog with monotonous regularity and fearful atrocities were committed which produced the lasting legacy of our time. The following description of the actions of one Elizabethan officer in the late sixteenth century would now land him in front of a war crimes tribunal:

> . . . his manner was that the heads of all those which were killed in the day should be cut off from their bodies and brought to the place where he encamped at night and should be laid on the ground by each side of the way leading to his own tent so none could come into his tent for any cause but commonly he must pass through a line of heads which he used ad terroram, the dead feeling nothing the more pains thereby and yet it did bring greater terror to the people when they saw the heads of their dead fathers, brothers, kinsfolk and friends lie on the ground before their faces when they came to speak with the said Colonel.[34]

Even in the brutal world of the late sixteenth century, the conduct of the English troops in Ireland was particularly barbaric.

Essex floundered around Ireland in fruitless pursuit of the rebel leader Tyrone. The Earl became progressively more angry and disillusioned with the Queen's apparent lack of interest in his endeavours and unexpectedly returned to England without permission, bursting in on the Queen unannounced while she was still in her nightgown, looking decidedly unregal. The Earl's ill-considered action was highly embarrassing to Elizabeth and signalled the beginning of the end for the Queen's last great favourite in the final years of her reign.

Elizabeth was invariably quick to face up to her mistakes and Essex was speedily replaced as her commander in Ireland by his one-time friend and colleague in arms, Sir Charles Blount. They had previously campaigned together and Blount had been on Essex's ill-fated Islands Voyage in 1597, the Earl's sister, Lady Penelope Rich, being at one time Blount's mistress. Blount had now become Lord Mountjoy. He had first served under the Earl of Leicester at the age of fifteen in the Low Countries, had fought with 'Black John' Norris in France and been a member of the English fleet which overcame the Armada.

Appointing Mountjoy to take charge of her military effort in Ireland heralded a return of the Queen's instinctive ability to pick good men to undertake difficult tasks on her behalf. First, he defeated a substantial Spanish invasion force in Munster during 1601 and following three years' relentless effort, he was able to flush Tyrone and his troops out into the open for a decisive battle near Kinsale, where the rebel leader was comprehensively defeated. Peace was finally restored in Ireland after many years of bloody but inconclusive conflict, there having been 'an Irish problem' for the English since Norman times. Elizabeth had given Mountjoy her unswerving support throughout his arduous campaign. Thus it was sad that the news of his triumph was received in England several days after the Queen's death. Mountjoy later became the Earl of Devonshire and married Lettice Knollys, the attractive widow of the Earl of Leicester.

These numerous long-running conflicts involving English forces both on land and sea inevitably took a heavy toll on Elizabeth's men at war, as one by one they were struck down in battle. Grenville died on his ship *The Revenge*, while single-handedly engaging an entire Spanish fleet off the Azores in 1591; Frobisher was mortally wounded when storming a Spanish-held fort in Brittany the following year. The greatest of the Queen's sea captains, Hawkins and Drake, both perished on the Spanish Main some four years later. Thus in a period of barely five years Elizabeth had lost the services of almost all her most capable combat veterans. The professionals were gone, leaving only gentlemen playing at soldiers, the likes of Ralegh and Cumberland, who fought the good fight with rather more enthusiasm than skill.

The glory days were well and truly over for Elizabeth's men at arms. The English sovereign had lost most of her outstanding sword-bearers along with her most eminent statesmen, all dead and gone, no longer serving Queen and country. Time was also running out for Elizabeth – the Tudor age was finally drawing to a close, as its last and arguably most able monarch lay dying at her favourite palace at Richmond:

This yeere Queene Elizabeth departed this mortall life at Richemonde, the xxiiijth daie of March and in the morninge and that same daie by nyne of the clocke James the Kinge of Scotlande was pclaimed in London to be oure Kinge . . . at which tyme here was great trivmphe with Bondfiers, gunnes and ringinge of bells with other kinds of musicke.[35]

The Queen was dead. Long live the King.

NOTES

ABBREVIATIONS

BL   British Library
CSPD   *Calendar of State Papers, Domestic Series*
CSPF   *Calendar of State Papers, Foreign Series*
CSPSc. *Calendar of State Papers, relating to Scotland*
CSPSp. *Calendar of State Papers, Spanish*
CSPV   *Calendar of State Papers, Venetian*
HMC   Historical Manuscripts Commission
MSS   Manuscripts
PRO   Public Record Office, Kew
SP   State Papers in the Public Record Office, Kew

1. The Tudor Kingdom

1. *Sudeley Castle and Gardens*, 'A Queen's Castle'. By kind permission of Lady Ashcombe.
2. *CSPD*, 11/4, number 1.
3. Foxe, *Acts and Monuments*, 1877 edn, Vol. VIII, p. 610.
4. *CSPD*, 1547–80, Vol. III, p. 61.
5. Foxe, *Acts and Monuments*, 1562–3, 1570 edn, p. 1937.
6. Harington, *Nugae Antiquae*, Vol. II, p. 15.
7. Naunton, *Fragmenta Regalia*, p. 7.

2. At the Royal Court

1. Harington, *Nugae Antiquae*, Vol. 1, p. 358.
2. *Penshurst Place and Gardens*, p. 11. By kind permission of Viscount de L'Isle.
3. Harington, *Nugae Antiquae*, Vol. I, p. 362.
4. *CSPF*, XX1(3), p. 233.
5. Naunton, *Fragmenta Regalia*, p. 109.

6. Fuller, *History of the Worthies of England*, 1662.
7. Naunton, *Fragmenta Regalia*, p. 109.
8. PRO, 13/280/82.
9. Dekker, 'Old Fortunatus'.
10. de Maisse, *Journal*, p. 95.
11. d'Ewes, *Journal of all the Parliaments during the reign of Queen Elizabeth*, 1693 edn.
12. *CSPD*, Vol. CCLXIV, p. 474.
13. de Maisse, *Journal*, p. 59.
14. *Hampton Court Palace*, p. 11. By kind permission of Historic Royal Palaces.
15. de Maisse, *Journal*, p. 11.
16. Ibid., p. 3.
17. Ibid.
18. William Shakespeare, *Henry the Fifth*, Chorus, Act I.

3. Portrait of a Queen

1. *CSPV*, 1556–7, p. 1058.
2. Naunton, *Fragmenta Regalia*, p. 10.
3. *CSPSp.*, Vol. I, p. 263.
4. Ibid.
5. Ibid.

6. *CSPD*, Vol. CLIX, p. 98, March 1583.
7. Ibid., Vol. CCXXIV, p. 601.
8. de Maisse, *Journal*, p. 93.
9. *CSPV*, 1581–91, Vol. VIII, pp. 344–5.

4. The Statesmen

1. Harington, *Nugae Antique*, Vol. I, p. 67.
2. Ibid., pp. 86–7.
3. Chamberlain, *Sayings of Queen Elizabeth*, 1923.
4. Talbot, MSS, Longleat.
5. Naunton, *Fragmenta Regalia*, p. 49.
6. de Maisse, *Journal*, p. 3.
7. Camden, *Annals*.
8. Haigh, *The Reign of Elizabeth I*, p. 77.
9. *CSPD*, 1586 Vol. CXCV, p. 372.
10. Ibid., Vol. CCVIII, p. 457.
11. Ibid., Vol. CCIII, p. 414.
12. *Caquets de l'Accouchée*, 1621. Attributed to Henry IV of France in conversation with his minister Sully.
13. *CSPD*, Vol. CCI, p. 414.
14. de Maisse, *Journal*, p. 80.
15. Ibid., Addenda, Vol. XXX, p. 241.
16. BL, Harleian, MSS, p. 133.
17. *CSPD*, Vol. CCLXXXVII, p. 241.
18. Haigh, *The Reign of Elizabeth I*, p. 26.
19. PRO, SP, 12/278/23.
20. *CSPD*, Vol. CCLXXXVII, p. 298.
21. Ibid.
22. Ibid.
23. Green, *A Short History of English People*, 1874, ch. VII.

5. The Seafarers

1. Corbett, *Drake and the Tudor Navy*, Vol. I, p. 78.
2. Ibid., p. 400.
3. PRO, SP. Dom., 10–15–13.

4. Corbett, *Drake and the Tudor Navy*, Vol. I.
5. Ibid.
6. Ibid., Vol. 2, p. 391.
7. Ibid.
8. CSPSp., 1580–86, Vol. 3, p. 75.
9. Bacon, *Considerations Touching a War with Spain*, 1629.
10. *CSPD*, Vol. CCXIV, p. 528.
11. Ibid.
12. Ibid., Vol. CCXXIV, p. 600.
13. Ibid., p. 595.
14. Laughton, 'Armada Papers', Vol. 2, p. 62.
15. *CSPD*, Vol. CCLIII, p. 91.
16. Corbett, *Drake and the Tudor Navy*, Vol. 2, p. 400.
17. Ibid.
18. Laughton, 'Armada Papers', Vol. 2, p. 3.
19. Corbett, *Drake and the Tudor Navy*, Vol. 2, p. 361.
20. Ibid., p. 362.
21. Hakluyt, *Principal Navigations*, Vol. VII, p. 218.
22. Ibid., p. 248.
23. Duro, *La Armada Invencible*, Vol. I, p. 13.
24. *CSPD*, Vol. CCXI, p. 488.
25. Brandon, *Plymouth Armada Heroes*, p. 90.
26. Laughton, 'Armada Papers', Vol. 1, p. 256.
27. Ibid., p. 190.
28. Ibid., p. 202.
29. Ibid., p. 274.
30. Ibid., p. 288.

6. The Explorers

1. Hakluyt, *Principal Navigations*, Vol. II, p. 457.
2. Ibid., Vol. III, p. 196.
3. Ibid., Vol. II, p. 336.
4. Ibid., p. 246.
5. Ibid., Vol. VII, pp. 211–12.

6. Ibid., p. 214.
7. Ibid., p. 220.
8. Ibid., pp. 217–18
9. National Trust, *Compton Castle*, pp. 26–7. By kind permission of the National Trust.
10. Hakluyt, *Principal Navigations*, Vol. VIII, p. 67.
11. Ibid., p. 74.
12. Ibid., p. 75.
13. Ibid., p. 310.
14. Ibid., Vol. X, p. 63.
15. Ibid., Vol. VII, p. 204.
16. Ibid., Vol. XI, p. 293.
17. Ibid., p. 392.
18. Ibid., Vol. VII, p. 230.
19. Ibid., Vol. XI, p. 116.
20. Ibid., Vol. VI, p. 156.
21. Ibid., pp. 164–5.
22. Ibid., Vol. XI, p. 23.
23. Ibid., Vol. VI, p. 176.
24. Corbett, *Drake and the Tudor Navy*, Vol. I, p. 118.
25. Worth, *Calendar of the Plymouth Municipal Records* ('The Black Book').
26. Hakluyt, *Principal Navigations*, Vol. XI, p. 101.
27. Ibid.
28. Ibid., p. 110.
29. Ibid., p. 111.
30. Ibid., p. 123.
31. Housed in the Library of the University of California.
32. Hakluyt, *Principal Navigations*, Vol. XI, p. 129.
33. Ibid., p. 132.
34. *CSPSp.*, Vol. III, p. 28.
35. National Trust, *Compton Castle*, p. 28.
36. Navy Records Society (1898), Vol. II, p. 134.

7. The Suitors

1. *CSPV*, 1581–91, Vol. VIII, pp. 344–5.
2. *CSPD*, 14, p. 190.
3. Ibid., Vol. CCXV, p. 538.
4. Ibid., Vol. CXCIV, p. 362.
5. *CSPF*, Vol. VII, p. 21.
6. *CSPSp.*, 1580–86, p. 226.
7. Ibid.
8. Naunton, *Framenta Regalia*, p. 9.
9. *CSPD*, Vol. CXLVIII, p. 12.
10. *Memorials of the Bagot Family*, p. 39.

8. Men of God

1. Dobson, *The Jewel of Salisbury*, p. 9.
2. *CSPV*, Vol. VII, pp. 22–3.
3. Spedding, *Works of Francis Bacon*, 1862, Vol. 8, p. 98.
4. *CSPD*, 1547–80, p. 48.
5. Ibid., Vol. 7. p. 142.
6. Count Feria Don Gomez Suarez de Figueroa.
7. Harington, *Nugae Antiquae*, Vol. II, ch. 4.
8. PRO, SP, 12/113/17.
9. de Maisse, *Journal*, p. 22.
10. Bishop John Jewel, *An Apology of the Church of England*, 1562.
11. Dobson, *The Jewel of Salisbury*, p. 4.
12. Ibid., p. 12.
13. Ibid., p. 15.
14. Ibid., p. 19.
15. The Right Reverend David S. Stancliffe, Bishop of Salisbury, introduction to Dobson's *The Jewel of Salisbury*.
16. Hooker, *The Laws of Ecclesiastical Polity*.
17. Ibid.

9. The Scholars

1. Ascham, *English Works*, London, 1761.
2. Ibid.
3. Aubrey, *Lives of Eminent Men*, 1813.

4. Bacon, 'Essays', 1625.
5. Hakluyt, *Principal Navigations*, dedication to Sir Francis Walsingham, 1st edn.
6. Ibid., Vol. IX, p. 398.
7. Bacon, *Advancement of Learning*.
8. Pope, *An Essay on Man*, Epistle 4 (1734).
9. Camden, *Britannia*, p. 57.
10. Trevelyan, *Trinity College, an Historical Sketch*, p. 21. Courtesy of Trinity College Library.
11. Ibid.
12. Rowse, *The England of Elizabeth*, p. 531.

10. Cambridge Connections

1. Rowse, *The England of Elizabeth*, p. 515.
2. Trevelyan, *Trinity College, an Historical Sketch*, p. 18.

11. The Creators

1. de Maisse, *Journal*, p. 21.
2. Archives of Penshurst Place. By kind permission of Viscount de L'Isle.
3. Records of the building of Longleat, The Thynne Papers, Vol. 3, p. 61.
4. Camden, *Britannia*.
5. William Shakespeare, *Richard III*, Act 1, Scene 1.
6. Dr Robin Robbins, Wadham College, Oxford, 3 March 1999.
7. Gildon, *The Works of Mr William Shakespear*, 1710, Vol. VII, p. 291.
8. Ryan, *Dramatic Table Talk*, 1825, Vol. II, pp. 156–7.
9. Spenser, *Prothalamion*, 1596.
10. Birch, *The Life of Mr Edmund Spenser*, 1751.

11. Donne, *Go and Catch a Falling Star*.
12. Drayton, *Polyolbion*.
13. Brochure, *Penshurst Place and Gardens*, p. 13.
14. Ibid.
15. d'Ewes, 'The Golden Speech', 1601, *The Journals of all the Parliaments during the reign of Queen Elizabeth*, 1682, p. 659.

12. Men at War

1. CSPD, Vol. CXCIV. p. 362.
2. Corbett, *Papers relating to the Navy during the Spanish War, 1585–87*, p. 104.
3. Ibid., p. 101
4. Worth, *Calendar of the Plymouth Municipal Records* ('The Black Book').
5. Ibid.
6. Laughton, 'Armada Papers', Vol. I. p. 205.
7. HMC, MSS of the Marquess of Bath, Vol. II, p. 28.
8. Duro, *La Armada Invencible*.
9. *CSPD*, Vol. CCXIII, p. 511.
10. Ibid., p. 513.
11. Ibid., Vol. CCXI, p. 492.
12. Ibid.
13. Laughton, 'Armada Papers', Vol. I, p. 192.
14. Ibid., p. 204.
15. Corbett *Drake and the Tudor Navy*, Vol. II, p. 176.
16. *CSPD*, Vol. CCXII, p. 507.
17. Camden, *Annals*, p. 411.
18. *CSPD*, Vol. CCXIII, p. 517.
19. Ibid., Vol. CCXIV, p. 522.
20. Ibid., Vol. CCXIII, p. 516.
21. Ibid., Vol. CCXII, p. 508.
22. Somers, *A Third Collection of Scarce and Valuable Tracts*, 1751, p. 196.
23. *CSPD*, Vol. CCXIII, p. 517.

24. Ibid., Vol. CCXVI, p. 543.
25. Laughton, 'Armada Papers', Vol. II, p. 286.
26. Balthasar Porreno, *Biographer of King Philip the Second of Spain.*
27. *CSPD*, Vol. CCXIV, p. 529
28. Ibid., p. 527.
29. Laughton, 'Armada Papers', Vol. II, p. 69.
30. *CSPD*, Vol. CCXV, p. 533.
31. Duro, *La Armada Invencible,* Vol. II, p. 296.
32. Emanuel van Meteren, *History of the Low Countries.*
33. *Caquets de l'Accouchée,* 1622. Henry IV in conversation with his minister, Sully.
34. Churchyard, *General Rehearsals of War,* 1579.
35. Worth, *Calendar of the Plymouth Municipal Records* ('The Black Book').

BIBLIOGRAPHY

Ascham, Roger, *English Works, of Roger Ascham*, London, 1761
Aubrey, John, *Lives of Eminent Men*, 1813
Beckinsale, B.W., *Burghley, Tudor Statesman*, 1967
Birch, Thomas, *The Life of Mr Edmund Spenser*, 1751
Black, J.B., *The Reign of Elizabeth*, OUP, Oxford, 1936
Brandon, William, *Plymouth Armada Heroes*
Calendar of State Papers, Domestic Series, ed. Robert Lemon, 1856–77
Calendar of State Papers relating to Mary Queen of Scots, ed. Joseph Bain, Edinburgh, 1898
Calendar of State Papers relating to English Affairs, in the Archives of Simancas, ed. Martin Hume, 1892–9
Calendar of State Papers, Foreign Series, ed. Arthur John Butler, 1907–14
Calendar of State Papers in the Archives of Venice, ed. Rawdon Brown, 1864–98
Camden, William, *Annals of Queen Elizabeth*, 1616
Chamberlain, F., *Sayings of Queen Elizabeth*, 1923
Churchill, Winston, S., *A History of the English-Speaking Peoples*, Volume II, 'The New World', Cassell & Company, 1956
Churchyard, Thomas, *General Rehearsals of War*, 1579
Corbett, Julian, *Drake and the Tudor Navy*, 2 vols, Longmans Green, 1898
——, *Papers Relating to the Navy During the Spanish War, 1585–1587*, Navy Records Society, 1898
Dobson, Clifford, B., *The Jewel of Salisbury*, R.J.L. Smith & Associates for the Dean and Chapter of Salisbury Cathedral, Much Wenlock, 1996
Duro, Cesareo Fernandez, *La Armada Invencible*, 2 vols, Madrid, 1884
d'Ewes, Simonds, *The Journals of all the Parliaments during the reign of Queen Elizabeth*, 1682
Foxe, John, *Acts and Monuments*, 4th edn, 1877
Fuller, Reverend Thomas, *History of the Worthies of England*, 1662
Gildon, Charles, *The Works of Mr William Shakespear*, 1710
Girouard, Mark, *Robert Smythson & The Elizabethan Country House*, Yale University Press, New Haven & London, 1983
——, *Robert Smythson & the Architecture of the Elizabethan Era*, Yale University Press, New Haven & London, 1967
Green, *A Short History of the English People*, 1874
Haigh, Christopher, *The Reign Of Elizabeth I*, ed. Christopher Haigh, Macmillan Publishers Ltd, Basingstoke, 1984
Haigh, Christopher, *Elizabeth I*, 2nd edn, Addison Wesley Longman Ltd, 1988
Hakluyt, Richard, *Principal Navigations, Voyages, Traffiques and Discoveries of the English Nation*, 1903

Hale, John Richard, *The Story of the Great Armada*, Thomas Nelson & Sons Ltd

Harington, John, *Nugae Antiquae*, 2 vols, ed. Henry Harington, 1836

Hibbert, Christopher, *The Virgin Queen*, Penguin Books, 1990

Honan, Park, *Shakespeare, A Life*, OUP, Oxford, 1998

Jewel, Bishop John, *An Apology of the Church of England*, 1562

Kelsey, Harry, *Sir Francis Drake, The Queen's Pirate*, Yale University Press, New Haven & London, 1998

Laughton, John Knox, *State Papers relating to the defeat of the Spanish Armada* (the 'Armada Papers'), Navy Records Society, Vols 1 and 2, 1894

MacCaffrey, Wallace, *Elizabeth I*, Edward Arnold, 1993

de Maisse, André Hurault, *A Journal of all that was accomplished by Monsieur de Maisse, Ambassador in England from King Henri IV to Queen Elizabeth, 1597*, ed. and tr. G.B. Harrison and R.A. Jones, 1931

Manningham, John, *Diary of John Manningham*, Camden Society, 1868

Marshall, Rosalind K., *Elizabeth I*, HMSO, 1991

Martin, Colin and Parker, Geoffrey, *The Spanish Armada*, Penguin Books, 1989

Mattingly, Garrett, *The Defeat of the Spanish Armada*, Cape, 1959

Naunton, Robert, *Fragmenta Regalia*, 1824

Read, Conyers, *Lord Burghley and Queen Elizabeth*, Cape, 1960

——, *Mr Secretary Walsingham and the Policy of Queen Elizabeth*, 3 vols, Cambridge, Mass., 1925

——, *Mr Secretary Cecil and Queen Elizabeth*, Cape, 1967

Rowse, A.L., *The England of Elizabeth*, Macmillan & Co., 1950

——, *Eminent Elizabethans*, Macmillan & Co., 1983

Ryan, Richard, *Dramatic Table Talk*, 1828

Schoenbaum, S. *William Shakespeare, A Documentary Life*, The Clarendon Press, Oxford, 1975

Somers, Lord, *A Third Collection of Scarce and Valuable Tracts*, 1751

Somerset, Anne, *Elizabeth I*, Weidenfeld & Nicolson, 1991

Starkey, David (ed.), *The English Court from the War of the Roses to the Civil War*, Longman, 1987

Stow, John, *Annals*, 1631

Strong, Roy, *Gloriana, The Portraits of Queen Elizabeth*, Thames and Hudson, 1987

——, *The Elizabethan Image*, The Tate Gallery, 1969

Trevelyan, G.M., *Trinity College, An Historical Sketch*, Cambridge Trinity College, 1983

Williams, Neville, *All the Queen's Men*, Weidenfeld & Nicolson, 1972

Williamson, J.A., *The Age of Drake*, Black, 1938

——, *Hawkins of Plymouth*, Black, 1968

Winter, Carl, *Elizabethan Miniatures*, Penguin Books, 1955

Winton, J., *Sir Walter Ralegh*, Michael Joseph, 1975

Worth, R.N., *Calendar of Plymouth Municipal Records* ('The Black Book'), William Brendon & Sons, 1893

INDEX

Bold numbers indicate main or significant entries.

Act of Supremacy 117, 124
Act of Uniformity 117, 119, 124
Alençon, François, Duke of **103–6**, 172
Allen, Cardinal 124
Alva, Duke of 153, 171
Anne of Cleves 3
architecture **14**, **25–6**, **154–8**
Ark Royal (ship) 66, 175, 178
Armada *see* Spanish Armada
Armada Portrait, the 32, 45, 154
Arundel, Earl of 44, 96, 115
Ascham, Roger 15, 114, 129, **130–2**, 146
Ashley, Kat 5, 23, 24, 108–9
Aubrey, John 133
Audley, Lord Thomas 139
Azores 68, 72, 176, 185

Babington Plot 57
Bacon, Anthony 135, 142, 146
Bacon, Francis 27, 58, 61, **135–6**, 141, 142, 165, 167
quoted 46, 115, 133, 135
Bacon, Lady 126
Bacon, Sir Nicholas 44, 46, 135, 146
Beaufort, Lady Margaret 147
Bedford, Francis Russell, Earl of 44, 45, 140
Bedingfield, Sir Henry 10
Bertendona, Martin de 71
Bess of Hardwick 9, 158
Bible 158–9
Blois Château 14
Bodley, Thomas 138
Boleyn, Anne 3, 12, 20, 116
Borrough, William 73
Bosworth, battle of 1, 2, 47
Bothwell, James Hepburn, Earl of 99
Bray, Vicar of 118

Bruno, Giordano 137
Brydges, Sir John (Lord Chandos) 8
Buckland Abbey 70, 92
Bull, Dr John 29, 39, 142, 151
Burbage, James 162
Burbage, Richard 161
Burghley House 47, 156
Burghley, William Cecil, Lord
    14–15, 26, 34, 37, **46–9**, 57, 58, 130
    cultural life 94, 113, 131, 135, 136, 141, 146
    and Elizabeth 56, 59–60, 96, 100, 104
    quoted 64, 164
    also mentioned 19, 21, 23, 24, 31, 39, 44, 50, 65, 90, 118, 120, 122, 178
Byrd, William 29, 39, 115

Cabot, John 76–7
Cabot, Sebastian 77
Cadiz 72, 73, 173–4, 185
Caius, Dr 139
Calais 14
Calvin, Jean 113, 118
Cambridge University 113, 115, **138–41**, **145–50**
    Emmanuel College 139, 149
    Gonville and Caius College 139
    King's College Chapel 141
    Magdalene College 139, 149
    Queen's College 145
    St John's College 146, 147, 149
    Sidney Sussex College 139, 148, 149
    Trinity College **129–30**, **139–41**, 145, 147–8, 149–50
Camden, William 26, 104, **136–7**, 167, 180

Campion, Edmund 124, **125**, 146
Canada 79, 93
Cartier, Jacques 78, 134
cartography 94
Cartwright, Thomas 123, 124, 147
Catherine of Aragon 2, 3, 12, 97
Catherine de Medici 14, 35, 36, 87, 97, 103
Cavendish, Thomas 93
Cecil, David 47
Cecil family 2
Cecil, Sir Robert 21, 24, 40–1, 53, **59–62**, 146, 152, 153, 157, 185
    quoted 31, 181
Cecil, Sir William *see* Burghley
Cervantes, Miguel de 167, 176, 184
Chambord Château 14
Chancellor, Richard 73, 77, 78
Charles, Archduke of Austria 96, 98
Charles I of England 168, 185
Charles II of England 184
Charles IX of France 103
Charles V of Spain 14
Cheke, Mary 130
Cheke, Sir John 130, 146
Chenonceau Château 14
Church of England
    Elizabeth and **112–28**
    Henry VIII breaks with Rome 2–3, 112
Church of Scotland 113, **118–19**
Clement VII, Pope 2, 3
Clifford, George *see* Cumberland
Cobham, Lady Frances 22, 23, 103
Cobham, Lord Henry 22, 25
Coke, Sir Edward 135, 146
Columbus, Christopher 2, 76, 78
Copernicus, Nicholaus 137
Corsham Court 110, 156
Courtenay, Edward *see* Devon
Coverdale, Miles 113, 116
Cranmer, Archbishop Thomas 10, 11, 113, 145, 147
Critz, John de 54, 60, 152, 153
Croft, Sir James 8–9, 9, 115
Cromwell, Oliver 119, 131, 139, 148
Cromwell, Thomas 3, 4, 130
Cumberland, George Clifford, Earl of 28, 73, 149, 187

Darnley, Henry Stuart, Lord 99
Davis, John 73, 93
Davison, William 57
de Vere, Edward *see* Oxford
Dee, Dr John **132–3**, 149
Dekker, Thomas 28, 161
Delight (ship) 83
Devereux, Robert *see* Essex
Devon, Edward Courtenay, Earl of 7, 10
Devonshire, Charles Blount, Earl of 186–7
Ditchley Portrait, the 27, 152
Donne, John 142, 165
Doughty, Thomas 90
Drake, Sir Francis 63–4, **66–71**, 73, 78, 79–80, 85, 86, **87–93**, 95, 153, 170, **173–5**, 176, **177–9**, 185, 187
Drayton, Michael 165
Dryden, John 168
Dudley, John *see* Northumberland
Dudley, Lord Guildford 6
Dudley, Robert *see* Leicester

education 143
Edward III of England 129
Edward IV of England 1
Edward VI of England 3, 4, 6, 45
Egerton, Sir Thomas 165
Elizabeth I of England
    character 15–16, 17–18, 30–1, 32, 34–6, **37–43**, 46, 181
    cult of Gloriana 27, 28, 108, 149
    death 187
    early years **3–11**, **14–16**
    education 129, **130**
    love of arts 29–30, 151, **161–2**, **168–9**
    marriage intentions 37, 96–111
    portraits 32, 33–4, 40, 110–11, 145, 152, 154
    religion **112–28**
    smallpox 36–7
English language 169
Erasmus 137, 145, 146
Eric XIV of Sweden 96, 98
Ermine Portrait, The 32, 40, 154
Essex, 1st Earl of 102
Essex, Robert Devereux, 2nd Earl of

21, 24, 27–8, **58–9**, 135, 141, 146
downfall 18, 21, 39, **61**, 151
and Elizabeth 18, 102, 110, 111, 162–3
naval exploits 68, 73, 185, 185–6
portraits 45
Eworth, Hans 13, 33, 129–30

Fenelon, Bertrand de 31
Fenner, Thomas 72–3
Fenton, Edward 73, 174
Ferdinand I, Emperor 98
Ferdinand of Spain 2, 78
Fisher, Bishop John 146–7
Fitton, Lady Mary 23, 166
Fitzroy, Henry 109
Fitzwilliam, Sir William 182
Fletcher, Francis 90
Fletcher, John 163, 164
Foxe, John 113
France 2, 13–14, 30, 31, 54, 155, 185–6
    Elizabeth's French suitors **103–7**
François I of France 14, 30, 78, 155
François II of France 99, 103
Frobisher, Sir Martin 68, **72**, 73, 74, **79–81**, 132, 187

Galileo Galilei 137
Gama, Vasco da 2, 76, 78
Gardiner, Bishop Stephen 9
Gerard, John 124, 125
Gheeraerts, Marcus, the Younger 27–8, 40, 145, 152, 153
Gilbert, Sir Humphrey **81–3**, 93–4, 132, 141
Globe Theatre 161, 164
Golden Hind (ship) 83, 89–92 *passim*
Gower, George 32, 45, 102, 153, 154
Greene, Robert 149, 160
Greenwich Palace 25, 26
Gregorian calendar 133
Grenville, Roger 70
Grenville, Sir Richard **70–2**, 92, 93, 187
Gresham College 142
Gresham, Sir Thomas 142
Grey, Lady Jane 6, 7, 79
Grey, Lady Mary 23

Grindal, Archbishop Edward 113, **120–3**, 133, 147, 148
Grindal, William 15, 130, 146

Hakluyt, Richard 132, **133–5**, 167
Hampton Court Palace 4, 25, 26, 32
Hardwick Hall 9, 156, 157–8
Harington, Sir John 18, 149
Harvard, John 139
Hatfield House 6, 10, 14–15, 31, 153
Hatton, Sir Christopher 18, 30, **52–3**, 56, 58, 89, 102–3, 105–6, 110, 141, 142, 156
Hawkins, Sir John **63–6**, 69, 74, 85, 86, 87, 88, 170, 174–6, 180, 182–3, 187
Hawkins, William 63, 87
Hawkins, William Jr. 89, 180
Heneage, Sir Thomas 22, 102, 110
Henry II of France 14, 97, 97–8
Henry III of France (Duke of Anjou) 19, 103, 185
Henry IV of France 57, 185–6
Henry the Navigator 78
Henry VII of England (Tudor) 1–2, 47, 76–7
Henry VIII of England **2–5**, 5, 30, 44, 70, 77, 109, 112, 129, 155
    portraits/statue 129–30, 168
Hilliard, Nicholas 28, 41, **152–4**, 157
Holbein, Hans 129–30, 153
Holy Roman Empire 2
Hooker, Richard 126, **128**
Howard, Catherine 3
Howard, Charles, Lord Howard of Effingham 44, 66, **72–5**, 134, **176–85** *passim*
Howard, Lady Margaret 22
Howard, Lord Thomas *see* Norfolk
Howard, Lord William 9
Hunsdon, Lord George 58, 149
Hunsdon, Lord Henry 24, 58, 65, 152, 161

Inns of Court 142
Ireland 51, 182, **186–7**
Ivan the Terrible, Tsar 77, 96

James I and VI 30, 57, 61, 148, 154, 157, 187

Jenkinson, Anthony 73, 77, 78, 132
Jesuits **124–6**, 146
Jewel, Bishop John 126–8
Jones, Inigo 155, 157, 158, 169
Jonson, Ben 161, 163, 164

Kenilworth Castle 156
Keys, Thomas 23
Knollys, Sir Francis 39, 45, 58, 102
Knollys, Lettice 102, 104, 154, 187
Knox, John 40, 113, 118–19
Kyd, Thomas 161, 164

Latimer, Bishop Hugh **10–11**, 113,
    127
Laud, Archbishop William 139
Lee, Laurie 165
Lee, Sir Henry 27–8, 152
Lee, Thomas 28
Leicester, Robert Dudley, Earl of 6,
    21, 24, **99–102**, 111, 141, 156,
    171–2, 181
    death 58, 183
    and Elizabeth 29–30, 36–7, 52–3,
        108, 110
    and Mary Queen of Scots 97
    portraits 152, 153
    Privy Councillor 49–50, 56, 87, 89,
        104
    quoted 18, 178
    and theatre 151–2, 161–2
Leonardo da Vinci 14, 155
Lepanto, Battle of 176
Lincoln, Lord 65, 89
literature **169**
    see also poetry; theatre
Longleat 156, 157–8
Louis XI of France 2
Lovell, Humphrey 157
Lulworth Castle 158
Luther, Martin 40, 113
Lyminge, Robert 157

Madre de Dios (ship) 185
Magellan, Ferdinand 2, 78
Maisse, André de 29, 31–2, 42–3, 154
Marlowe, Christopher 55, 149, 161,
    163–4
Marprelate tracts 123
martyrs **10–12**, 113, **124–5**, 127

Mary I (Tudor) of England **10–15**, 35,
    42, 44, 97, 129
    and young Elizabeth 3, 6–7
Mary, Queen of Scots 30, 35, **56–7**,
    97, **98–9**, 107, 118, 171, 173
Mary Rose (ship) 70
Maximilian I, Emperor 2, 132
Medina Sidonia, Alonso, Duke of 177,
    179, 181, 183–4
Mendoza, Bernardino de 31, 67, 92,
    105, 107
Mercator, Gerardus 94, 132
Mexico 64, 84
Middleton, Thomas 163, 164
Mildmay, Sir Walter 25, 57, 58, 65,
    131, 138, 149
Millais, Sir John Everett 84
Milton, John 137, 149, 168
Montacute House 158
Mor, Antonio 13
More, Sir Thomas 4, 8, 137, 148,
    159
Muelen, Steven van der 98, 101, 152

Napoleon Bonaparte 178
Nashe, Thomas 148, 160
Nelson, Lord Horatio 79, 177
Netherlands 14, 106, 152, 153,
    171–3, 184, 185
Nevile, Thomas **140**, 148
Neville family 52
'New Learning' 137, 146
Newman, Mary 92
Newton, Sir Isaac 141, 148
Nonpareil (ship) 72
Nonsuch Palace 26, 171
Norfolk, Thomas Howard, Duke of
    49, 66, 73
Norris, Henry 20
Norris, Sir John 18, 39, 68, 171, 185
North America 2, **78–9**, **82–4**, **91**
Northeast passage 77
Northumberland, John Dudley, Duke
    of 6, 48
Northwest passage 72, 80, 92, 93
Nottingham, Charles Howard, Earl of
    9–10
Nuestra Señora de la Concepciòn
    (ship) 90
Nuestra Señora del Rosario (ship) 68

Ogelthorpe, Bishop 114
Oliver, Isaac 152, 153
Ortelius, Abraham 94, 132
Ottoman Empire 77
Owen, Wilfred 166
Oxford, Edward de Vere, Earl of 18, 23, 30, 102–3, 110, 115, 146
Oxford University 126, 127, 131, **138**, 141, 145–6, 148
  Bodleian Library 49, 138

Panama 69, 70
Parker, Archbishop Matthew 113, **115–16**, 117, 120
Parker, Margaret 120
Parma, Alexander Farnese, Duke of 171, 176, 177, 180–1
Parr, Anne 45
Parr, Katherine **4–5**, 107, 113, 114, 129, 130
Parry, Blanche 23, 24
Parry, Thomas 24
Parsons, Robert 124
Peake, Robert 153, 154
Pembroke, Mary, Countess of 165
Pembroke, William Herbert, 1st Earl of 44, 45, 87
Pembroke, William Herbert, 3rd Earl of 23, 166
Penshurst Place 29, 157
Percy family 52
Petrach 159
Petre, Sir William 44
Philip II of Spain 14, 40, 54, 67, 92, 168
  and Armada 115, 177, 182, 184, 185
  and Elizabeth 96, 97, 107, 170
  and Mary Tudor 6, 12
  portraits 45
Pickering, Sir William 96
Pizarro, Francisco 78, 84
Plymouth 85–8 *passim*, 92, 179, 180
poetry **165–6**
Poitiers, Diane de 14, 97
Pole, Cardinal Reginald 115, 117, 148
Pope, Aklexander 136
Portugal 68, 72, 78–9, 106, 177, 185

Presbyterianism **118–19**, 147
Privy Council **34**, **44**, 115, 123, 141, 146, 170–1
prophesying **121–2**
public schools 143, 150
Puritanism 40, 119, 120, 122, 123–4, 131, 139, 147, 151, 161

Quadra, Alvaro de la 36
'Queen's Men' (actors) 162

Rainbow Portrait, the 40, 153
Ralegh, Sir Walter 18, 19, 22, 101, 132, 142, 150
  and Elizabeth **21**, **53–4**, 93–4, 110
  naval career 63, 70–1, 72, **83–4**, 92, 175, 185, 187
Ralegh, Walter (author) 134
Recalde, Juan Martinez de 73
Reformation *see* Church of England; Church of Scotland
Renaissance 2, 138, 143, 146, 155
Revenge (ship) 65, 71–2, 187
Richard III of England 1, 47, 59
Richmond Palace 26, 187
Ridley, Bishop Nicholas **10–11**, 113, 127, 145, 147
Ridolfi Plot 50, 57
Robsart, Amy 99, 101
Roman Catholicism 11–12, 39–40, 107, **124–6**, 138
Rowse, A.L. 41, 146
Russell, Bertrand 140
Russia 77, 96

Sackville, Sir Richard 44, 131
St Bartholomew's Day Massacre 31, 54
St Loe, Sir William 8, 9
Salisbury, Countess of 12
San Felipe (ship) 174
San Juan de Ulua 64, 66, 87
Santa Cruz, Marquis 73
Scotland 2–3, 48, 118–19, 182
  see also Mary, Queen of Scots
Scrots, William 4, 6, 33
Segar, William 32, 40, 154
Sen, Professor Amartya 150
Seymour, Jane 3
Seymour, Lord Edward *see* Somerset

Seymour, Lord Henry 71, 73, 177, 181, 183
Seymour, Lord Thomas **4–5**, 109
Shakespeare, William 23, 55, 59, 142, 159, 161, **162–4**, **166–7**
quoted 1, 32
Sheemakers 166
Sheffield, Lord 66, 73, 74
Shrewsbury, Earl of 115, 158
Shrewsbury, Mary, Countess of 149
Sidney, Lady Frances 139
Sidney, Sir Henry 17, 81, 166
Sidney, Lady Mary 22, 37
Sidney, Sir Philip 17, 25, 29, 104, 134, 142, 158, 165–6, **172**
Sixtus V, Pope 43, 96, 171
slave trade 87
Smith, Sir Thomas 31, 103, 146
Smythson, Robert 157, 158
Somerset, Edward Seymour, Duke of 4, 5, 6, 48
South America 13, 78–9, 87, 90–1
Southampton, Earl of 146, 163
Southwell, Robert (Jesuit) 124–5
Southwell, Sir Robert 74
Spain
colonial power 13, 41, **78–9**
culture 69, 167–8
and England 2, 40, 64, 66–8, 71–2, 87–91 *passim*, 106, **170–4**
and Netherlands 14, 106, **171–3**
Spanish Armada 66, 68, **72–5**, 115, 170, **174–6**
aftermath 184–6, 187
Spenser, Edmund 149, 158, 161, 163, 164
Stafford, Sir Edward 134
Stowe, John 132, 167
Strange, Lord 161, 162
Strong, Sir Roy 154
Stubbs, John 104
Sudeley Castle 5, 7–8
Sussex, Thomas Radcliffe, Earl of 7, 7–8, 50, 51–2, 102

Tallis, Thomas 39, 151
theatre 142–3, **158–65**
Theobalds 47, 157
Throckmorton, Beth 22, 53, 101

Throckmorton, Sir Nicholas 15, 31, 101
Tilt Yard Tournaments **27–8**
Topcliffe, Richard 125
Tower of London **7–10**, 26
Trevelyan, G.M. 140, 148
Trinity College *see* Cambridge
Triumph (ship) 72, 74
Tyrone, Hugh O'Neill, Earl of 186–7

Valdes, Diego Flores de 184
Valdès, Pedro de 68
Vavasour, Anne 23
Vega, Lope de 69
Verrazano, Giovanni da 78
Vespucci, Amerigo 76
Victory (ship) 74

Wales, Charles, Prince of 140
Walsingham, Frances 25
Walsingham, Sir Francis 18, 20, 21, 25, **54–7**, 58, 89, 122, 133, 146, 152, 153, 178, **183**
Webster, John 164
Wentworth, Peter 123
Westminster Palace 25
Whitehall Palace 25–6
Whitgift, Archbishop John 45, 113, **123–4**, 141, 147
Willoughby, Lord 185
Willoughby, Sir Hugh 73, 77, 78
Wilmot, James 136
Wilton House 45
Winchester, Marquess of 7, 44, 115
Windsor Castle 26
Woburn Abbey 28, 45
Wollaton Hall 156, 157–8
Wolsey, Cardinal 25, 26, 44, 148
Woodstock House 10
Wooton, Sir Henry 165
Worksop Manor 158
Wren, Sir Christopher 140, 142, 155
Wyatt, Sir Thomas 6–7, 8–9

York, Sir John 79

Zuccaro, Federigo 152
Zutphen 172
Zwingli, Ulrich 113